Run The Mile You're In

One Founder's Journey
Through Success, Loss,
and Reinvention

Kettia Etienne Ming

This work reflects actual events in the life of the author as truthfully as recollection permits. Some events have been compressed, and some dialogue has been recreated. While all persons within are actual individuals, names and identifying characteristics have been changed to protect their privacy.

Copyright 2026 by Kettia Etienne Ming

All rights reserved. No part of this book may be reproduced or used in any manner without written permission of the copyright owner except for the use of quotations in a book review.

For more information, address:

mingkettia@gmail.com

Paperback ISBN: **979-8-9946392-0-7**

Ebook ISBN: **979-8-9946392-2-1**

Hardcover ISBN: **979-8-9946392-1-4**

Dedication

To my mom and dad, Abner and Jeannine Etienne: you are the axis upon which I spin. To my children, Alexi, Chloe, and Sophie: you are my purpose. And to Robert: for what we built together.

Contents

Prologue 8

As the Crow Flies 8

Chapter 1: The Silence Was Wrong 13

Chapter 2: The Midnight Idea 25

Chapter 3: Breaking Free 57

Chapter 4: Open by 8! 65

Chapter 5: The Deal of a Lifetime 129

Chapter 6: The 100-Foot Fight 159

Chapter 7: Keeping the Doors Open 199

Chapter 8: Run the Mile You're In 209

Chapter 9: Doing Business While Black 233

Chapter 10: Parallel Lives 251

Chapter 11: The Cost of Showing Up 273

Chapter 12: The Surrender Strategy 313

Chapter 13: When the Magic Showed Up 335

Chapter 14: Closure 373

EPILOGUE: The Becoming 391

PROLOGUE

As the Crow Flies

I'm on the Amtrak from Boston to New York, fresh off the Boston Marathon. It's the day after Patriots' Day, 2016. I'm sore. Marathon sore. The kind where waddling feels like an Olympic event and sitting on the toilet requires strategy and upper-body strength. But it's the good kind of sore, the kind that says: *You did it.*

The Boston Marathon is the granddaddy of them all. It is the hill, pun intended, that runners, recreational or pros, are willing to die on. One of the things I love most about running is how democratic it is. I, a weekend warrior, can toe the same line as Desiree Linden, Kara Goucher or Shalane Flanagan, all because I qualified to be there. It doesn't matter what I look like, how much I make, or what kind of gear I've got. What matters is that I put in the work. That I earned my spot.

And let me tell you, 99 percent of that work happens when no one is watching. At 5 a.m. or 8 p.m., through rain, sleet, or snow. No crowds. No cowbells. No finish-line glory. You have to want it. No one is making you do this. You have no chance of winning. The victory is all inside you.

Boston was my North Star. My dangling carrot. My ultimate finish line. I had trained for that qualifier like it was a second job, as if I needed a second job! But you couldn't tell me I wasn't going to make it there.

I first learned about Boston from my earliest running partner, Lodz. She and my sister Martine worked together, and Martine casually mentioned that her sister was a runner. Lodz reached out, we met up, and that was that. An instant connection. Lodz was a fellow first-generation Haitian woman navigating two spaces that weren't exactly built with her in mind. At that time she was working as a global health professional and getting her masters in midwifery at Columbia University and somehow also found time to train for marathons.

We bonded quickly and started training together. I remember one day, we were doing Harlem Hill repeats, a favorite for runners chasing strength. It was February and the kind of cold winter day that finds most normal people indoors or bundled up to their eyeballs if they had to step foot outside. Our breath hung in the air like clouds and our lungs were struggling to warm up the frozen air. Somewhere between gasps, she said, "These hills will help when we qualify for Boston."

"Boston?" I said. "What do you mean?"

"The Boston Marathon," she replied. "I'm going to qualify. I want that damn jacket."

"There's a jacket?"

She laughed. "Yeah. Like the Masters. It's a thing."

The only reason I even knew about the Masters was because Tiger Woods was dominating the sport at the time. But something about the way she said it—a jacket as proof of grit, as proof of passage—struck me. I was intrigued.

"Okay," I said. "Let's sign up."

She looked at me sideways. "You have to qualify. It's by age group. You have to hit a certain time just to register."

I was hooked. I didn't even know I needed this challenge until she said it. And it sounded scary as hell, which meant I had to do it. I learned that for my age group, I would need to run the race in 3 hours 45 minutes just to qualify. Up to that point I had run one whole marathon in 5 hours and 55 minutes. What made me think I could run that distance in 2 hours and 10 minutes faster?

Challenge accepted.

Stupid? Maybe. But is there any other way to meet a challenge?

Spoiler alert: I did it! Sure, it took me six years and 11 marathons to finally qualify but on April 18th, 2016, I turned left on Boylston Street and got my Boston.

Riding that post-race high, I sank into the train seat, casually scrolling through emails on my phone, half-distracted. My legs were still shaking from the adrenaline, and I was savoring that unique combination of exhaustion and euphoria that only comes after crossing a finish line you've been chasing for six years.

And then I saw it—an email from the president of Bright Horizons, the company that bought my first two childcare centers.

The message read something like:

"We understand you're opening a childcare center at 99 John Street. This would be in violation of your non-compete clause, as it is too close to the nearest Bright Horizons location."

I didn't even finish reading it. I immediately forwarded it to my attorney.

She replied quickly:

"This is absurd. They're just trying to block you from doing business again. Don't worry, we've got this."

Over the next few days the emails kept coming. Each one was more direct, more aggressive. What at first seemed like a bluff quickly escalated into a threat—and then a full-blown lawsuit.

They're suing me. Over 100 feet. Not a block. Not a building. Just 100 feet, as the crow flies.

I remember reading that phrase and thinking, *What the hell does that even mean?* Turns out, it's a legal way of measuring distance in a straight line, point to point, regardless of streets, buildings, or actual walking paths. A crow could fly it, sure.

But no parent dropping off a toddler in a stroller is flying like a damn bird.

That 100 feet became the rope they used to pull me into court and tie up my future.

I'm in shock. My head is spinning. My phone is buzzing. I've got a thousand decisions to make, a new business hanging in the balance, and suddenly, the finish line I thought I crossed feels like a false summit.

And I can't help but ask myself: What is this really about? Is this about a contract—or about control?

CHAPTER 1

The Silence Was Wrong

I stood in the doorway of Ms. Elsie's living room, my heart sinking as I took in the scene. Four toddlers were scattered around the alphabet carpet, but none of them were making a sound. The enormous TV dominated the wall, cartoons flickering across the screen, but even that seemed muted. And there, in the corner by the toy kitchen, sat my fifteen-month-old daughter Sophie.

She wasn't crying. She wasn't fighting. She wasn't doing any of the things that made her Sophie. She was just sitting there, staring at nothing, her little shoulders slumped in a way that made my chest tight.

"How was her day?" I asked Ms. Elsie, though I could already see the answer written all over my daughter's face.

"Oh, she's fine," Ms. Elsie replied, not looking up from wiping down the coffee table. "They're all just tired. You know how it is."

But I didn't know how it was. I knew Sophie. And this quiet, resigned little person wasn't my child.

This was March 2002, and I was drowning. We all were.

My husband Robert and I were living in a cramped one-bedroom apartment in the Bronx with our three kids: Alexi, four; Chloe, two; and fifteen-month-old Sophie.

We had a crib in our bedroom for the baby, and Robert had converted the living room into a shared bedroom for Alexi and Chloe. It was always meant to be temporary. We were looking for an apartment in Manhattan but hadn't had much luck finding something that fit our budget.

Right before Chloe was born, we got it in our head that we should move out of the city like a responsible little family and settle somewhere in the suburbs like adults. When you're a young couple with a growing family, everyone has an opinion about what you should be doing. Robert's mom would call from Bermuda asking when we were going to "get the children a backyard where they can run around." The news was full of stories about crime rates and the so-called exodus of New Yorkers to places like New Jersey or Westchester. Good school districts and outdoor spaces were all people wanted to talk to us about, and everyone had an opinion.

The message was clear: real families lived in houses with driveways and swing sets, not cramped city apartments where your toddler's bedroom was also the living room.

We scraped together some savings and were lucky enough to have our parents contribute some funds towards the down payment so we could buy a loft in Jersey City. It was a beautiful loft that we nicknamed Shangri-La. It had 50-foot ceilings which I learned later were also known as cathedral ceilings. The building used to be a former Wells Fargo stable. Yep, *that* Wells Fargo. As part of their operations, they built this complex in 1890 in Hamilton Park, Jersey City, originally using it as stables and a storage facility for their horses and carts. It was now called the Wells Fargo Lofts. Our loft had an open floor plan with a massive living room, huge kitchen and the kind of skylight you would normally see in a church. We had two main bedrooms upstairs and a guest room with office space downstairs. But the beautiful staircase leading upstairs wasn't at all child-friendly. The handrails had these bars big enough for a child to slip through. We had a gate at the top and bottom of the stairs but we still wrestled with the idea of closing the gaps or even replacing the stairs entirely as soon as we could afford it.

I was about 8 ½ months pregnant with Chloe when an incident made us rethink our whole lives. I had slipped out on a quiet Saturday morning to the corner store to pick up some fresh bagels. Robert and Alexi were still sleeping upstairs. I don't remember being out that long but Alexi woke up and heard me at the door coming back in. He got excited and yelled "Mommy!" and pushed through the gate somehow. I saw him starting to come down the stairs as I turned the entrance corner. Then he tripped. I watched in horror as he tumbled right through one of those bars to a loud thud on the ground. That was about a 7 or 8 foot drop. To this day, I think the anxiety of that day sent me into labor with Chloe. Alexi was fine. He sprained an ankle. I went into labor two days later. Robert and I both aged about 10 years.

Three months later, I went back to work. We made the decision to sell the loft and move back into the city. Our loft sold before we could secure a place for us to move to, so we found this small apartment in the Bronx while we tried to figure out a long term home. A year later, I found out I was pregnant with Sophie, a surprise but we took it in stride. We still wanted to move back into Manhattan but decided to stay until after giving birth before we attempted another big transition.

Finding a space in Manhattan big enough for our growing family, and still remotely affordable, proved harder than we thought. Robert was working as a public relations manager for a men's skincare line, and I had taken on a brand new position as a chief of staff for a hedge fund manager. Between our full-time jobs and the kids, we could barely find the time to go apartment hunting. Still, we were desperate for a place to settle. The cramped living quarters started to get on our nerves.

Parenting was equal parts improvisation and panic. We loved our kids deeply, but everything felt like a fire drill. Diapers, milk, fevers, teething. I was always on the edge of burnout. Our parenting styles were wildly different. Robert was intuitive, hands-on, playful. The designated fun parent. And I was fine with that. Lord knows you can't have two fun parents—that would be a recipe for disaster.

We were both dreamers, but in very different ways. Robert moved through the world with ease, like the rules didn't apply to him, or maybe he just didn't care if they did. I, on the other hand, lived by the checklist. Pacifier, doctor's appointments, 401(k), sleep schedule, receipts. He'd throw together elaborate puppet shows with cereal boxes and pipe cleaners, but forget to pack a bottle on the way out of the door. I was logistics. Calendar alerts. Baby monitor turned all the way up. Where he floated, I anchored. But somehow, it worked.

We hired a nanny early on, someone who came highly recommended. But she was unreliable. She'd show up late or not at all. I once came home early to find her on the phone for what looked like hours while our baby chewed on a stray shoelace. Another one, also recommended, took Chloe to the park and anchored the stroller between her legs so she could nap. A concerned parent who witnessed the incident called and told me. Then there was the one who spanked Sophie for not finishing her dinner. Alexi and Chloe reported it to me as soon as I got home. So, she had to go.

Our only experience with a daycare center at that time had been for Chloe. It wasn't exactly positive. The center we tried was cold and overcrowded, an assembly line of children. The lights were too bright, the paint was too loud, and the place reeked of antiseptic. Drop-off felt like a battlefield. Pick-up was no better. Chloe would often throw herself to the floor as soon as I walked through the door in full dramatics, as if to say, "How could you leave me here all day?" Having gone through that already, I didn't even consider it as an option for Sophie.

Just when we were reaching our breaking point, in the fall of 2002, we found the apartment. Not just any apartment, but the holy grail of New York City rentals—a ground-floor duplex with a private garden, right off Columbus Avenue on West 74th Street. I had been working with several brokers, but only one stood out. Young, hella ambitious and a little aggressive, but I didn't mind. He was hungry, and that worked for me. I remember thinking, *if anyone's going to find me what I'm looking for, it's going to be this guy.*

He called me the second a listing came through. Most of them weren't right, too expensive, too small, wrong neighborhood, but he kept checking in until I was confident, he knew exactly what I needed. One day he called about a space that hadn't even hit the market yet. I saw it, loved it, and had my application in before the landlord could list it.

Technically, it was a one-bedroom duplex with a rec room downstairs and a small side room attached. But the real luxuries were the private garden and the half bath downstairs. Our kids had space to play, to run, to just be. It felt like we had won the real estate lottery.

Alexi was in preschool at that point and since Chloe would turn three that August she could start in the fall. It might sound strange now, but back then, childcare options didn't really begin until age three when preschool kicked in. Before then, you were mostly on your own, navigating a world of nannies, family members, or home daycares you heard about in the back pages of newspapers. Nowadays you can find childcare options starting at six weeks.

Now that Sophie wouldn't have a sibling with her, I didn't feel comfortable leaving her home alone with a nanny—not after everything we had been through. I wanted her to have social interaction. I also wanted accountability.

I saw an ad for a home daycare. Where, I don't remember, but it sounded ideal. A small group, with the right amount of structure. I called the center excited to set up an appointment with the provider, Ms. Elsie.

She was warm and friendly. She answered my list of questions, and seemed pretty knowledgeable with this age group. Ms. Elsie, in turn, asked me questions about Sophie's milestones. I felt comfortable there. The kitchen area was spotless and Ms. Elsie showed us where all the edges had been childproofed. The play area for the kids was right in her living room and I could tell that she put some thought into the plushy alphabet carpet and plenty of age-appropriate toys. Her home was clean, licensed, and seemed to check all the boxes, though I couldn't ignore the enormous 60-inch TV dominating her living room, the kind that looked like it played cartoons from breakfast to pick-up. Still, we were desperate and she had the full-time availability we needed. So, we signed Sophie up.

My daughter's first day was brutal.

I can still hear her cries echoing down the hallway as I walked toward the elevator. That wail, that 'mama, don't leave me' sob, followed me all the way to my desk at work. Granted she was 15-months-old and separation anxiety was a normal developmental stage in babies and toddlers, and peaks around 14 to 18 months. I never believed Sophie was being mistreated or that she was in danger. She was being a toddler and I was a working mom who felt like a bad parent for leaving her kid with strangers to go to work. Technically everyone is a stranger until you get to know them.

"Sophie, baby," I said, kneeling down beside her. "Mama's here."

She looked up at me with those big eyes, and I wanted her to cry. I wanted her to scream. I wanted her to throw herself into my arms and wail about her terrible day. Instead, she just reached up silently, like she'd given up on expecting anyone to understand what she needed.

Something in me broke. I knew right then and there I wouldn't bring her back. I just couldn't do it. I know my kids. All three of them have very distinct personalities. They may share genetics, but their traits are their own. For example, I am pretty sure Alexi came out of the womb knowing how to read.

No one ever tested that theory because up until age 2, he couldn't really talk. But once he found the right words, we discovered his love for language. It was evident when he read *Goodnight Moon* cover to cover while putting him to bed one night. Neither of us ever formally taught him. Surprised, we assumed he memorized the story since it was a favorite book to read before bedtime. So we skipped pages and quizzed him on different words out of order. At 6 years old, he was the backseat driver telling us to slow down if we were as little as five miles over the speed limit. By 10 years old, he was listing the dangers of alcohol as we poured our normal glass of wine with dinner, so much so that a lot of times we would wait until after their bedtime to enjoy a glass without judgment.

Chloe was dramatic from the minute she came out screaming bloody murder, squinting at the hospital lights like somehow she really screwed up in a past life to end up here. She was the tiniest of my babies, born just under 6 pounds, but the loudest crier. She wailed day and night for the first two weeks of her life. It wasn't until she was almost a month old, I realized she cried to be put down. She didn't like to be held all the time. One day she was crying her head off and I was over it. I thought to myself, *let me put this girl down before I lose it*. The second I put her down in her crib, she stopped, instantly. The next time she screamed after being fed and dry and all that jazz, I put her down. Again, she stopped. It was my first lesson in actually listening to what my children were telling me, instead of assuming I knew what they needed.

Sophie was always loud and energetic, not in a "all toddlers are rambunctious" kind of way. She moved to her own rhythm. Her volume was always on high whether it was in disapproval or squealing in delight. She was quiet only when she slept. Even then sometimes you could hear her giggle in her dreams like she was sharing some inside joke with the universe. Her expressions were priceless. She was a ball of energy. Even if she came down with something, she never became listless or despondent as you see sometimes with sick kids. She would fight sleep or a cold or anything that she thought was trying to take her out of the party that is life. When she was unhappy, she cried like someone was trying to kill her.

So when I picked her up at Ms. Elsie's on that third day, she was completely despondent, like she had no fight left in her. I wasn't just concerned, I was heartbroken. At that moment, I wanted her to go back to crying because that was the child I knew. I couldn't handle this quiet resignation. I wanted her to go back to fighting. I felt like I had failed her.

I called out sick from work and stayed home with no real plans of what I was going to do the next day.

Robert and I often stayed up late after the kids went to bed, just the two of us on the couch. That was the only quiet time we had. We'd watch a little TV, but mostly we just talked—me venting about my boss, him nodding along and throwing in a few jokes to make me feel better. He was good like that. He always showed up for the debrief.

Late that night with no childcare for the next day, faced with the reality that I must call out again, the thought just came to me sometime around midnight, both of us half-awake and half-listening to whatever was on in the background, "Why couldn't I just turn this place into a daycare? I mean if this woman can run a daycare out of her home, why can't I?"

Let me be clear: I had zero business ambitions at that moment. I wasn't trying to be an entrepreneur. I just needed a solution. And God bless Robert. He didn't blink. No hesitation. He just looked at me and said, "Okay. So how do we do that?"

I don't know if he just said that because he knew I was spinning and wanted to make me feel better. If agreeing to something that sounded slightly insane was going to make me feel better in that moment, then that's what he was going to do.

By the way, I am pretty sure that's how I ended up running my first marathon. I had started running on the treadmill at the gym to lose a bit of post-pregnancy weight after Sophie was born. I built up myself from one to two miles to four to six without stopping. This took a few months but I saw a difference in my clothes so I kept going. I remember the first time I ran six miles, without stopping. I couldn't wait to get home from the gym to tell Robert. I burst through the apartment and said, "Honey, guess what? I just ran six whole miles without stopping!!"

"Wow, that's great," he replied. "You could probably run a marathon now."

"You're right. I can. I think I will." Yep, that's how I decided I was going to run my first marathon.

It was that simple.

When I look back, I laugh because it was in that same spirit that Robert said, "Yeah honey, let's open a daycare in our home with our three children under five and two full time jobs!"

But anyway, that was the beginning of Smarter Toddler.

CHAPTER 2

The Midnight Idea

Robert and I met in a retail distribution class at the American College in London, one of those courses where design and commerce collide. He was pursuing a double major in fashion design and merchandising; I was focused on fashion merchandising. But it was in that classroom, debating the intersection of creativity and business, that we first recognized something in each other. He was tall, dark, and handsome in that effortless way some men just are. Lean build, perfectly sculpted face, but it was the dimples that got me. Deep, pronounced dimples that lit up his entire face when he smiled. The kind of dimples you'd normally see on a beautiful woman, which somehow made this gorgeous man even more appealing.

He was from Bermuda, an island I'd only ever associated with mysterious disappearances and triangle theories. Even coming from the melting pot that is New York, Robert felt exotic to me. His mother was Bermudian, his stepfather Trinidadian, and Robert himself was the product of a brief college romance between his mother and a Ghanaian engineering student at Columbia University. While he was born in New York during his mother's time at Teachers College, he moved to Bermuda with her as a baby. His biological father, returned to Ghana for an arranged marriage. After marrying his mother, his stepfather, Fred, adopted him, but Robert maintained dual citizenship, a detail that would help him years later when we eventually settled down in New York.

Where I was practical, Robert was purely creative. He interned at John Galliano and other prestigious British design houses while I worked at Browns, one of London's most exclusive boutiques. This was the early '90s, when Pucci and Romeo Gigli and Christian Lacroix ruled the fashion world. I remember strutting through London in a bright citron Gigli coat that would probably break Instagram today, feeling like fashion royalty.

Our plan was simple: graduate and land jobs at major fashion labels, preferably in Paris. Robert was always more artist than commerce, but fashion design felt like a practical way to channel his creativity, something he could explain to his parents without them worrying about a starving artist son.

For my graduation, Robert designed and sewed my outfit himself–a bright lime green Yves Saint Laurent-inspired linen pantsuit, tailored to absolute perfection. When I walked across the stage to collect my degree, the entire graduating class rose to their feet, cheering and applauding. That was Robert: never content with good enough, always creating something that stopped people in their tracks.

He'd graduated two years ahead of me and moved to Paris, landing a job in Sentier, the city's fashion district. After my graduation, I joined him, and we spent two glorious years bumming around Europe—working, traveling, living entirely in the present tense, the way only people in their early twenties can manage.

In the fall of 1994, we decided to return to the States. While I'd never had trouble finding work in European fashion, New York proved almost impossible. I'd send in my resume and have employers gushing over the phone, only to meet me in person and suddenly hear about budget cuts or hiring freezes. Robert faced the same walls. It was my first real education in systemic racism—the way opportunities could evaporate the moment you walked into a room.

While holding out for fashion careers, we survived on retail jobs and office temp work. But Robert never stopped creating. He designed lines of hats, gloves, and candles. We entered home goods trade shows at the Javits Center. He created a collection of mirrors that were really art installations—including one piece that reimagined a Maasai spear and shield in glass, with intricate etchings depicting tribal life. That mirror got coverage in Vogue, The New York Times Home section, and Essence. I still own it.

It's almost too simplistic to call Robert an artist. He's never been just "an artist." He's a multi-disciplinary creative visionary who's been thinking outside conventional boxes as long as I have known him. From the beginning, his mindset was never about a traditional 9-to-5. He always dreamed bigger, saw possibilities where others saw limitations. Our start in New York was bumpy when it came to job hunting, but our confidence in our talent and capacity never wavered.

That fall, he proposed to me at the Obelisk, also known as Cleopatra's Needle in Central Park, one of the oldest outdoor monuments in New York City standing between the Great Lawn and the Met. It was gifted to the U.S. by the Egyptian government in 1879. We'd spent countless hours near that spot, walking the paths around Cat Hill, dreaming out loud about our future.

When I said yes, I wasn't just saying yes to marriage. I was saying yes to a life built on the belief that we could create anything we could envision.

That same vision, that belief we could create something beautiful from nothing, is what Robert carried down the narrow stairs to our basement rec room in early 2003. The same creative partnership that had carried us through fashion sketches in Paris and mirror installations in our early days in New York was about to transform a random space into something revolutionary. When I told him I needed to start a daycare, he didn't just see a childcare solution. He saw an opportunity for us to build something that had never existed before. And it all started with paint chips.

The paint chips were spread across our kitchen table like a designer's fever dream—dozens of small rectangles in every shade of white, cream and gray imaginable. Robert held one up to the light streaming through our window, then another, squinting as if he were choosing the perfect fabric for a couture gown.

"This one," he said, tapping a chip labeled 'Dove Wing.' "No, wait." He picked up another. "Maybe 'Morning Mist.'"

I looked at both samples. They appeared identical to me, two very expensive ways to say 'off-white.'

"Robert, they're the same color."

He gave me the look. The same look he'd given me in Paris when I suggested we could buy curtains at Monoprix instead of having him design them from scratch. It was patient but pitiful–the look of an artist trying to explain color theory to someone who thought beige was a personality trait.

"Honey, look at the undertones." He held both chips side by side. "Dove Wing has warm gray undertones. Morning Mist leans cool. In the afternoon light in that basement room, warm undertones will make the space feel cozy. Cool undertones will make it feel like a morgue."

It was early 2003, and we'd been living in our Upper West Side "duplex" for about six months. What the real estate listing generously called a "garden duplex" was really a ground-floor apartment with a basement that previous tenants had used as storage. But Robert saw something else entirely when we first walked down those narrow stairs.

"This could work," he said, running his hands along the walls like he was reading braille. "Good bones. Natural light from those windows." He pointed to two small windows near the ceiling that let in slivers of street-level light. "We'd need to brighten everything, but the proportions are right."

Now, three weeks after my meltdown about Sophie's daycare situation, he was approaching the transformation of that basement with the same intensity he'd brought to his fashion design work in Paris. The same focus that had gotten him coverage in Vogue for those stunning mirrors he'd created—each one, a piece of art that happened to show your reflection.

"What about the floors?" I asked, watching him make notes in a small sketchbook. Everything with Robert started with sketches.

"We'll need to add more rugs," he said, looking at the beautiful area rugs he'd already chosen for our family space. "What we have works perfectly for our three kids, but for twelve children spending ten hours a day here, we'll need additional coverage. More jute rugs for the high-traffic areas, extra wool ones for comfort zones."

He grinned and continued drawing. "We'll layer them strategically; create defined spaces while keeping that warm, homey feeling we've already established."

The Midnight Idea

"I'm thinking we section the space with furniture instead of walls," he continued. "Create different zones like a reading corner, art station, dramatic play area."

I watched him work, remembering how he'd designed my graduation outfit that last night in London, pins between his teeth, adjusting the fit until 2 a.m. because "good enough" wasn't in his vocabulary. He approached everything from hemlines to home design like he was creating something that had never existed before.

"Alright, show me what you're thinking," I said.

He led me downstairs to the basement that had been our children's playroom for months. Robert had already transformed this space into something special—warm rugs covering the cold concrete, carefully chosen furniture, artwork at child height. It was beautiful, but it was designed for three children who lived here, not twelve children who would be learning and playing here all day.

He was moving through the space like he was envisioning the enhanced version he could already see.

"Picture this," he said, standing in the center of the room. "We keep the foundation of what we've created but elevate it. More strategic rug placement for traffic flow, additional storage that doubles as seating, expanded art areas."

He gestured toward the corner where we already had some low shelving. "We expand the reading nook, add more built-in storage. Make everything accessible but organized for twelve little ones."

He walked to the opposite corner. "Art station here gets upgraded—proper work surfaces, supply storage, easy cleanup near the utility sink." He paused by the small windows where we already had sheer curtains. "And we maximize every bit of natural light with additional mirrors positioned to reflect light deeper into the space."

I could see it starting to take shape in my mind. It was not a complete overhaul, but a thoughtful evolution of what we'd already created.

"The furniture needs to stay real," he continued, gesturing to the wooden pieces he'd already chosen for our family. "Nothing plastic. Real wood, real fabric."

This was vintage Robert. When we'd lived in Paris, he'd furnished our tiny studio apartment with pieces he'd found at flea markets and refinished himself. Nothing matched in the traditional sense, but everything worked together like a 1950s armchair reupholstered in deep burgundy velvet, a distressed wooden table he'd painted the color of sea glass, vintage jazz posters he'd had professionally framed.

"What about safety?" I asked, the practical side of me kicking in. "Licensing requirements?"

Robert laughed and waved his hand dismissively. "Oh, I'm leaving all that fun stuff to you."

I rolled my eyes. "Wait, you know we can't just wing the licensing process."

"I know, I know," he said, still grinning. "But whatever the requirements are: corner guards, outlet covers, cabinet locks—we can do all of that without making the space look like a padded cell."

He pulled out his phone and showed me photos of some daycares he'd found online. "Look at these places," he said, flipping through the images. "Primary colors everywhere. Plastic furniture. Cartoon characters screaming from every wall. Why hasn't childcare evolved?"

"So you did do some research," I said.

"Visual research," he corrected. "I researched what not to do. You can handle finding out what we have to do."

I studied the photos. He was right. Every daycare looked exactly the same—bright, loud, chaotic.

"What about music?" I asked. Robert and I were both serious music lovers. Our apartment was always filled with everything from Nina Simone to Stan Getz, Massive Attack to Miles Davis, and everything in between. "I want music to be played throughout the day, like we do at home."

Robert's face lit up. "Yes! We should get a built-in sound system. We'll run speakers through the walls. I want the music to feel like it's just...there. Part of the atmosphere. And we'll play our own stuff so the adults don't feel left out."

He was already sketching again, drawing sight lines and traffic patterns like he was designing a fashion show runway. "I want parents to walk in here and forget they're in a basement. I want them to feel like they're dropping their child off at a friend's beautiful home."

I got caught up in the excitement and mused out loud, "Sophie's gonna lose her mind when this is done."

He stopped sketching and looked at me. "Yeah, they all will. Alexi and Chloe are gonna want to stay home with her now," we both laughed.

He looked around our rec room and continued, "But seriously, I want her to understand that beauty and culture aren't luxuries reserved for fancy schools or wealthy families. They're necessities and every child deserves them."

Over the next hour, Robert measured every inch of the space. He made notes about electrical outlets, ventilation, even the angle of light at different times of day. He approached this transformation the same way he'd approached everything else– as an artist who refused to compromise his vision, even when the canvas was a suburban basement.

"How long do you think this will take?" I asked as we headed back upstairs.

"If we do it right?" He flipped through his sketches. "Six weeks for the major work. Then another two weeks for the details—the art, the books, the finishing touches."

"And if we don't do it right?"

He smiled, the same smile he'd given me when I'd worried about the cost of those custom curtains in Paris. "Hey, we don't know how to do anything except right."

That night, after the kids were asleep, Robert spread his sketches across our bed. The basement transformation had evolved into something bigger, a complete philosophy of what early childhood education could look like when you started with beauty instead of efficiency.

"You know what this is?" he said, pointing to his drawings. "This is us refusing to accept that good enough is good enough."

And I realized he was right. We weren't just creating a daycare. We were meeting a demand, sure, but we were also creating a space that hadn't yet existed in this form. The kind of place where learning felt like play, where every detail mattered, where children understood instinctively that they deserved to grow and thrive in beautiful spaces.

Robert had taken my desperate need for childcare and turned it into a vision. Now all I had to do was bring it to life.

The Midnight Idea

Finding the right teachers felt as crucial as choosing the right paint colors. I wasn't just looking for someone to watch children–I needed people who understood that I was creating something entirely different.

I'd posted the job listing on a few education websites, being very specific about what I was looking for: "Seeking early childhood educators who believe beautiful spaces matter, who understand that children deserve respect and intentionality, who want to be part of something revolutionary."

The responses fell into two categories: people who thought "revolutionary" sounded like too much work, and people who wanted to know more.

Sarah was in the second category.

She arrived for her interview wearing a soft gray cardigan and carrying a worn leather portfolio. While I talked her through our vision–the music, the art, the natural materials. She nodded like she'd been waiting her whole career for someone to say these things.

"I've worked at three different centers," she said, opening her portfolio to show photos of classroom setups. "Every single one looked exactly the same. Children were treated like products on an assembly line instead of the whole, complete human beings they actually are."

She showed me a photo of a reading corner she'd created in her last position: a cozy nook with real books, a vintage rug, plants on low shelves. "My director made me take down the plants. Said they were 'unnecessary.' I quit two weeks later."

That's when I knew I'd found my first teacher.

The second teacher was harder to find. I interviewed candidates for weeks, and most of them seemed confused by my questions. When I asked how they'd incorporate art into daily activities, they talked about finger painting and construction paper crafts. When I asked about creating calm environments, they suggested more colorful posters.

Then Maria walked in.

She was older than the other candidates, maybe late forties. She had kind eyes and calloused hands that suggested she wasn't afraid of real work. She'd been teaching for fifteen years, mostly in public programs, but something in our job description had caught her attention.

"Tell me about your philosophy," I said, the same question I'd asked everyone else.

Maria was quiet for a moment, looking around our living room—at the books on the shelves, the plants in the windows, the art on the walls.

"Children know when adults respect them," she said finally. "They know when you are talking to them and not at them.

They understand and appreciate when you've put thought into their space. Most places don't think children notice these things. But children notice everything."

Robert and I exchanged a look. This was exactly what I'd been hoping to hear but hadn't known how to ask for.

"What would you want to change about traditional daycare?" Robert asked.

"The noise," she said immediately. "Every center I've worked in is so loud. Children screaming, TVs blaring, teachers shouting over the chaos. Children need quiet spaces, too. They need to hear themselves think." Maria paused for a moment. "Oh, and the food," she added with a slight smile. "I'd love to work somewhere that serves real food. Not just crackers and juice boxes."

Maria talked about creating rhythm in the day; quiet activities followed by active ones, time for reflection built into every routine. She talked about real conversations with children, not just the constant chatter about colors and numbers that filled most programs. Something else on her resume had caught my attention. Her training was in Reggio Emilia. This was the first time I had heard of it. I looked it up briefly before her interview and asked her to tell me about it.

As Maria started explaining the Reggio Emilia approach, I felt that strange sensation of hearing something completely new that somehow sounded completely familiar.

"It's an educational philosophy that started in Italy after World War II," she said. "The core belief is that children are capable of constructing their own learning, and that the environment itself becomes the third teacher."

I leaned forward. "What do you mean, the third teacher?"

"Think about it," Maria said, her eyes lighting up. "The first teacher is the adult, the second is the other children, but the third teacher is the space itself. A beautiful, thoughtfully designed environment that invites exploration and respects children as capable human beings."

A Reggio Emilia inspired space respects children as capable by providing them with authentic materials and tools.

Think about the difference between giving a child a plastic toy hammer versus a real, child-sized wooden hammer. Or offering actual glass cups instead of sippy cups to a three-year-old who's ready for the responsibility. Reggio environments trust children with real paintbrushes instead of foam brushes, actual plants to care for instead of plastic flowers, real wooden blocks instead of foam alternatives.

It's about believing that children can handle beauty, fragility, and responsibility when we give them the chance. When you hand a toddler a real ceramic bowl instead of a plastic one, you're telling them, "I trust you to be careful. I believe you're capable of handling something precious." And children rise to meet that expectation in ways that constantly surprise adults.

The Midnight Idea

This philosophy extends beyond materials to how we talk to children, how we set up their environments, how we approach their questions and ideas. Instead of dumbing things down, we elevate our expectations and watch children exceed them.

My mind immediately went to our kids' bedrooms. The way Robert had designed each corner with purpose. The Calder mobiles that had hung over their cribs as babies, slowly rotating and casting gentle shadows. The framed photos of Miles Davis and Thelonious Monk on the walls, the Basquiat print that Alexi would stare at for long stretches, pointing out details we'd never noticed. Jazz music playing softly as they fell asleep, their nervous systems calmed by those soothing tones instead of overstimulated by bright primary colors and chaotic sounds.

"And then there's what we call the Hundred Languages of Children," Maria continued. "It's a metaphor for all the diverse ways children learn and communicate. Not just through reading and math, but through drawing, sculpting, dramatic play, music, movement. Every child has their own unique way of making sense of the world."

That's when it hit me. The aha moment that made everything click.

I thought about Robert teaching Alexi to count using his toy keyboard, turning numbers into music. I thought about Sophie and Chloe in their dramatic play corner, putting on elaborate performances for us, working through emotions and ideas through storytelling and movement. I thought about the small plants in their room that they'd learned to water and care for, understanding responsibility and growth through touch and routine.

I even thought about myself, arriving in New York from Haiti at twelve years old, not speaking a word of English. While my parents worked, I'd sit in front of our small TV watching *Sesame Street*, learning the language through songs and stories and puppets. Big Bird and Cookie Monster had been my English teachers, and it had worked.

"This is what we've been doing at home," I said, the excitement building in my voice. "I just didn't know there was a name for it."

Maria smiled. "Most parents who really pay attention to their children end up discovering these principles naturally. You've been creating an environment where your kids feel respected and capable, where they can explore and learn in ways that make sense to them."

The Reggio Emilia approach became the foundation of everything we built at Smarter Toddler. Not because I read about it in a manual, but because Maria helped me realize that the instincts Robert and I had been following as parents, the way we'd designed our home and our children's spaces, had a name and a philosophy behind it. We'd been honoring our children's capacity for learning and growth all along. Now we just had the language to be more intentional about it.

By the end of her interview, Robert and Maria were talking to each other like old friends, already planning how they'd organize the space, what materials Maria would need, how she would handle transitions between activities.

"When can you start?" I asked.

She looked around the space, then back at me.

"Tomorrow?" she said. "I mean, if you'll have me."

And just like that, I had my team.

The next step was to submit a license application. Teachers are a part of the licensing process. You can't apply without having your teachers on the application. Their fingerprints and background are also a part of this process. It's all running simultaneously. You just cross your fingers and hope everything comes back in time for final approval.

What I didn't realize until I was knee deep in it is that the licensing process is designed to crush your soul before you even serve your first snack.

I thought I was ready. I had the vision, the space, the teachers, the enthusiasm. How hard could it be to get a piece of paper saying I was allowed to care for children?

The answer: soul-crushingly, mind-numbingly, bureaucratically hard.

My first clue should have been when the woman at the Department of Health and Mental Hygiene (DOH) handed me a thick binder and said, "This is Article 47. It's your Bible now."

Article 47 of the New York City Health Code. Two hundred and thirty-seven pages of regulations governing the operation of child care programs. Everything from the exact temperature water had to be (between 105 and 120 degrees Fahrenheit) to the required square footage per child (35 square feet of indoor space, plus additional outdoor space requirements that made my head spin).

One of the challenges is that there are several agencies involved and they don't talk to each other.

My first contact was with the Office of Children and Family Services (OCFS) where I signed up to take the Child Day Care orientation. I then scheduled a preliminary inspection to assess the feasibility of the space. OCFS would do their inspection and create a detailed report. I'd also need a Department of Buildings inspection but I had to get a manual copy of my preliminary because there's no shared database between the agencies and the DOB will need that report. The Fire Department operated in their own universe entirely. And the Department of Health and Mental Hygiene, the agency that trumps them all, the one that will ultimately grant the license, seemed to exist in a parallel dimension where none of the other agencies' findings mattered.

I became a human filing cabinet, carrying folders between agencies, trying to manually connect dots that should have been connected by some basic computer system.

This was just the beginning. This bureaucratic maze, this feeling of swimming upstream against systems that seemed designed to exhaust you into giving up. This would become a recurring theme in everything I tried to build. The licensing process was teaching me something I'd need to know for the next twelve years: that sometimes the biggest obstacle to creating something meaningful isn't lack of vision or resources or demand. Sometimes the biggest obstacle is simply the unnecessarily complicated machinery of institutions that have forgotten why they exist in the first place.

The folders I was carrying between agencies were preparing me for the folders I'd carry between banks when I needed financing for expansion. The circular conversations with inspectors who couldn't talk to each other were training me for the circular conversations I'd have with insurance companies who couldn't coordinate their own departments. The feeling of being one person trying to navigate systems built for corporations with legal teams and administrative assistants, that feeling would follow me through every growth phase, every challenge, every attempt to scale something that started in my basement.

But I didn't know any of that yet. All I knew was that I had a vision, a beautiful space, and two incredible teachers, and somehow I had to make all the pieces fit together, even when the pieces seemed to come from entirely different puzzles.

"Did the fire department approve your emergency exits?" the DOH inspector asked.

"They haven't inspected yet. They're waiting for your clearance."

"I can't clear you until I see fire department approval."

"But they won't inspect until you clear me."

She shrugged. "Not my problem."

The breaking point came with the egress requirements. Two means of egress, both leading directly to the street. Not to a yard, not to a hallway, not to another room. To the street.

My beautiful basement had one obvious exit, the stairs leading up to our main apartment. The backyard door of our garden apartment, which I'd assumed would count as a second exit, was immediately rejected.

"Leads to an enclosed space," Frank, the fire inspector said, making another note on his clipboard of doom. "Children could be trapped in the yard if there's a fire in the building."

"But it's outside," I said. "Fresh air. Open space."

"Enclosed by fences. Doesn't count."

The Midnight Idea

So I had to create a second exit. Easier said than done. It had to come from the basement to the street.

Robert and I spent weeks figuring out how to cut a new entrance in the wall that would lead directly to the sidewalk. I had to hire a structural engineer to make sure I wasn't compromising the building's integrity. I had to get permits from the Department of Buildings. I had to coordinate with the city about sidewalk access.

"Mrs. Ming," the DOH inspector said during her third visit, "your soap dispensers are the wrong height."

I looked at the soap dispensers Robert had carefully installed at child height so the kids could wash their hands independently.

"Child height is good," she continued, "but you also need adult-height dispensers for staff. Article 47, section 12.3.2."

I wanted to cry. I could feel myself tearing up out of pure frustration right there in front of her, standing next to our beautiful reading corner that now needed to be reconfigured because the bookshelves were apparently a "climbing hazard."

"How does anyone ever open a daycare?" I asked.

She looked at me with something that might have been sympathy.

"Most people give up," she said. "The ones who make it through? They really, really want it."

Oh, but there's more, and this is where it got really fun: I was a renter.

All these modifications I was making to create that second egress? I needed my landlord's permission to cut a hole in the wall of their building.

I called our property management company, explaining what I needed to do and why.

"Absolutely not," was their immediate response. "You want to cut a hole in the foundation? That's structural. That's permanent. That's...that's probably illegal."

"I hired an engineer. He already inspected it and confirmed it's not structural and I have permits," I said. "The city is requiring this for my license."

"Not our problem. The lease doesn't allow for structural modifications."

"But it's not structural."

"No."

I hung up and stared at the ceiling. I'd already spent so much on permits, an engineer and a contractor. Not to mention the money spent on revamping the basement. Now I was stuck because my landlord wouldn't let me create the exit that the city required for me to operate.

For two weeks, I called every day. Different people, same answer. No modifications. Period.

Then, three weeks later, my phone rang.

"Mrs. Ming? This is Janet from Riverside Property Management. I've been thinking about your request."

My heart jumped. Maybe they'd changed their minds. Maybe they'd realized I was a good tenant who just wanted to run a legitimate business.

"I'm willing to consider it," Janet continued, "but there would need to be an adjustment to your lease terms."

"What kind of adjustment?"

"A rent increase. Significant modifications to the property require...compensation for the added risk and value."

I grabbed a pen. "How much?"

"Seven hundred dollars a month."

Seven hundred dollars! An extra seven hundred dollars per month?

For permission to cut an exit that I was paying for, that I was required by law to have, that would actually make their building safer in case of emergency.

"That's..." I started to say "outrageous," but stopped myself. I was so close. I'd come too far to give up now.

"That's a big increase," I said instead.

"Take it or leave it," Janet replied. "And we'll need the first year of the increase paid upfront. As a good faith deposit for the modifications."

So not only did they want $700 more per month, they wanted $8,400 up front.

These costs were becoming astronomical. The timeline kept extending. And every day that passed was another day I couldn't open, another day of paying rent and salaries with no income.

Let me break down what "astronomical" actually meant in real numbers, because nobody warns you about this part when you're dreaming about starting your own business.

By the time I was four months into the licensing process, I was hemorrhaging money at a rate that would have made my hedge fund boss proud, if it had been anyone else's money. Our monthly burn rate was crushing: $4,500 in rent, plus now the additional $700 from our extortion-friendly landlord. Another $500 for utilities. Then there were the teacher salaries: Sarah and Maria were making $6,500 combined per month, and I needed them for licensing, but that was money going out with zero coming in.

The one-time costs were even more brutal. We'd spent about $12,000 on the aesthetic renovation and children's furniture, all those beautiful rugs and real wood pieces that Robert had insisted on. The permits and various fees added up to around $1,000, which sounds reasonable until you realize that's just the paperwork cost, not including the actual work the permits allowed you to do.

The engineer alone cost $5,000. Five thousand dollars for someone to tell the city that cutting a hole in my basement wall wouldn't bring down the building. Then there was the contractor to actually cut the hole. And don't forget that $8,400 upfront payment to my landlord for the privilege of making their building safer.

Oh, and insurance. Fourteen thousand dollars a year for the security to operate a business that might never open.

All of this money was coming from our savings, which disappeared faster than I thought possible. When that ran out, we turned to credit cards. When I started losing sleep over the credit card balances, Robert launched what he called his "robust eBay side hustle"—selling designer clothing and handbags we'd brought back from our time in Europe. Pieces that had seemed so important in our Paris apartment suddenly became survival tools in our New York reality.

"Look at it this way," Robert said one evening as he photographed a vintage Gaultier jacket for eBay. "These clothes got us through our fashion phase. Now they're getting us through our entrepreneur phase."

When that wasn't enough, I did something I'd sworn I'd never do: I dipped into my 401(k). Taking money from your retirement to fund a dream feels like betting your future on your present, which is basically what starting a business is. Seeing those numbers disappear from my retirement account made it terrifyingly real.

The math was simple and brutal. Four months of expenses with zero revenue. Over $50,000 out the door before I could legally accept my first child.

"How does anyone survive this?" I asked Robert one night as we sat at our kitchen table, surrounded by bills and bank statements.

"Most people don't," he said quietly. "Most people give up before they get to this point."

What saved us, ironically, was the faith other parents had in what we were building. Families were so eager to secure spots that they were willing to prepay a month's deposit when they enrolled, even though we couldn't give them a firm opening date. That advance money became the lifeline to our business, the difference between making it to the finish line and having to shut down before we ever opened.

I hung up and called Robert.

"They want what?" he said.

"$8,400 now, plus $700 more every month for the rest of our lease."

"For permission to make their building safer?"

"Apparently."

Robert and I sat in silence on the phone. This was money I didn't have. Money that would eat into my operating budget before I even opened. Money that represented months of potential profit.

But what choice did I have? Start over somewhere else? Lose all the work I'd already done? Abandon the families who were counting on me to open?

If you're reading this as someone who's thinking about starting your own business, let me pause here and share what I wish I'd known before I signed that first lease.

Do your research before you invest a single dollar.

I went into this with passion, vision, and determination, but I was woefully unprepared for the actual mechanics of opening a licensed childcare business in New York City. I knew I wanted to create something beautiful and meaningful. I knew there was demand. I knew I had the right team. But I didn't know about Article 47. I didn't know about egress requirements. I didn't know that every agency would want their piece, and that none of them would talk to each other.

The Midnight Idea

I wish I'd spent weeks researching the licensing process before I ever considered my space. I wish I'd called other daycare owners and asked them about their startup costs, their timeline, their biggest unexpected expenses. I wish I'd understood that "preliminary approval" doesn't mean what you think it means, and that your landlord can hold your entire business hostage if they want to.

Most importantly, I wish I'd built realistic financial projections that included a buffer for bureaucratic insanity.

Here's what I should have done, and what you should do if you're starting any business that requires licensing, permits, or significant modifications to a space:

- Research the full licensing process first. Don't just read the overview on the website. Get the actual manual. Talk to other business owners who've been through it. Find out what each agency requires, how long they typically take, and what kinds of unexpected issues come up.

- Triple your timeline estimates. If someone tells you licensing takes six weeks, plan for eighteen weeks. If the contractor says two weeks for modifications, plan for six weeks. Everything takes longer than anyone tells you it will.

- Quadruple your budget for modifications and compliance. That $5,000 you budgeted for "miscellaneous startup costs?" Make it $20,000. There will be requirements you didn't know about, modifications you didn't anticipate, and fees that appear out of nowhere.

- Understand your landlord's power over your business. Read your lease with a lawyer before you sign it. Know what modifications you're allowed to make, what approvals you'll need, and what happens if the city requires changes your landlord doesn't want to allow. If possible, get permission for potential modifications in writing before you commit to the space.

- Have multiple funding sources. Don't rely on just your savings, or just a loan, or just investor money. You'll need more than you think, and you'll need it faster than you expect. Have backup plans for your backup plans.

- Connect with others who've done what you're trying to do. Join industry associations, find mentorship programs, attend networking events. Other business owners are usually generous with advice if you approach them respectfully and specifically.

- Build relationships with the agencies you'll be dealing with. If possible, go to informational sessions, ask questions early, get to know the process and the people before you're in crisis mode.

The hard truth is passion and vision aren't enough. You need systems, research, preparation and financial cushions that feel excessive until you need them.

I made it through, but it was much harder and more expensive than it needed to be. And there were moments, standing in that basement with yet another inspector telling me about yet another requirement I'd never heard of, when I seriously considered walking away from the whole thing.

The families who were counting on me, the teachers who'd committed to the vision, the money I'd already invested, and Robert's unwavering support kept me going. But if I'd done my homework properly from the beginning, I could have saved myself months of stress and thousands of dollars.

So, do the homework. All of it. Before you fall in love with a space, before you quit your day job, before you invest your life savings in a dream.

Because once you're in it, once you've made commitments and signed leases and hired people, walking away becomes almost impossible, even when every rational part of your brain is screaming that you should cut your losses.

"Let's do it," Robert said finally. "I mean what's the alternative? We have to do it, right?"

I agreed to the increase. And got permission to cut my hole leading to the street.

"Congrats," Janet said when I signed the amended lease. "Hope your daycare works out."

By the time I finally got my license—four months and approximately almost fifty thousand dollars in modifications, permits, and extortion later—I understood something fundamental about running a business in New York City: everyone wants a piece of your dream. The city wants permits. The landlord wants rent increases. The inspectors want compliance.

But if you want it badly enough, you figure out how to give them what they want while still holding onto what you're building.

I wanted it. Despite the circular paperwork, despite the egress requirements, despite Frank and his clipboard of doom, I wanted it badly enough to make it work.

The day the license arrived in the mail, Robert and I sat in my kitchen, staring at the official document like it was made of gold.

"I can't believe it," I said.

"You survived Article 47," he replied.

And somehow, that felt like the biggest victory yet.

CHAPTER 3

Breaking Free

Here's the part I haven't mentioned: at that time, I was still working my 9-to-5.

I was chief of staff for a hedge fund bro who, to put it mildly, had all the cliché makings of a rom-com villain. The kind who only dated Victoria's Secret models and went through them like, well, Victoria's Secret undies. He liked his cars fast, his relationships brief, and I'm pretty sure he singlehandedly kept the local florist in business with his nonstop orders of huge Casablanca lily arrangements. He had a bouquet for every occasion: breakup, make-up, made-another-mistake.

I remember one particular situation when he called me at 7 a.m. in a panic.

"Kettia, I need you to handle something urgent," he said. I could hear the stress in his voice. I grabbed a pen, ready for some market crisis or client emergency.

"The florist screwed up my order. Sent roses instead of lilies. Giselle, or was it Gabrielle? She specifically said she hated roses after that thing with her ex. Can you fix this?"

I stared at my phone. "You want me to...fix your flower situation?"

"It's a disaster. She's coming to the Hamptons this weekend. If she sees roses, she'll think I wasn't listening when she told me that story."

I spent the next hour of my morning calling every high-end florist in the Hamptons, explaining that my boss needed an emergency lily intervention for his weekend romance. This was my life. This was what my expensive education and years of fashion industry experience had led to: flower crisis management for a man who couldn't remember his girlfriend's name but could recite the closing prices of every stock in his portfolio.

And all the while, my phone was buzzing with texts from Robert and Sarah about the daycare.

"Sophie had a great morning! She's obsessed with the new art station."

"We need more construction paper and maybe some new books for the reading corner."

"Two more families called asking about enrollment."

It was a crazy time. I was working full-time for a demanding, erratic boss, juggling high-maintenance clients, managing chaos at work while also managing chaos at home. But the chaos at home was the good kind, the kind that comes from building something meaningful. The chaos at work was just...chaos.

By now, Sarah and Maria had been with me for about six months, and they were everything I'd hoped for and more. Meanwhile, Robert was stepping into his new role as manager with love and grace, and I was backseat driving with spreadsheets and text messages between meetings.

I'd created a whole system for staying connected to the daycare from my office. I had a shared doc where Sarah and Maria could update me on daily activities, incidents and supplies I needed. I reviewed enrollment applications during my lunch breaks. I returned parent phone calls from the bathroom, whispering updates about their child's day while pretending to use the facilities.

The irony wasn't lost on me. I was spending my days managing the personal life of a man who treated relationships like stock trades, while my own life's work was happening thirty blocks away without me.

On paper, I was doing really well. Great money. Excellent healthcare. Stability. The daycare was generating modest income, but not enough to replace my corporate salary, not yet. And with three young children, walking away from health insurance felt like playing Russian roulette with our family's future.

I was hella scared to quit.

What if the daycare didn't work out? What if the waitlist disappeared overnight? What about the health insurance? Because when you've got little kids, it's not just about the paycheck. It's about the coverage. You're one ear infection, one ER visit, one freak accident away from a financial tailspin.

But I was also tortured by the thought of staying. What was the point of starting this business in the first place if I couldn't even be present for it? I had created this beautiful, intentional, nurturing space but I was still spending most of my days answering emails for a man-child with a Ferrari and a Rolodex of supermodels.

The breaking point was building for weeks before I recognized it.

And then it came.

It was June. The last week of school. Alexi's kindergarten class was having their end-of-year showcase, a moving up ceremony that signals the transition to grade school. It's one of those precious, tiny moments you can't get back. It was scheduled right in the middle of the day, around 11 a.m.

I'd known about it for weeks. It was written on our family calendar in red ink, circled twice. I'd even mentioned it to my boss a month earlier during one of our weekly check-ins.

"I'll need to step out for a couple hours on the 15th," I said casually. "My son's kindergarten graduation."

He nodded absently, scrolling through emails on his phone. "Sure, sure. Whatever you need."

But that Tuesday morning, as I was gathering my things to leave for the showcase, he appeared at my desk with a stack of papers and that particular expression that meant someone else's emergency was about to become my problem.

"I need you to stay," he said, dropping the papers in front of me. "The Singapore client moved up their call. They want to review the entire portfolio before markets open there."

I looked at the clock. 10:30 a.m.; he caught me just as I was throwing my bag over my shoulder to head out. The showcase started in thirty minutes.

"I can't," I said, stepping aside and pushing my chair under my desk. "I told you about this. My son's graduation."

He looked at me like I'd suggested burning down the office.

"Kettia, this is a twenty-million-dollar client. Your kid will have other graduations."

The words hung in the air between us. Other graduations. As if a five-year-old's first major school milestone was some interchangeable commodity. As if the look of pride on my son's face when he saw me in the audience could be replicated on demand.

"No," I said, surprising myself with how steady my voice sounded. "Actually, he won't have other kindergarten graduations. This is it. This is the only time he'll be 5 years old, wearing that construction paper cap he made, looking for his mom in the crowd."

My boss's face was turning that particular shade of red that usually preceded someone getting fired or a toddler's tantrum.

"I need you here," he said, his voice getting harder. "This is your job."

"And that," I said, walking toward the elevator, "is my son."

I could feel the entire office watching as I waited for the elevator doors to open. My heart was pounding so hard I was sure everyone could hear it. Part of me was already calculating how long it would take to find another job, whether I could afford COBRA for health insurance, what I'd do if I couldn't find something quickly.

But a bigger part of me, the part that had spent four months watching Sarah and Maria love other people's children the way I wanted to love my own, knew I couldn't turn around.

The elevator doors opened, and I stepped inside.

Twenty minutes later, I was sitting in the auditorium at PS9, watching Alexi march across a makeshift stage in his handmade graduation cap. When he spotted me in the audience, his entire face lit up. He waved so enthusiastically he nearly knocked over the girl next to him.

"That's my mom!" I heard him whisper to his teacher, pointing directly at me.

That's when I knew. This wasn't just about missing a kindergarten graduation. This was about what I was teaching my children about priorities, about showing up, about what mattered. Here I was, running a business dedicated to nurturing children, to creating beautiful spaces where kids felt valued and loved, and I was missing my own child's milestones to manage flower deliveries for a man who couldn't remember his girlfriend's name.

After the ceremony, Alexi ran to me, still wearing his paper cap.

"Mom, did you see me walk across the stage? Did you hear what I said about the solar system?"

"I saw everything," I told him, and I meant it. For the first time in months, I had seen everything. I was completely present, completely there.

Walking out of that school, holding Alexi's hand while he chatted about summer plans and first grade, I made a decision.

I wasn't going back to that office.

I walked out of that kindergarten classroom, my son beaming with pride, and I knew: this was my job now. This business. These children. My family. My vision. I had made the decision, finally. Or maybe the decision had made me.

Ready or not, I was going to run this business. And I was going to make it work.

CHAPTER 4

Open by 8!

Running a home daycare meant my day started before sunrise and ended well after the last child went home.

Every night, after Robert and I got our own kids to bed, I went downstairs and transformed our basement back into its morning perfection. Toys sorted into their designated baskets. Art supplies restocked. Surfaces wiped down with the special non-toxic cleaner the health department required. The reading corner fluffed and arranged just so.

By 10:00 p.m., the space looked like a magazine spread again. By 4:30 a.m., my alarm went off.

The morning routine was like choreographing a small orchestra. Get Chloe and Alexi fed, dressed, and ready for their respective schools. Pack their lunches, check their backpacks, make sure homework was signed and permission slips were tucked into folders. Then race them through their morning routines and out the door for drop-offs.

By 7:45 a.m., I was back home, transforming myself from "school mom" to "daycare director." Fresh clothes, fresh energy, fresh smile. At 8:00 a.m. sharp, my first little student would arrive.

Open by 8!

Flynn was always first.

He was the fifteen-month-old son of my neighbor Julia, and in many ways, he was the other reason, besides Sophie, that Smarter Toddler existed. Julia and I had met on the playground a few months earlier, both of us pushing our toddlers on swings, both of us venting about the impossible childcare situation in Manhattan. Julia wasn't just a playground acquaintance, she was my neighbor. I didn't even realize we lived in the same building until we started commiserating about childcare struggles during our regular playground visits.

It was an unusually warm day for January in New York. The playground was more packed than usual. Parents who'd normally be cooped up inside this time of year were taking advantage of a spring-like day and came out to soak up the sunshine while their kids ran wild after weeks of indoor energy.

Julia and I claimed a bench near the swings, both of us in that familiar parent mode of half-watching our toddlers while trying to steal a few minutes of adult conversation. Flynn was in his rebellious shoe phase, constantly trying to kick them off the moment Julia got them on.

"Flynn, honey, shoes stay on at the playground," Julia said for the third time, wrestling a tiny sneaker back onto his squirming foot. She looked up at me with that exasperated parent expression I knew so well. "I'm desperate, Kettia. I literally fired my sitter last week."

"What happened?" I asked, pulling Sophie back from a collision course with the monkey bars.

Julia secured Flynn's shoe with a double knot and sat back with a sigh. "She was stealing my clothes. For months, apparently. I only figured it out when she showed up wearing this very specific blouse my sister-in-law brought me from a street market in Portugal. It wasn't from some store where we might have bought the same thing. It was completely one-of-a-kind."

"Oh my God, that's awful," I said, watching Flynn toddle toward the slide while Julia kept one eye on him.

"So I went looking," she continued, her voice getting more animated as the story unfolded. "A pair of Louboutins—can you imagine? My only pair, gone! As if I would never notice. A cashmere shawl that was an anniversary gift. Some jewelry. She was strategic about it, taking things I wouldn't miss right away."

Flynn had made it to the bottom of the slide and was clapping for himself. Julia waved at him proudly before turning back to me.

"Now I can't trust anyone alone in my house with my baby," she said, her voice getting quieter. "I don't know what I'm going to do for childcare."

That's when I told her about the daycare I was planning to start in my basement.

"Really?" Her whole face lit up. "Can I see it?"

A week later, she was standing in our transformed rec room, Flynn on her hip, both of them taking in the space Robert and I had created.

"This is beautiful," she said, running her hand along the smooth wooden edge of our low shelving. "It doesn't look like any daycare I've ever seen."

Flynn was already squirming to get down, drawn to the basket of wooden blocks near the art station. "When can we start?" she asked.

I laughed, "Soon. Going through licensing. Say a prayer for me!"

This was back in January, and I was still working my full time job and doing tours one evening a week at 6 p.m.. Julia enrolled Flynn on the spot and became my unofficial marketing team. She told every mom at the playground, every parent at music class, every neighbor in our building. Some of these families signed up without even seeing the space, just on her recommendation.

By the time our license finally came through that April of 2003, I had my twelve slots filled and a waiting list of almost a dozen more families.

Open by 8!

One of those early enrollees was a sweet, shy little girl named Margaret.

She arrived on a Tuesday morning in early May, clutching something I'd never seen before: a Nelson Mandela doll. I didn't even know they made them. She was tiny for her age, with wispy blonde hair and enormous blue eyes that seemed to take in everything.

Her father walked her down our basement stairs, and I saw the apprehension in both their faces. Most toddlers her age struggled with separation anxiety. I'd built transition periods into our enrollment process—short visits at first, gradually building up to full days.

I knelt down to Margaret's eye level.

"Hi, Margaret," I said softly. "I'm Miss Kettia. Welcome to our school."

What happened next surprised everyone.

Margaret let go of her father's hand, walked straight to me, and wrapped her tiny arms around my neck in the biggest hug. Not a scared, clingy hug but a welcome hug. Like she was greeting an old friend she hadn't seen in a while.

Over her head, I caught her father's eye. He shrugged with a smile that said, 'Your guess is as good as mine.'

"She doesn't usually do that," he said. "She's pretty shy with new people."

Margaret had already pulled back from our hug and looked around the room with those wide blue eyes, still clutching her Nelson Mandela doll.

"This is where I'm going to play?" she asked in her small, clear voice.

"This is where you're going to learn and play and make friends," I told her.

She nodded solemnly, like we'd just made an important business agreement.

As the weeks went by, I got to know Margaret and her family better. Her father was one of the kindest men I'd ever met—soft-spoken, thoughtful, the kind of parent who listened when his child spoke instead of just waiting for his turn to talk.

Every morning, his goodbye ritual was the same.

"I love you, Margaret," he'd say, kneeling down for one last hug.

"I love you too, Daddy."

"Be kind today, okay?"

Most parents said "I love you" or "See you later" or "Be good." But Margaret's father always said "Be kind." Margaret shook her head, like he'd given her the most important assignment in the world.

Watching her throughout the day, I saw how that simple daily reminder shaped her interactions with the other children. Margaret was the one who noticed when someone was sad. She shared her snacks without being asked. She helped younger kids reach toys on higher shelves. But whenever I was in the room she wouldn't leave my side. She followed me everywhere. Strangely enough, my own daughter Sophie didn't care. When daycare was in session, Sophie forgot I was her mother. She was so preoccupied with new friends that weren't her siblings, teachers doting on her, activities that took all her energy that by the end of the day she could barely keep her eyes open through dinner.

That Nelson Mandela doll came to school with Margaret every day, and gradually I learned the story behind it. Margaret's family believed in teaching children about heroes and changemakers from the very beginning. The doll wasn't just a toy—it was a conversation starter, a way to talk about kindness and justice and standing up for what's right.

"She asked for it specifically," her father told me one morning. "We were at the toy store, and she saw it and said, 'He looks kind, Daddy. Like you.'"

These were the families filling our little basement daycare. Parents who thought about the messages they were sending, who cared about more than just having somewhere safe to leave their children while they worked. They wanted partners in raising thoughtful, curious, kind human beings.

I'd created a space that attracted exactly those people.

It turned out that other parents had been longing for exactly this kind of experience for their children, even if they couldn't quite describe what was missing from the traditional daycare model. They knew it when they walked into our space—this feeling of, "Yes, this is what I wanted for my child but couldn't find anywhere else."

That's when I knew this wasn't just about solving our childcare problem. I was creating something that had never existed before, a daycare that looked like a page from a home magazine but functioned like the most nurturing home you could imagine.

By October, just four months after I'd quit my corporate job, it became obvious I had a problem.

A good problem, but still a problem.

I was standing in our basement at 6 p.m. on a Wednesday, watching the last parent collect their child, when I really looked at our space for the first time in weeks. Twelve toddlers had been living, learning, and playing in this room for ten hours. Despite our best efforts to maintain order, it looked like a toy store had exploded.

Every basket was overflowing. Every shelf was packed. The reading corner that had seemed so spacious in the beginning now felt cramped when more than three children tried to use it at once. During active play time, I was practically stacking kids on top of each other.

"We need more space," Sarah said, reading my mind as she gathered scattered blocks into a basket.

It wasn't just the physical space that was bursting at the seams. The waiting list Julia had helped me build through playground word-of-mouth had taken on a life of its own.

Parents were calling daily. They weren't just neighbors or friends of current families but referrals from pediatricians, from other parents at music classes across the Upper West Side, from nannies who'd heard about us in the park.

"I got a call today from a family in Tribeca," I told Robert that night as we cleaned up from dinner. "Tribeca. They're willing to commute all the way up here because they heard about what we're doing here."

The waiting list had grown to over forty families. For twelve spots.

What we created had clearly struck a nerve. But I was also hitting a wall that felt impossible to break through. I could either accept the limitations of a home-based program, or I could figure out how to take this to the next level.

Robert was right when he reminded me that we had never settled for good enough. Not in London, not in Paris, not in New York. Together we'd always believed we could create something better. That's what brought us from fashion dreams in Europe to basement daycare innovation in Manhattan. And that's what would carry us forward now.

If I wanted to serve more families, I had to move to a commercial space.

I started keeping a notebook of comments from tours:

"This feels like a home, not an institution."

"My daughter's current daycare looks like a fast food playspace. This looks like somewhere I'd want to spend time."

"You can see the thought that went into every detail."

"Finally, someone who actually thinks about the space where children are spending most of their time."

The feedback was intoxicating but also overwhelming. Every "yes" meant disappointing three other families. Every enrollment call meant having to tell someone else I had no space.

During pickup time, I watched parents linger in our basement, reluctant to leave. Margaret's father arrived early just to sit in our reading corner and flip through books with her. Flynn's mom, Julia brought coffee for Sarah and Maria, turning pickup into a mini social hour. In the beginning, I kept a big bowl of snacks like mini trail bars and pistachios on a table for the parents and teachers. Then I realized that was extending pickup even more, so I stopped supplying. This way, people wouldn't linger.

Open by 8!

"This place reminds me so much of preschools in Denmark," one expat mom told me during a particularly chaotic Friday pickup. "Really glad I found you guys. My daughter talks about her school friends all weekend. She's excited to come back on Monday."

The children were thriving in ways that surprised even me. Margaret had gone from shy and clingy to confident and social, organizing elaborate tea parties with her Mandela doll and whoever wanted to join. Flynn, barely eighteen months old, was already showing signs of the empathy and gentleness that our environment seemed to nurture.

But success brought its own pressures.

I was operating at capacity every single day. No room for error, no space for growth, no ability to accommodate even one more family. And the licensing regulations were clear: twelve children maximum in a home-based program.

If I wanted to serve more families, I had to move to a commercial space.

One evening, seven months after opening, I told Robert, "I need to start looking."

The idea of commercial real estate felt like jumping from a kiddie pool into the ocean. Everything would be bigger, more expensive, more complicated. It wasn't that there were additional expenses I hadn't considered. It was that every single expense would multiply. Residential rent was $3,200 a month. Commercial spaces I was looking at started at $8,000 and went up from there.

Rent was just the beginning. Instead of two teachers, I'd need ten to twelve staff members. Instead of furnishing one basement room, I'd be outfitting 4,500 square feet of specialized learning spaces. Instead of general liability insurance for twelve children, I'd need coverage for fifty-five kids and a dozen adults. Everything was relative to scale, but the scale was enormous.

On paper, the practical answer was obvious: this was too much, too fast, too risky. We'd only been operating for eight months. But I wasn't thinking practically. I was thinking inevitably. From the moment we opened at capacity with a growing waitlist, the question wasn't if we'd expand, but when. I had this deep, almost spiritual certainty that this was exactly what I was meant to be doing. I didn't know where the funding would come from, but I knew it would come. You have to have the stomach for risk in entrepreneurship. It's not for the weak. And sometimes, you have to proceed on faith that the path will reveal itself as you walk it.

"Do we even know how to do this?" Robert asked, scrolling through commercial listings online.

We didn't. Neither of us had ever leased commercial space, nor negotiated with landlords who spoke in terms of triple net leases and percentage rent. I didn't have a traditional business degree, nor connections in commercial real estate. We had no track record beyond six months of running a basement daycare.

But I had something else: a waiting list of families who believed in what I was building, and the growing certainty that I'd created something worth expanding.

My first commercial space tour was a ground-floor retail location on Columbus Avenue. The landlord's agent, a sharp-suited man named Dave, met us at the door with a handshake and a smile that didn't quite reach his eyes.

"So you want to open a daycare," he said, looking around like he was trying to picture finger paintings on the pristine white walls.

"An early childhood education center," I corrected, already sensing this wasn't going well.

The space was beautiful—high ceilings, great natural light, perfect location. But as Dave walked us through the details, the obstacles multiplied.

"You'll need special licensing for this use," he said. "Health department approval, fire department signoff, zoning verification. That could take months."

Robert and I exchanged glances. I'd already been through licensing hell once so that part didn't scare me.

"And the rent?" I asked.

"Twelve thousand a month, triple net. Plus first and last month, security deposit, and broker fee. You're looking at about fifty thousand to get in."

Fifty thousand dollars. Just to get in the door!

"I'll need to see three years of financial records," Dave continued, "plus personal guarantees from both of you."

"I've been operating for about 8 months," I said.

His smile became even more strained. "Then I'll need to see other proof of financial stability. Assets, credit reports, letters of recommendation from business partners."

What he didn't say, but what hung in the air between us, was: *What makes you think you can afford this?*

I toured six more spaces over the next month. Each one followed the same pattern: initial enthusiasm from the listing agent, followed by growing skepticism once they understood who I was and what I was trying to do.

"First-time commercial tenants are risky," one broker told me bluntly. "Especially in childcare. High liability, lots of regulations, frequent turnover."

Another landlord took one look at my seven-month financial history and said, "Come back when you've been in business for at least two years."

By December, I panicked. My waiting list continued growing, but I was stuck in a basement that couldn't legally hold even one more child. Parents were calling daily, asking when I might have openings. There was a sense of growth or bust.

"Maybe I'm thinking too big," I said to Robert one night, dejected after another rejection. "Maybe I should just be content with what I have."

"Honey, don't think like that," he said, looking up from his sketchbook where he'd been drawing plans for a larger space. "When have we ever been content with what other people think you should have?"

The space hunting process stretched another three months. I looked at more than a dozen different properties across Manhattan–from cramped basement spaces in Midtown to overpriced storefronts in both Upper East and Upper West Sides. Each viewing was an education in just how unprepared I was for the commercial real estate world.

Robert and I arrived at each appointment nervous but hopeful, clutching our folder of financial documents and licensing paperwork like armor. I peered through windows, measuring spaces with my eyes, imagining where the reading corner would go, how the natural light would hit the art station.

Most landlords took one look at the short operating history and politely declined. A few were more direct.

"You need at least two years in business before I'd consider you," one broker told me flatly. "Childcare is high-risk. Too much liability, too many regulations."

Others were intrigued by my waitlist but concerned about my lack of collateral.

"What happens if the business fails?" a landlord in Chelsea asked. "Who's going to pay the rent?"

The process was draining, but giving up wasn't an option. Every rejection just meant I had to find another way forward.

Eventually, I found a space that felt like destiny.

It was a ground-floor corner unit on West 89th Street, just a few blocks from our apartment. Beautiful natural light streamed through large windows. High ceilings made the space feel open and airy. A layout perfect for my vision. I could already see where each learning area would go.

The realtor's name was Ted. He was from a family-owned real estate development group based out of Briarwood, Queens. They owned several buildings in this Upper West Side neighborhood, most of them ground floor commercial properties of high-end condos. During our initial walkthrough, he seemed genuinely interested in my concept.

"My granddaughter goes to one of those chain daycares," he told us, running his hand along the window frame. "Looks like a doctor's office. What you're describing sounds much better."

I put in my application immediately. Three days later, the landlord's assistant called to say he wanted to move forward. I sent over my financials, my licensing documentation, letters of recommendation from current families. Everything they had requested.

The phone calls that followed were promising. I mostly dealt with the landlord's rep, a gentleman named Joe who I had not met in person. He asked thoughtful questions about my curriculum, my safety protocols, and my plans for growth. He appreciated that I wasn't just looking for the cheapest space available. I wanted a partnership with a landlord who understood my mission.

"I think this could work," he said during our final phone conversation. "Let me draw up a lease."

When that lease arrived in my inbox, Robert and I sat at our kitchen table, reading every line like it was a love letter. The rent was higher than I'd hoped but within my stretched budget. The terms were fair. This was really happening.

I was ecstatic. This was the culmination of months of dreaming and planning, of late-night conversations about what the expanded program could become. I could already picture the grand opening, the ribbon cutting, the excited faces of all those families on my waiting list.

"The landlord is sending his foreman to meet us at the space to do a final walkthrough." I told Robert after getting off the phone with the landlord's office. "Tomorrow at 2 p.m.. Then we can sign the lease."

That night, I barely slept. I kept imagining walking through my new space, seeing it through the eyes of the children who would soon fill it with laughter and learning.

The next afternoon, Robert and I arrived at the building fifteen minutes early. I stood on the sidewalk, holding hands with Robert, both of us practically vibrating with nervous energy.

"I can't believe this is really happening," I whispered.

Robert squeezed my hand. "You did it, babe. You actually did it."

Nope. "We did it!" I declared.

At exactly 2 p.m., a pickup truck pulled up to the curb. Out stepped a man in his forties wearing work boots and a flannel shirt. This had to be him. I was holding my breath, and silently told myself to breathe. I reminded myself he's only here to meet us and assess any modifications I might need for my licensing requirements.

Robert and I walked toward him with huge smiles, extending my hand. "Hi, I'm Kettia, and this is Robert. We're so excited to—"

He stopped mid-stride. His smile faltered, then disappeared entirely. He looked from me to Robert, then back to me, his expression shifting from friendly anticipation to something much colder.

"You're the...the daycare people?" he asked, though he clearly already knew the answer.

The way he said "daycare people" made it sound like we were some other species he'd never encountered before.

"That's us," Robert said, his voice still warm despite the obvious shift in energy.

Let me explain something: with our last name, Ming, most people assume we're Asian. And more often than not, when I show up in person, I am met with surprise—sometimes curiosity, sometimes confusion, and on occasions like this, an unmistakable coldness that spoke volumes about their assumptions.

Being Black shaped our interactions in ways that were far from subtle, especially in moments when people had already formed expectations about who we were supposed to be.

Joe recovered quickly, forcing his professional smile back into place, but the damage was done. We could all feel it.

"Right, well, let's take a look at the space," he said, fumbling with his keys.

The walkthrough that should have been celebratory became awkward and tense. Every question Robert asked about electrical outlets was met with curt, minimal answers. When I mentioned my plans for natural lighting, the foreman barely responded.

I kept trying to engage him, asking about the neighborhood, the building's history, anything to rebuild the friendly rapport I thought I was walking into. But Joe's responses were clipped, professional, and distinctly cold.

"The space looks perfect for what we're planning," I said as we finished the tour, hoping to end on a positive note.

"Uh-huh," he replied, already heading toward the door. "I'll let Mr. Petrosky know how it went."

Robert and I walked back toward Columbus Avenue in confused silence.

"That was weird, right?" I finally said. "The way he just...changed when he saw us?"

"Yeah," Robert said quietly. "That was definitely weird."

But I pushed the uncomfortable feeling aside. I'd gotten this far. The lease was drawn up. The foreman's personal reaction didn't matter as long as the space worked for my needs.

Less than two hours later, my phone rang.

"Ms. Ming? This is Lynn from Mr. Petrosky's office."

"Hi Lynn! Are we all set for the lease signing?" I replied.

There was a pause that made my stomach drop.

"I'm afraid there's been a development. We received another application this afternoon, a very strong application. The new applicant came through with everything. Mr. Petrosky has decided to move forward with them instead."

The words hit me like a physical blow. "I'm sorry, what?"

"The space is no longer available. I'm sorry for any inconvenience."

"But I already went through the application process. I had the walkthrough. You sent me a lease."

"The other applicant's offer was just...more attractive. I'm sure you understand."

I didn't understand. What I understood was that two hours after a foreman met us in person, my "attractive" application had suddenly become inadequate.

Just like that. No warning. No counter-offer. No chance to match whatever this mysterious "more attractive" application had offered.

Gone.

I hung up and immediately called Robert.

"They gave it to someone else," I said, my voice barely above a whisper.

"What? How is that possible?"

"Another application. Apparently more attractive than mine."

We were both quiet for a long moment.

"You think it was because of...?" Robert started.

"I don't know," I said, though deep down, I did know. "Maybe. Probably."

That night, Robert and I sat on our couch, sharing a bottle of wine, trying to process what had happened. Disappointed didn't begin to cover it. I was furious, but it was a complicated kind of anger mixed with humiliation, disbelief, and a familiar rage that I'd felt before but never quite this sharply. How to process being rejected not for your qualifications, but for your skin color? Especially when it wasn't just my dream on the line anymore. I had others counting on me, and I felt like I was letting them down.

"We had everything they asked for," Robert said, staring at the lease papers I'd printed out but would never sign. "Our credit was good. Your business plan was solid and the references were stellar."

"Everything except the right skin color," I said.

The words hung in the air between us. We both knew it was true, but saying it out loud made it real in a way that was both liberating and devastating.

"So what do we do now?" Robert asked.

I looked around our living room, thinking about the families on my waiting list, the children who were counting on me to expand, the teachers who believed in my vision.

"We keep looking," I said. "But next time, we're going to be smarter about it."

That's when I decided to take matters into my own hands. If the traditional real estate world wasn't going to welcome me with open arms, maybe it was time to find someone who understood exactly what I was up against.

Back in those days, if you needed help with anything–finding an apartment, a date, or an investor–you turned to the classifieds. The Village Voice, The New York Times, Daily News. It was a Wild West of opportunity and scammers, but often you found exactly what you needed.

I decided to place an ad in The Village Voice and The Times: "Small business seeking commercial real estate guidance. Established daycare looking to expand. Serious inquiries only."

The responses were...educational.

My rule of thumb was simple: I'm not paying anyone upfront to find me money. If someone asked for fees before delivering results, they were out. There were plenty of fraudsters trolling those classifieds, and I had to be patient enough to kiss a lot of frogs before finding my prince.

I also had my own screening method: I looked at their shoes.

Call it superficial, but people with real money invest in quality footwear. This wasn't some random hunch I'd developed. It was ten years of fashion education talking: four years of high school at Fashion Industries, four years of college studying fashion merchandising, two years in Paris completely immersed at the highest levels of fashion, and now married to one of the most fashion-conscious men I know. Some things become universal laws when you've lived and breathed the industry that long.

It's like Elle Woods in *Legally Blonde*, when she breaks the case wide open by knowing that a straight guy wouldn't know the difference between her black shoes and last season's designer ones. When you've spent that much time around fashion, you develop an eye for authenticity that goes way beyond clothes.

Real money whispers; it doesn't shout. Someone with genuine wealth invests in good Italian leather shoes that are built to last, not flashy designer logos or whatever's trending on Instagram. They understand the difference between price and value, between quality and marketing. And they take care of their investments—well-maintained leather, proper shoe trees, resoled when necessary.

Fake money? Fake money buys whatever looks expensive.

This theory was confirmed when one potential "investor" showed up to meet me wearing shoes that appeared to be made of vinyl. The synthetic material was actually cracking where the laces met the side of the shoe, creating these sad little fissures that I found so distracting I could barely focus on his pitch.

"I've helped dozens of small businesses get off the ground," he was saying, while I stared at his deteriorating footwear. "My specialty is finding creative financing solutions."

Then he mentioned, almost as an aside, that he was currently living with his mother to "save money for investments."

Robert and I shared a look across the coffee shop table. This was definitely not our guy.

After a decade in fashion, you learn to read people through their choices. And someone who can't invest in decent shoes for a business meeting probably can't invest in your business either.

Three weeks and seven questionable meetings later, my phone rang.

"Is this the lady with the daycare ad?" The voice was gravelly, distinctly Queens.

"Yes, that's me."

"George Gordon. I do real estate deals. Been in the business thirty years. You looking for space or money?"

"Space first, then probably money."

"Where you at now?"

"Upper West Side. Home-based program, but I'm outgrowing it."

"How many kids?"

"Twelve now, but I've got a waiting list of fifty families."

There was a pause. "Fifty families? For twelve spots? What the hell are you doing over there?"

I laughed. "Something different, apparently."

"All right. Meet me tomorrow. And bring your financials—real ones, not some bullshit projections."

The next day, Robert and I stood outside a corner Starbucks on West 73rd Street and Columbus Avenue, where I took all my meetings, waiting for George Gordon to arrive. A black Town Car pulled up, and out stepped a man in his sixties wearing a perfectly tailored navy suit and beautiful leather shoes. Italian. Well-maintained. The kind that cost more than some people's rent.

"You the daycare people?" he asked, extending a firm handshake.

George Gordon looked like central casting's version of an old-school New York real estate guy. Sharp suit, sharper wit, and a Rolodex that probably contained half the landlords in Manhattan. I told him everything. About my growing daycare, my impossible waitlist, and especially about the humiliating experience on West 89th Street.

"Let me get this straight," George said, leaning back in his chair after I'd finished the story. "You had the lease in hand, passed the walkthrough, and then suddenly there's a 'better offer' two hours after the foreman met you?"

"That's exactly what happened."

George's expression darkened. "What's the address?"

I told him. He wrote it down in his little notebook.

"That space still available?"

"As far as I know, yes. Why?"

"Because that's your space," he said with a big grin, "They just don't know it yet."

I looked at him skeptically. "George, they already rejected me. Why would they..."

"They rejected you because you played by their rules. I don't play by their rules. So, tell me about this waitlist," he said.

I explained how I'd built my program, the kind of families I attracted, the word-of-mouth referrals that had created more demand than I could handle.

George was quiet for a long moment as he looked around the coffee shop.

"You know what I like about you?" he said finally. "You're not trying to sell me some pie-in-the-sky dream. You've already got customers lined up. That's real business."

He looked out the large windows facing the street.

"I think I can help you. But fair warning: it's not going to be cheap, and it's not going to be easy. New York doesn't make it easy for people like you to get ahead."

"People like me?" I asked.

George's smile was knowing but not unkind. "First-time commercial tenants. No family money. No connections. Just hustle and a good idea."

What he didn't say, but what I was about to learn was that for people who looked like me, the obstacles would be even greater.

What happened next was like watching a master class in old-school New York real estate warfare. For two weeks, George tried calling Mr. Petrosky's office. Every call went unreturned. His emails disappeared into the void. The man who had once been so responsive to my family-friendly daycare concept had apparently vanished.

"They're screening my calls," George told me after a week of radio silence. "But that's okay. I know where they eat lunch."

George had done his homework. Apparently he'd figured out that Mr. Petrosky's office staff ordered from the same deli every Tuesday and Thursday. So George started showing up with lunch. For everyone.

"I walked in with bags," he told me later, laughing. "Sandwiches, soup, cookies, coffee. Enough food for the whole office. They started looking forward to my visits."

For two weeks straight, George appeared at their office with lunch, sat in their reception area, and made himself indispensable. He'd chat with the staff about their kids, their weekend plans, their favorite restaurants. He'd talk about whatever game was happening. He'd help move boxes.

"I became furniture," he said. "They stopped seeing me as an intruder and started seeing me as part of the office."

The breakthrough came on a late afternoon. Mr. Petrosky was rushing out to his car when George intercepted him in the parking garage.

"Mr. Petrosky! George Gordon. I've been trying to reach you about that corner space on 89th Street."

"The space is leased," Mr. Petrosky said, not slowing down.

"Funny thing about that," George said, matching his pace. "My contacts at the city tell me no new certificate of occupancy has been filed. No permits pulled. Nothing that suggests anyone's actually moving in."

Mr. Petrosky stopped walking.

"The deal fell through last week," he admitted. "Tenants got cold feet."

"Well then," George said, "I've got the perfect tenant for you. Already licensed, already operating, already proven she can navigate city bureaucracy. And she's ready to sign today."

Open by 8!

That's how George Gordon got me my lease. Not through connections or family money or institutional backing. Through persistence, charm, and the strategic deployment of Zabar's sandwiches.

But it came at a price.

A high price.

That's when I learned about the Black Tax.

George had worked his magic, but getting me approved required assembling what he called "the package." Three small-time investors would act as guarantors on the lease, people George knew believed in my concept but wanted something in return for taking the risk.

"Here's the deal," George explained, laying out the papers on his desk. "They'll guarantee your lease, which gives Petrosky the security he wants. In exchange, they get a monthly fee and 2% of your gross revenue."

"For how long?" I asked.

"In perpetuity."

Let that sink in.

Two percent of everything I'd ever make, forever, just for the privilege of getting a lease that should have been mine in the first place.

"I can't sign that. We have to negotiate that down," I asked.

We got them down to ten years. The lease itself was fifteen years, so I had five years at the end without that payment.

I went home that night and ran the numbers. Over ten years, that 2% would cost me hundreds of thousands of dollars. Money that could have gone toward teacher salaries, better materials, facility improvements, or simply my own family's security.

But what choice did I have?

I remember calling one of our friends to talk through the decision. When I explained the terms, he just shook his head and let out a long, low whistle.

"Whew," he said. "Girl, you're paying that Black tax."

And I was.

The Black Tax: the extra cost of doing business while Black. The premium I pay for access to opportunities that others get as a matter of course. The investors I need because banks won't lend to me. The guarantors I require because landlords don't trust me. The additional hoops I jump through because my word, my credit, my track record somehow isn't enough.

But I signed the lease. Because I didn't have a choice. I had families on a waitlist who'd been waiting months for me to expand. I had teachers depending on me for employment. I had children whose names I already knew, whose parents called weekly asking when I'd have space.

And I had a vision I could see so clearly, I could practically smell the paint drying.

So I paid the Black Tax.

Because the alternative—giving up, staying small, accepting limitations—wasn't acceptable.

"At least now you own something," George said as I signed the papers. "Even with the extra costs, you're building equity in your business. That's more than most people ever get."

He was right. I was building something. But I was building it with a tax that my white competitors would never have to pay.

Still, I had my lease. I had my vision. And now I had to turn an empty shell into the kind of space that would justify every extra dollar I'd been forced to spend just to get in the door.

The space had previously housed a medical practice, with a spacious waiting area and multiple small examination rooms branching off from a central hallway. I needed to completely demolish the existing layout and reimagine it as a warm, welcoming space for children. I was definitely feeling the pressure to create something that would take this vision to the next level from the basement daycare. And then, just when I thought the pressure couldn't get any heavier, I met someone else who would play a major role in keeping my dream alive.

His name was Angelo.

Open by 8!

Robert discovered him by accident. Every morning and afternoon, walking our kids to and from school, Robert passed by an Eileen Fisher store under construction on Columbus Avenue. Day after day, Robert watched the work in progress.

"The craftsmanship was incredible," Robert told me one evening. "These weren't just construction workers throwing up drywall. These guys were artists."

The attention to detail caught his eye. The precise angles of the display cases, the seamless integration of lighting, the way every surface seemed to flow into the next. Robert had worked in high-end fashion retail in Europe; he knew quality when he saw it.

One day, instead of just walking past, he went in.

"Excuse me," he said to one of the workers. "Who's your contractor? This work is beautiful."

That's how he got Angelo's information.

Robert reached out immediately and arranged to meet Angelo on-site the next week. I'm not sure what Robert was expecting, maybe a local contractor who specialized in retail. What he found was something much bigger.

Angelo Michilli was a contractor with a serious pedigree. He'd built out flagship locations for every major Italian designer lining Madison Avenue. Valentino. Gianfranco Ferré. Armani.

When those luxury brands needed their New York flagship stores to match their European standards, they called Angelo.

Angelo was a soft-spoken first-generation Italian-American who spoke fluent Italian. His wife worked in education, so he immediately understood what we were trying to create for children. But what really sealed the deal was his connection with Robert. They bonded over their shared love of design and high-end fashion. Robert could talk to him about Gianfranco Ferré's construction techniques or Armani's approach to retail spaces, and Angelo knew exactly what he meant. It felt like destiny: finding a contractor who understood both the educational vision and the aesthetic standards we demanded.

"We speak the same language," Robert told me after their first meeting, his eyes lit up with excitement. "This guy understands that every detail matters. He gets what we're trying to do."

Robert spent an hour walking Angelo through our vision—the natural materials, the child-height furniture, the way we wanted beauty and functionality to work together. Angelo listened, asked thoughtful questions, and by the end of the conversation, agreed to come see our space.

I'd already received bids from several other contractors. Most came in impossibly high, the kind of numbers that would eat my entire budget before I installed a single light fixture. A few came in suspiciously low, which was almost worse. When you're doing a buildout that has to meet dozens of city codes and licensing requirements, cheap usually means corners get cut.

Angelo's bid was high, not as high as the luxury retail guys, but definitely at the top of my range. The space was 4,500 square feet and would be licensed for 55 children. This wasn't a simple renovation; it was a complete transformation.

But Robert and I both knew he was our guy. The quality, the craftsmanship, the understanding of our vision—everything I needed to create the kind of center I was imagining.

"The question is," I said to Robert after I'd reviewed all the bids, "how do we afford him?"

That's when Robert came up with the idea that would change everything.

"What if we don't pay him?" Robert said one night as we sat in bed going over the numbers for the hundredth time.

"What if we make him a partner? He does the buildout, and he gets equity in the company."

It was brilliant. And risky. But it solved the immediate cash flow problem while bringing someone onto our team who understood quality at the level we were working with.

I had a lawyer draw up a proposal: Angelo would handle the complete buildout in exchange for 20% of the company.

When Robert presented it to him, Angelo didn't say no. But he didn't say yes either.

"I need to think about it," he said.

Days passed. Then a week. Meanwhile, my free rent period was ticking away. Every day delayed was money out of my pocket.

"Maybe he's not interested," I said to Robert.

"Or maybe he's just not good at negotiating," Robert replied.

He decided to push a little harder. Robert called Angelo directly.

"Look, we really want to work with you," he said. "What would it take to make this happen?"

More silence. More thinking. More time passing.

Finally, Robert had a realization: "He's not countering because he doesn't know how to counter. He's a craftsman, not a dealmaker."

So we came up with an idea to sweeten the deal.

With my free rent rapidly disappearing and the pressure mounting to get construction started, Robert and I invited Angelo to dinner at Arte, an old-school Italian spot on the Upper West Side. We had already offered him twenty percent of the company to do the build-out on the first location, but he still hadn't committed.

And we couldn't wait anymore.

That night, over pasta and red wine, we came prepared to make a final offer.

"We've got the lease, we've got families ready," I said, stirring my iced tea. "We just need the walls. The permits. The plumbing. The damn floors."

Angelo was more interested in talking about our time in Europe and his favorite restaurants in Italy. Finally, he turned to Robert and said "Guys, it's not the concept. I believe in the concept. I told you my wife is a preschool teacher, she loves what you're doing here."

"So what's the issue?" Robert asked.

"It's just…twenty percent feels a little thin for the risk."

I looked at Robert, then back at Angelo.

"Why didn't you say that all this time? We'll give you forty," I said.

Angelo sat back in his chair, surprised.

"Forty percent?" he repeated, like he was giving us a chance to take it back.

"You'll handle the full build-out. You'll be on standby for the second location when the time comes. Forty percent for both centers. Are you in?"

Angelo didn't answer right away. He took a sip of water. I could feel my body buzzing, part adrenaline, part something else. A deeper discomfort.

"I'll be right back," I said, standing up.

I walked down the hallway to the restroom, and as soon as I closed the stall door, I knew immediately something was wrong. The bleeding was heavy, sudden, and completely unexpected. I froze and just stared. I tried to breathe. I had just found out I was pregnant two weeks earlier. It was a surprise. A hard one. I cried when I saw the test, not out of joy or fear exactly, but from the sheer weight of it. Another baby. On top of everything else. Robert had held me and said, "We'll figure it out."

And now I was sitting in a bathroom stall at Arte, bleeding. I already knew what it meant. There was no need for confirmation. I sat there for a moment, trying to process what was happening to my body while the sounds of the restaurant continued outside. Clinking glasses, muted conversations. Life going on as normal while mine was quietly falling apart.

Two weeks of secretly panicking about how we'd manage another baby while launching a major expansion into our first commercial space. Two weeks of thinking, *This is terrible timing.* Two weeks of feeling guilty for not being immediately overjoyed.

Now, staring at the evidence that I was losing this pregnancy, I felt something completely different. Devastation. And worse:

the crushing thought that maybe I'd somehow wished this into happening.

I cleaned up the best I could, splashed water on my face, and stared at myself in the mirror. My reflection looked stressed. I told myself, *just get through the rest of dinner. You can fall apart later.*

When I got back to the table, Robert looked at me. He noticed something. He gave me a small, quiet check-in with his eyes.

I shook my head, just barely.

"You good?" Angelo asked, taking a sip of wine.

"All good," I said.

We finished dinner. We talked timelines. He agreed to the deal. Forty percent. I exhaled like it was my last breath.

The second we stepped outside, I pulled Robert to the side.

"I think I just had a miscarriage."

He stopped. "Wait, what?"

"In the bathroom. I didn't say anything in there. I couldn't."

"I knew something was wrong. You came out of the bathroom looking like you had seen a ghost." He sighed heavily and just held me. Right there, on the sidewalk outside Arte. The street noise, the headlights, the clink of glasses from the restaurant window. I cried into his coat, quietly, like I didn't want to disturb the city.

"Do we need to go to the hospital?" he asked.

"I think it's over," I said. "I think it already happened."

"I am so sorry. What can I do? What do you need?"

"Take me home, please," I whispered.

"Okay. Let's go home. We'll call the doctor in the morning."

As we walked the couple of blocks home, Robert kept his arm around me, steadying me when I stumbled slightly.

"Should we tell the kids?" he asked.

"Tell them what? They didn't know I was pregnant. I don't think we need to put them through this, too."

"Whatever you think is best."

That night, lying in bed, I stared at the ceiling while Robert held me.

"I don't know how I'm going to run around tomorrow and pretend everything's normal," I said.

"You don't have to pretend anything."

"Yes, I do," I said. I can't fall apart now, Robert. Too many people are counting on us. We just got ourselves a new partner.

We have an open house on Thursday. The accountant set up a meeting with the new banker next week."

"Honey, the business can wait."

"No, it can't. And honestly? I think I need it not to wait. I think I need to keep moving or I'll just fall apart completely."

Robert was quiet for a moment. "Then we keep moving," he said. "But we do it together."

We never told the kids. We hadn't told them about the pregnancy, so it didn't make sense to tell them about the loss. That story stayed between us. Just another thing I carried while keeping everything else running.

Giving away 40% of the company to our new partner and contractor might have seemed insane to some people, but I knew we had made the right choice as I watched Angelo transform the empty shell into something magical over the next three months.

In true high fashion, he didn't just build a daycare. He built something that looked like a high-end boutique. Instead of mannequins, I had three-year-olds.

The buildout process was like watching two artists collaborate on a canvas that happened to be 4,500 square feet. Angelo and Robert spoke the same language when it came to design. The two of them walked through the space discussing details that would never occur to most people.

"The reading corner needs softer acoustics," Robert said, running his hand along the wall where Angelo planned to install built-in bookshelves.

"Sound-absorbing panels behind the shelving," Angelo replied without missing a beat. "Covered in fabric that matches your color scheme."

Angelo understood that every choice mattered because children would be experiencing this space for up to ten hours a day. The height of door handles. The radius of corner edges. The way light would hit different areas throughout the day.

"Most contractors build for adults who visit occasionally," Angelo told me one afternoon as he showed me samples of child-safe finishes. "We're building for little people who live here."

The attention to detail was extraordinary. He created custom storage that doubled as seating areas. He built a stroller room that could easily have passed for a comfortable sitting area with dark wood panels and a bench to sit and organize your child's belongings before going into the classroom.

"This corner gets direct sunlight from 2 p.m. to 4 p.m.," he explained, marking where the art station would go. "Perfect for afternoon creative time, but we'll need UV-filtering film on the windows to protect the children's eyes."

Open by 8!

Robert was in heaven. He finally had someone who shared his obsession with getting every detail right. They spent entire afternoons debating the perfect shade of paint for the bathroom doors or the exact angle for installing coat hooks.

"Six inches lower," Robert said.

"But then the adults can't reach them comfortably," Angelo countered.

"Then we install two sets. One for kids, one for teachers."

And that's exactly what they did.

The transformation happened gradually, then all at once. One day I had empty walls and concrete floors. The next, I had a space that looked like it belonged in a design magazine but felt like the most welcoming home you'd ever visited.

Even with Angelo's expertise, I was racing against time. My target opening date was September, giving families time to transition from summer arrangements. By mid-August, I was still weeks away from being ready.

"We're going to make it," Angelo assured me, as his men worked around the clock to meet the looming deadlines.

"And if we don't?" I asked.

"Then we'll have to sneak in and work through the weekend. I've never missed a deadline, and I'm not starting with this project."

While construction was underway, I worked on licensing and staffing. Strangely enough, licensing the commercial space was far less grueling than it had been for the home daycare. Maybe I was just better prepared this time, knowing what to expect. Or maybe it was because I'd learned to build in extra time for surprises and the inevitable bureaucratic hurdles that would pop up along the way.

I knew exactly which forms to file when and which agencies to contact in what order. Angelo's expertise with building codes meant our fire department inspection went smoothly from the start, unlike the basement egress nightmare.

But staffing? That was a completely different challenge. I went from hiring two teachers serving twelve children to needing ten to twelve staff members for fifty-five kids. The math was daunting, but what I discovered was that success breeds success.

"I heard through the grapevine that you're opening a new location," was how most of my staffing conversations started. Teachers from other programs reached out to me, not the other way around. Sarah and Maria talked about our program within their professional networks, and word was spreading about this place that treated teachers like professionals and children like whole human beings.

"My friend Sarah referred me to you," one candidate told me during an interview." She says that she really loves how teachers are nurtured here as much as the kids."

That was Alinda, who became one of my lead preschool teachers. Alinda was Haitian and she shared my maiden last name, Etienne. We joked we were probably related knowing Haitian fathers. That wasn't the reason she got the job. In addition to her credentials, she embodied this warmth and gentleness about her that made me trust her with my own children. She'd been working at a daycare chain where teachers weren't allowed to teach outside of scripted lesson plans, even when children showed interest in something completely different.

"I had a group of four-year-olds who became obsessed with the construction happening outside our window," she told me. "They wanted to know everything—how cranes work, why workers wear hard hats, what all the machines were for. But we weren't allowed to deviate from the curriculum even when the kids got bored with the lesson plans and showed interest in learning something new."

I knew immediately she was perfect for us.

The hardest position to fill was my assistant director. I needed someone with both educational credentials and management experience, someone who could help me run a program nearly five times larger than what I'd been doing in my basement.

That's when Sarah suggested her former colleague from graduate school, Jessica, who'd been working as a curriculum coordinator at a Montessori school on the Upper East Side.

"She's brilliant," Sarah told me. "But she's frustrated. Her current school is super focused on parent expectations. Everything becomes academic pressure and children's natural development is an afterthought."

Jessica came in for an interview on a Friday morning while Angelo's crew was installing the reading loft. She walked through the space asking thoughtful questions about my philosophy, my approach to discipline, how I handled parent communication.

"How would you respond to a parent complaining that their three-year-old wasn't reading yet?" she asked.

"I'd ask them what they hope their child will remember about being three," I replied. "The joy of discovery, or the stress of meeting artificial milestones."

She smiled. "Really?"

By opening day, I had assembled a team of twelve educators who understood that their job wasn't crowd control—it was cultivation. Teachers who saw art projects as opportunities for expression, not picture-worthy bulletin board displays. Educators who valued children's questions more than their ability to recite the right answers.

The ratio requirements meant I needed almost six times as many staff members as the basement location, but the caliber of people who wanted to work with us had elevated significantly. My biggest challenge wasn't finding qualified candidates. It was choosing among all the excellent teachers who wanted to be part of what we were building.

Opening day felt slightly surreal. I had an out-of-body experience, like I was watching myself move through the space rather than actually being there. I looked down the hallway that had been transformed from dingy doctor's offices and couldn't believe what Robert and Angelo had accomplished. The space was breathtaking.

The transformation from medical offices to early childhood paradise was complete. Angelo had created five distinct classrooms, each designed for different age groups and learning styles. The infant room had soft lighting and cozy nursing nooks for mothers. The toddler space featured child-height sinks and toilets that actually worked properly. The preschool classroom had a reading loft that felt like a treehouse, complete with built-in cushioned seating.

But it was the central courtyard that really took my breath away. Angelo had enclosed what used to be a light well, creating an indoor-outdoor space where children could garden, paint, and play regardless of weather. Natural light streamed through the glass ceiling, and Robert had filled it with child-safe plants and a small fountain that provided the gentle sound of running water throughout the building.

I'd always imagined just me and Robert popping champagne the night before, toasting this incredible milestone. Now all I wanted was quiet time to soak it all in.

We dropped off our kids at school, which was now only four blocks from our new space, then walked over to handle last-minute details. While Robert attended to final touches, I found myself just wandering through the rooms, trying not to pinch myself. I felt like Alice in Wonderland, dropped into this magical space, thinking *Is this really mine?*

The emotions hit me all at once: pride, awe, and a little imposter syndrome. Could I really do this? I didn't have much time to spiral because my staff was arriving in thirty minutes. The children were expected in an hour.

At 9:00 a.m. exactly, Julia walked through my front door with Flynn.

"Ready for this?" she asked, looking around at my beautiful new space.

I smiled and said, "I've been ready for months."

The space filled with children's voices and parents' conversations. Angelo's beautiful craftsmanship provided the backdrop for exactly what I'd envisioned: a place where learning felt like play, where beauty wasn't a luxury but a necessity.

By lunchtime, the morning's nerves felt like a distant memory. By pickup time, I was standing in the middle of the 3-year-old classroom, watching Margaret carefully place her Mandela doll in his designated cubby, thinking: *I actually did it.*

Not that long ago, this was just a dream sketched in Robert's notebook. Now it was real, full of real children who would grow and learn and create memories within these walls.

But that's when the real work began.

Because this wasn't just about paint and pillows and licensing. This was about community.

The home-based daycare planted the roots for my vision to create community and a loving space for local kids. The commercial space helped expand that vision, and my responsibility to the neighborhood. I wasn't just caring for twelve children in my basement anymore. I was now a pillar of the community, taking care of neighborhood families, employing local teachers, and nurturing up to 55 children every single day.

The weight of that responsibility was both exhilarating and terrifying. Some mornings I walked through my beautiful space and thought, "I can't believe this is mine. I built this." Other mornings I'd lie awake at 4 a.m. thinking about payroll for twelve employees, insurance premiums, lease payments, and the fifty-five little faces counting on me to keep their world stable and safe.

It was a far cry from the woman who'd had a meltdown over Sophie's daycare situation just eighteen months earlier. Back then, I was just trying to solve my own problem. Now I was solving problems for dozens of families, creating jobs, and contributing to the local economy.

It felt like I was stewarding something bigger than myself, something that touched the lives of everyone who walked through my doors. The responsibility felt enormous, but so did the privilege of being trusted with something so important.

The families that became part of my family. The teachers who trusted me with their careers. The children I promised to protect, love, and guide every single day.

What I discovered quickly was that parents were hungry for exactly what I'd created, even if they hadn't been able to articulate it before they saw it.

"This feels different," one mother told me during her first pickup, lingering in my lobby while her daughter Madison finished putting on her shoes. "This feels like...like somewhere I'd want to spend time."

That became a common refrain. Parents didn't just drop off and run. They stayed. They asked questions about the art on the walls, the music playing softly in the background, the way I'd arranged the furniture to create intimate conversation spaces even in a large room.

Even the playlist was intentional. A journey. The vibe was everything. Whether it was Jobim's "Girl from Ipanema" or

Nina Simone's "Little Girl Blue," you were going to feel something.

At drop-off one morning, Paul, one of the dads, was in the stroller room folding up his child's stroller. He paused, looked up, and started tearing up. I wasn't sure if he was having a personal moment or if I should say something. Then he turned to me and said:

"For a second, I was back home in France. My mother played this record nonstop. I knew every word. I used to be so tired of her playing this but for a few seconds just now, I had her back."

His mother had passed away the year before.

The song playing that morning over the speakers was Charles Aznavour's "La Bohème." On a random weekday morning, in a stroller room in Manhattan, something Robert chose made this man cry with memory. That was the vibe he created.

The children were responding to the environment in ways that surprised even me. Margaret, who had been shy and clingy during my basement days, had discovered her artistic voice. She'd spend all her free time at our art station, creating elaborate paintings and narrating her artistic process to anyone who would listen, explaining why she chose purple for the sky or what her squiggly lines represented.

Flynn, now almost three, became my unofficial tour guide. When new families came to visit, he'd take their children by the hand and show them around.

"This is the art place," he'd say, pointing to my carefully organized supply station. "And this is where we read stories. And this is my favorite spot," he'd add, leading them to a cozy corner where Angelo had built a child-sized window seat overlooking the street.

Another parent pulled me aside during pickup one evening. "I need to tell you something. My son started drawing at home. Real drawing, not just scribbles. Your art teacher showed him how to look at shadows and light. He's four years old, and he's talking about shadows and light."

During pickup time, my lobby became an unofficial social hour for parents. Families who lived in the same neighborhood but had never met were suddenly organizing playdates and dinner parties. My space had become a community hub in ways I'd never anticipated.

"You know how they say it takes a village?" one Japanese mother said to me as she watched her daughter give goodbye hugs to three different friends. "You've given us a village. We don't have family here, and this place makes me feel like I have someone to call if something ever happens. My daughter has more meaningful friendships at three than I had in elementary school."

Our space had also become an unexpected expat hub. Families from Denmark, Japan, France, and Australia somehow found each other at Smarter Toddler. Word of mouth traveled fast within these international communities. Sometimes a family would return home and tell someone back in France exactly where to go when they got transferred to New York. That's how our expat community grew, one referral at a time.

These families were building their own support networks through our daycare, creating connections that went far beyond pickup and drop-off. They were finding their tribe in a city that could feel overwhelming and isolating, especially when you're far from home with young children.

The teachers were thriving too. Sarah and Maria, who had followed me from the home daycare, were joined by new educators who brought their own expertise and passion. They all shared a respect for children's intelligence and an understanding that their job wasn't just supervision, it was cultivation.

"I wake up excited to come to work," Alinda told me one morning as she was doing lesson prep for her classroom. "I've never worked anywhere that trusted me to make decisions about what the children need."

Three months after opening, I had a waiting list of over sixty families for the following year. Word was spreading not just through the neighborhood, but across Manhattan. Parents were calling from the Upper East Side, from Tribeca, asking if I had space.

"How did you hear about us?" I'd ask during phone inquiries.

"My friend's pediatrician recommended you," was a common response. Or, "I walked past the space and I want to take a tour."

Business was good. Really good.

By the end of my first year, I was operating at full capacity with a waiting list that continued to grow every month. The financial stress of those early months had given way to something I'd never experienced before: consistent profitability.

"Look at these numbers," I said to Robert one evening, reviewing my year-end financials. "We're not just breaking even. We're actually making money."

I'd found my rhythm, my families were thriving, and word-of-mouth referrals were bringing in more inquiries than I could handle.

"I have a problem," I told Robert by month fourteen.

"A good problem?"

"The best problem. I'm turning away three families for every one I can accept. These are amazing families who want exactly what I'm offering, and I have nowhere to put them."

That's when I started seriously discussing expansion.

The difference this time was that I wasn't desperately seeking help. Brokers who had ignored my calls two years earlier were now reaching out to me. But I didn't need to go hunting for my second location. I could just call George.

"I've got three spaces I want you to look at," he told me during one of our regular check-ins. "All prime locations, all perfect for what you're doing."

George had become more than just my real estate guy. After that brutal introduction to the Black Tax, I wasn't sure how to feel about him. He'd gotten me the space I needed, but at a cost that still stung every month when I wrote that 2% check. But George didn't disappear after the deal like I'd expected.

He started showing up. Not for money or business, just to see how things were going. Every few weeks, he stopped by around pickup time, chatted with parents in the lobby, watched the children play. He seemed genuinely invested in seeing the business succeed.

"I've done a lot of deals in the last forty years," he told me one afternoon as we watched parents filing in and out during pick up. "Most of them are just transactions. Money changes hands, everyone walks away. But this? This is something special. You're not just running a business, you're building community."

The check-ins became part of my routine. George would call once a month, sometimes every other month, not to sell me anything, but to hear how enrollment was going, whether I needed anything, if he could help with permits or vendor connections. When my boiler broke in the middle of winter, George knew exactly who to call. He showed up with the repair guy to make sure I wasn't getting overcharged.

"Look, I know the terms weren't ideal," he said once after I'd mentioned the ongoing 2% payments. "But you're building equity in something real. That matters more than people think."

Maybe it was guilt, or maybe I was too trusting, but George had evolved from dealmaker to mentor. He understood the game I was playing, and he wanted to see me win.

So when he said he'd curated options for me, I knew he'd already done the heavy lifting.

The first space was too small. The second had terrible natural light. But the third...

"This is it," I said to Robert the moment I walked into the ground-floor space on West 55th Street.

It was everything I'd dreamed of for a second Smarter Toddler. Spacious, bright, with the kind of architectural details that would complement our aesthetic perfectly. But what sealed the deal was the location itself.

"Look across the street," George said with a grin.

There it was: The Alvin Ailey American Dance Theater. A cultural icon that represented exactly the kind of arts integration we valued.

"The families are going to love this," Robert said, already envisioning how the energy of the dance studios across the street would influence programming.

The space was nearly twice the size of the first location, which meant we could serve more families while creating even more specialized learning environments. Robert was already sketching plans for expanded art studios, a dedicated courtyard, maybe even a small performance space where children could put on shows for their families.

"Are we ready for this?" I asked Robert as I stood in the empty space, imagining it filled with children's voices and laughter.

"We're more than ready," he said. "We've proven the model works. Now we get to do it again, but bigger and better."

For the first time since I'd started this journey, expansion felt like a choice rather than a necessity. I wasn't running from financial pressure or desperately seeking survival. I was growing from a position of strength, with the confidence that comes from knowing you've built something that truly works.

"Let's do it," I said to George. "Let's make this happen."

And right around that time, Bright Horizons came sniffing around.

Open by 8!

Bright Horizons is one of the largest childcare companies in the country. They operate hundreds of centers across the United States, primarily focused on corporate partnerships and employer-sponsored care. Think Verizon's on-site daycare or the childcare center in your office building's lobby. They were massive, well-funded, and had been steadily acquiring smaller operators to expand their reach.

The first contact came through what seemed like a casual conversation at a childcare industry conference I'd attended outside Boston in February 2007. I was there primarily for professional development, learning about subjects like new curriculum approaches and safety protocols. But these conferences are also where business happens, where people in the industry size each other up and make connections.

A well-dressed woman in her forties glanced at my name tag during the networking reception, then looked up with sudden recognition. "Oh, Smarter Toddler—you're the founder, right?" she said, extending her hand. "I'm Linda Chen from Bright Horizons. I've heard great things about your center."

It started off friendly enough. She asked about my business model, my expansion plans, and my approach to early childhood education. The kinds of questions you'd expect from someone in the industry who was genuinely curious about innovative programs.

"How are you handling the Manhattan market?" she asked. "It's notoriously difficult for independent operators."

"I'm doing well," I said, not wanting to reveal too much to someone I'd just met. "Strong enrollment, great families, solid finances."

"That's impressive," Linda said. "Have you ever thought about scaling beyond just two locations?"

There it was. The question that would change everything.

"I'm focused on getting my second center open first," I replied. "One step at a time."

But Linda wasn't done.

"Well, if you ever want to discuss growth opportunities, you should give me a call. We're always interested in partnering with quality operators who share our commitment to excellence."

She handed me her business card. Senior Vice President, Strategic Acquisitions. That title should have been my first clue about where this conversation was heading.

A few weeks later, she called.

"Hi Kettia, it's Linda from Bright Horizons. I've been thinking about our conversation in Boston. Would you be open to a more detailed discussion about your business?"

"What kind of discussion?"

"Just exploratory. We'd love to learn more about your model, and maybe share some insights about what we're seeing in the Manhattan market."

It seemed harmless enough. Market intelligence was always valuable, and I was curious about what a major player like Bright Horizons was planning for my area.

I met with them at a coffee shop near my West 89th Street location. Linda came with a colleague, a sharp-looking man in his thirties who introduced himself as their Director of Market Development.

"This is impressive," Linda said after I'd walked them through my program, my philosophy, my growth trajectory. "You've really found something special."

Looking back, I'm not entirely sure why I was so open with them. Maybe I was bored, maybe I was curious about their perspective, or maybe I was just proud of what I'd built and wanted to talk about it. But honestly? I didn't feel threatened by sharing the details.

Was any of it really proprietary? Not really. A massive chain like Bright Horizons wasn't about to suddenly convert their entire system to our hands-on, artisanal approach. Their whole business model was built on standardization and scale, the exact opposite of what made us special. You can't mass-produce the kind of intentional, relationship-based care we were providing.

I also never shared real numbers with them. They wouldn't have believed me if I had—our per-child revenue was probably double what they were used to seeing, and our waitlist-to-enrollment ratio would have seemed impossible to a corporate operation.

It felt like harmless conversation between industry colleagues. In exchange for my openness about our model, I was getting insights into how a major player viewed the Manhattan market. And I was curious—what did they see that I might be missing? What were their expansion plans for the area?

Was I trying to "out-suit the suits"? Maybe, or prove that a small operator could hold her own in conversations with corporate executives. Maybe I was just confident enough in what I'd built to know that even if they tried to replicate it, they'd never capture the essence of what made it work.

"Thank you," I said, still not sure where this was going.

"The question is," her colleague interjected, "Have you ever thought about selling?"

There it was. The real reason for the meeting.

It was a flat no.

"I appreciate the interest," I said, "but I just got started. I'm finally hitting my stride, and I'm about to open my second location. I have no interest in selling."

"Of course," Linda said smoothly. "We completely understand. But if you ever change your mind, or if you want to explore partnership opportunities that could help you scale faster, we'd love to stay in touch."

I said "sure" the way you say it to a neighbor who suggests you should get together sometime but you both know it's never going to happen.

My focus was on opening my second location. The vision was expanding, and I was just getting started, building something that could eventually become a small empire of beautiful, intentional early childhood spaces.

But Bright Horizons didn't go away.

Over the next few months, there were periodic check-ins. Casual emails asking how the expansion was going.

Honestly, it didn't bother me. I felt nothing about them, which was probably my saving grace. I don't waste mental energy on things that can easily be ignored, and since it was mostly emails —no phone calls or surprise drop-ins that would have been harder to dismiss—I could just delete and move on. Life went on, and I kept running my business.

Smarter Toddler was my baby. That's what made their attention feel more like noise than threat. When you're deeply connected to your purpose, when you know exactly why you're doing what you're doing, external validation becomes less important.

I didn't need Bright Horizons to tell me I'd built something special. I could see it every day in the faces of the children and families I served.

So I focused on what mattered: opening my second location and continuing to prove that there was a better way to care for children.

"They're persistent," I observed to Robert after I mentioned yet another Bright Horizons contact.

"They're patient," he corrected. "They're playing a long game."

What I didn't realize at the time was just how strategic their interest really was. They weren't just admiring my work from afar. They were studying me, understanding my model, and figuring out how I fit into their bigger plans for the Manhattan market.

As one of their executives would later tell me, "We want to fence in Manhattan." And I, apparently, was exactly the kind of fence post they were looking for.

CHAPTER 5

The Deal of a Lifetime

I was running late. Again.

It was a Friday evening in late spring 2014. I should have been home changing into something dressier for date night with Robert. Instead, I was still at the Hell's Kitchen location, dealing with a plumbing issue that decided to announce itself at 5:30 p.m., because of course it did. After almost twelve years of running two locations, I'd learned that emergencies don't check the clock.

Twelve years. It was hard to believe how much had changed since that first contact from Bright Horizons back in 2007, right before I'd opened our second location on 55th Street. Back then, I'd completely ignored their overtures. I was too busy, too focused on expansion, too uninterested in what some corporate chain wanted with my boutique operation.

Nothing happened for years. I kept running my business, living my life, watching my kids grow up. Then in 2012, they tried again. This time it was an acquisition executive named Don who kept reaching out with increasing persistence. Finally, I'd gotten curious enough to ask what they had in mind. I shared some basic financials, more to get him off my back than out of any real interest.

Their offer had been laughably weak. I'd declined and kept it moving, as I always did when something didn't serve my vision or my family.

But here we were in 2014, and they were back. This time with a new person in the acquisition role, someone who seemed to understand that I wasn't just another desperate small business owner looking for an exit strategy. This new contact had actually apologized for whatever had happened with Don, claiming they were serious this time.

Seven years of occasional check-ins, long silences, and corporate personnel changes had led to this moment. And honestly? I was finally ready to listen.

By the time I made it to the restaurant, Robert was already seated at our usual table, menu in hand. He looked up with that familiar smile, the one that said he knew exactly why I was late without me having to explain.

"HVAC or plumbing?" he asked as I slid into the booth.

"Plumbing. The usual suspect." I gratefully accepted the glass of wine he'd already ordered for me. "At least you got here first so we don't have to wait to order. I'm starving. I forgot to eat lunch again."

We ordered quickly, falling into our familiar Friday night rhythm. This was our sacred time, just the two of us, away from the controlled chaos of running two schools and raising three teenagers. But tonight, I had something on my mind.

"So," I said, taking a sip of wine, "I got another email from Morgan today."

Robert raised an eyebrow. Morgan had been our point of contact at Bright Horizons for the better part of two years, one of their business development executives who'd been courting us with the persistence of someone who genuinely believed in what we were doing. She followed my marathon training on Facebook, always sending congratulatory notes when I posted race results. It was all very surface-level, business-friendly stuff, but I appreciated the personal touch.

"Her boss is going to be in New York," I continued. "She asked if we'd be okay with him stopping by for a tour and maybe having a chat about our 'future together.'" I made air quotes around the last part. "I said yes, but I can always cancel if you think it's too soon."

The timing of her boss's visit was particularly interesting because Robert and I had actually been exploring another location ourselves. We'd found the perfect space in Chelsea for a third location and were deep into lease negotiations. Things were moving smoothly, the landlord was on board, and we were excited about the possibility. But Bright Horizons reaching out again made us wonder if we should at least hear what they had to say before committing to another major expansion.

Robert leaned back in his chair, considering. "Listen, we've been doing this fake dance with them for how long now? Two years? I'm fine with it if you are. We can always see what they want."

I nodded, feeling a mix of curiosity and apprehension. The truth was, I was tired. Deep-tired. The kind that doesn't go away with a weekend or a vacation. At nearly twelve years in, I was running on fumes most days. I had a staff of 36 people and over 160 families depending on me, and while I had an assistant and Robert as my partner, the division of labor wasn't exactly fifty-fifty.

Robert was brilliant at the big picture stuff: the vision, the concept, the magic that made Smarter Toddler special. He was like a museum curator, constantly reimagining our spaces, transforming them overnight for holidays and special occasions. I'll never forget that Mother's Day when parents walked in to find beautiful family photos hanging from the ceiling in glowing Japanese lanterns, each one featuring a different mom and her children. It looked like a festival of light, and the kids were absolutely mesmerized. His Chinese New Year and Halloween installations were legendary among our families.

But when it came to the daily grind (staff development, teacher ratios, licensing renewals, the broken dishwasher that flooded the kitchen, HVAC issues, insurance claims), that all fell to me. Robert was great at conceiving and birthing our ideas, but once that "baby" was here and walking around, his attention inevitably moved to the next creative project.

At home, things weren't much different. I still handled most of the administrative tasks of running our household while navigating the wonderful, exhausting world of teenage kids. Alexi was a high school senior, preparing to leave for college in the fall. Chloe was fifteen and testing every boundary she could find. Sophie, at thirteen, was somewhere between childhood and adolescence, trying to figure out where she fit in the family dynamic.

I loved my life, but I was drowning in it.

"You know what?" I said, reaching across the table to squeeze Robert's hand. "Let's do it. Let's see what they have to say. Maybe it's time we at least explored our options."

The school had become our fourth baby, and like all our children, it had grown beyond what we ever imagined when we first started. But maybe, just maybe, it was time to consider what came next.

The Bright Horizons executive arrived on a Tuesday morning, exactly one week later. I stood by the front door of our Hell's Kitchen location when I saw him approaching through the glass.

He was a tall man in an expensive navy suit, leather briefcase in hand, looking every inch like the corporate executive.

I opened the door with what I hoped was a confident smile, though my stomach was doing small flip-flops. "You must be David. I'm Kettia. Welcome to Smarter Toddler."

He stepped inside, and I watched his face as he took in our space. This was always the moment of truth with visitors. Would they get it, or would they see chaos where we saw carefully orchestrated learning?

Our Hell's Kitchen location was quintessentially us: bright, warm, and unmistakably child-centered. Colorful artwork covered the walls at toddler eye level. Reading nooks tucked into corners held baskets overflowing with picture books. A small greenhouse by the window housed our growing herbs and vegetables. Stuffed animals and soft toys were scattered strategically throughout the space, creating pockets of comfort and familiarity.

David's eyes moved slowly around the room, taking it all in. His expression shifted from polite professional interest to something that looked like genuine appreciation. "This is..." he paused, then smiled. "This is really something special."

I felt my shoulders relax slightly. "Thank you. Would you like the full tour? I'd love to show you what we've built here."

As we walked through both locations over the next two hours, I found myself seeing our spaces through his eyes. The carefully curated learning environments, the way our teachers moved seamlessly between activities, the obvious joy on the children's faces. It was good. Really good. And I could tell he knew it.

"Morgan mentioned you might be interested in some preliminary numbers," he said as we settled into my office at the West 89th Street location." Just to help us formulate a starting point for discussions."

This was it. The moment I'd been both anticipating and dreading. "Of course," I said, trying to keep my voice steady. "Though I have to tell you, this is just the beginning of our conversation."

He smiled. "I wouldn't expect anything less."

We said our goodbyes and I promised to send him some numbers and as I closed the door behind him, I thought about that conversation with Robert at dinner. We'd been dancing around this possibility for two years. Now, it seemed, the music was about to change.

That night at dinner, we couldn't even discuss the meeting. Our kids had established a strict "no Smarter Toddler talk at dinner" rule, and honestly, I couldn't blame them. After having the school dominate so many of our conversations for almost their lifetimes, they deserved to eat in peace. Instead, we listened to them argue about something trivial before we discussed the big transitions happening in all their lives.

Alexi only wanted to talk about college applications. He was throwing out different options and wanted to discuss the pros and cons of attending an HBCU, a Historically Black College or University. These institutions, founded primarily to serve African-American students during segregation, had become increasingly attractive to families like ours who valued both academic excellence and cultural connection.

Sophie was about to go through an application process, too—for high school. She only wanted a performing arts high school so her choices were fairly limited. We were deep in school options conversations bouncing from college to high school. Chloe didn't have any big changes for another two years when she would start the college process. It seemed like they were all growing up at warp speed, and these changes were happening faster than I was ready for.

The kids quickly retreated to their rooms as soon as dinner was over, finally giving Robert and me the privacy we needed.

"Okay," I said, settling back into my chair with a glass of wine. "Let's debrief."

I told him everything. How impressed David had been, how genuine his interest seemed, how he'd spent two full hours asking detailed questions about our operations and philosophy. We were both curious now, more than we'd expected to be.

"The thing is," Robert said, "we think we know what our company is worth, but it's not like we've ever sold a business before. How do we even get a proper assessment without retaining some expensive investment banker?"

That's when it hit me. "Karl."

Robert's face lit up. "Perfect. Karl is definitely our guy."

Karl was married to Angela, one of my oldest and dearest friends. Lucky for us, he was exactly the kind of person we needed. He was a financial analyst for a top firm based out of San Francisco, and he was tough. Karl talked fast in the way that some really smart people do, as if his words couldn't keep up with the pace of his brain. Half Japanese and half German, he spoke both languages fluently and looked like a Keanu Reeves doppelgänger. More importantly, he could eat guys like David for breakfast, smile while doing it, and ask for a croissant afterward. We were true family friends who had spent a great deal of quality time together over the years, and I knew I could trust him completely.

I emailed him that night, explaining what we were thinking. He immediately agreed to help.

"Send me your financials," he wrote back within an hour. "And connect me with their point person when they make contact again. I'll handle the rest."

The Deal of a Lifetime

At first, Robert and I thought maybe we'd just sell the smaller location, the West 89th Street school, and keep running the larger Hell's Kitchen space. We weren't ready to part completely with the company we'd built from scratch. I thought running one location wouldn't be as arduous, that I could manage that while still having more time for my family.

"We can test the waters," I told Robert. "See how it feels to work with them, what their offer looks like, whether they really understand what we've created here."

That became our game plan. We'd explore selling one location and see where it led us.

Life went on as usual after David's visit. I wasn't sitting around obsessing over the possibility or feeling desperate to make something happen. My state of mind was more curiosity than urgency. It was more like, *Wouldn't it be nice to not have these day-to-day obligations? To spend real time with my family? Maybe for Robert and I to travel again and explore a new chapter together?* These were all up-in-the-air ideas, nothing definite. I had more than just a job. I had a business I loved, a tight circle of family and friends, and I didn't want for anything. But that didn't mean I didn't dream of more.

About a week later, their offer arrived.

I was sitting in my office in Hell's Kitchen when the email came through. My heart rate picked up as I opened the attachment, but I forced myself to read through it slowly, carefully. Then I immediately forwarded it to Karl.

My phone rang twenty minutes later.

"Okay," Karl said without preamble, his voice moving at its usual rapid-fire pace. "I've looked at their offer. We need to talk."

"That bad?" I asked, though something in his tone told me I already knew the answer.

I learned from Karl that childcare businesses are typically valued using multiples of either Earnings Before Interest, Taxes, Depreciation, and Amortization, or revenue. "Let me put it this way," Karl said. "The childcare sector is normally valued at about two and a half times EBITDA. Looking at your numbers and the fact that you're not a motivated seller, I told them we're asking for 7x. They just offered you less than 3."

For 89th Street, licensed for under 100 children, we might get 2 to 3.5x EBITDA. Mid-sized like Hell's Kitchen, licensed for 100 to 200 children, could be 2 to 3.5x. For something licensed for 200 children, it could be worth 3 to 4x, or even higher. I felt my stomach drop. "So they lowballed us."

"Spectacularly," Karl confirmed. "But here's what I need from you before we respond. I need to know two things: what are you realistically expecting, and what's your lowest acceptable price?"

I was quiet for a moment, thinking. "Obviously I'm not going to tell them your lowest price," Karl continued. "I need to know it for myself during negotiations so I don't end up talking about something that isn't going to happen. I can't threaten to walk away if I don't at least know what your walk-away price is, just in case they're window shopping or just trying to get your information."

I needed to talk to Robert, so I just said, "Got it. Let me think about this and call you back."

But before I could even find Robert, Karl called again.

"Plot twist," he said when I picked up. "I just got off the phone with their team. When I told them the offer for 89th Street wasn't going to work, they asked about both locations."

"Both?" I said, puzzled.

"Yep. And suddenly, the math got very different. They're talking about a completely different multiple structure when we're discussing both properties."

I leaned back in my chair, trying to process this. "What kind of different?"

"The kind that makes you pay attention," Karl said. "They want to schedule a call with all of us. Are you and Robert available tomorrow afternoon?"

That night, I sat Robert down after the kids had gone to bed and explained the situation.

We sat in silence, both of us realizing this conversation had just taken a much more serious turn. We'd been testing the waters with one location, but now they were asking us to consider diving in completely.

"What do you think?" I asked.

Robert looked at me carefully. "I think we need to hear what they have to say. But babe, if we're going to consider this, like really consider this, we need to be prepared for what it means."

"You mean letting go of everything we've built?"

"Everything," he confirmed. "The question is: are we ready for that?"

The next afternoon, we hopped on a conference call. Karl had coached Robert and me beforehand: let him do most of the talking, don't show our hand too early, and remember that we weren't desperate to sell.

"We appreciate your interest in expanding the conversation," David said after the pleasantries were done. "When we look at both locations as a comprehensive acquisition, we can offer significantly more favorable terms."

"Define significantly," Karl said, his voice perfectly neutral.

"We're prepared to discuss a purchase price that reflects the true value of what Kettia and Robert have built. We're looking at this as our entry point into the Manhattan residential market, and we understand the premium that commands."

I caught Robert's eye across the room. This was really happening.

"We'll need to see those numbers in writing," Karl replied smoothly. "Along with a complete term sheet that outlines the structure of the deal."

"Of course. We'll get something to you by end of week."

After we hung up, we sat in my office, with Karl still on the phone, trying to process what had just happened.

"Well," Robert said finally. "I guess we're not just testing the waters anymore."

Karl laughed. "No, you're not. But here's the thing, they need you more than you need them. That's exactly where we want to be in these negotiations."

At the time, Bright Horizons was just breaching the Manhattan residential market. They were huge in corporate partnerships and employer-sponsored care, but they hadn't cracked the private, urban residential model in Manhattan. My West 89th Street location? That was going to be their first foothold.

One of their execs said to me, "We want to fence in Manhattan." And there it was.

They didn't just want to acquire my business—they wanted to claim territory. They saw Smarter Toddler as a way in. As a gateway. Later on in negotiations, a non-compete came in. Tightly worded. Carefully crafted. And very, very specific: I couldn't open another Smarter Toddler within the greater of one-third of a mile or six blocks north or south of an existing or in-development Bright Horizons location.

There were no restrictions on avenues–only streets.

And it applied to all of their locations, existing and future ones.

It was one of those clauses that looks harmless at first glance—until you realize how strategic it actually is. They were thinking ahead. They were already planning how to scale—and how to keep me out of their way.

Right before we began negotiations with Bright Horizons, we had found the perfect space in Chelsea and were deep into lease negotiations.

Then, just weeks into our discussions with Bright Horizons, the landlord suddenly pulled out. No warning. Just an abrupt end to what had felt like a done deal. We didn't know why at the time. But we later found out that Bright Horizons got the lease to that space.

They were already moving in. Quietly. Strategically. That clause? That wasn't just legal protection, it was tactical fencing. A corporate land grab. And that should've been my warning.

But at the time, I was still hopeful. Still giving them the benefit of the doubt.

"They're really good at this," Robert said one evening as we walked home from dinner. We'd spent an hour on the phone earlier in the afternoon with Bright Horizons' execs, listening to them paint pictures of how they'd preserve everything we'd built.

"What do you mean?" I asked, though something in his tone made me uneasy.

"The way they talk. Everything they say is exactly what we want to hear. They're going to keep all the teachers, maintain the programming, preserve the culture. It's like they have a script for anxious founders."

I was quiet for a moment, watching a couple push their toddler on a swing in the playground we passed. "Maybe they mean it," I said finally. "David seems genuinely different from other corporate types we've dealt with. And Morgan gets emotional when she talks about our programs."

Robert stopped walking and looked at me. "Or maybe they're just really good at telling us what we need to hear."

"You think they're lying?"

"I think they're telling us what we want to believe so we'll sign the papers," he said gently. "That's what good negotiators do."

I felt something sink in my stomach. "But the promises about keeping the teachers, the programming..."

"Cost them nothing to promise now. What happens after the deal closes is a different conversation."

"So you think we shouldn't do this?"

Robert took my hand as we started walking again. "I think the money is real, and the opportunity for us to step back and be present for our kids is real. But I also think we should go into this with our eyes wide open."

"Meaning?"

"Meaning whatever they're promising about preserving what we built, that's probably not going to happen. The question is: are we okay with that?"

I was quiet for a long moment, watching the playground as we passed. "I know it sounds terrible, but...yes. I think I am."

"It doesn't sound terrible. It sounds honest."

"The thing is," I said, the words coming out in a rush, "I'm exhausted, Robert. I'm tired of being responsible for everyone else's children, everyone else's livelihoods, everyone else's happiness. I want to be responsible for our kids. I want to go to Alexi's college tours without checking my phone every five minutes. I want to be present for Sophie's performances without worrying about payroll."

"And that's okay," he said gently.

"Is it? Because I feel guilty even thinking it. These families chose us specifically. They trust us. And I'm basically about to hand them over to everything they didn't want."

"You're not their parent, Kettia. You're not responsible for their choices after this."

I knew he was right, but it still felt like betrayal. "Deep down, I know they're going to change everything. The programming, probably some of the teachers, definitely the culture. But..."

"We still need to do what's best for us and our family."

"Exactly. And maybe that makes me selfish, but I've given twelve years to other people's children. I want to give the next few years to my own."

Robert squeezed my hand. "That doesn't make us selfish. That makes us human."

Walking home that night, I realized all the promises about preservation were making it easier for me to do what I already wanted to do. Sell the business, reclaim my life, and trust that everyone else would figure out their own path forward.

It was honest, if not exactly noble. But sometimes honest is all you can manage.

I loved what I had built. I knew the value of it. The numbers didn't lie—and neither did my instincts. I trusted both. I also knew they wanted us more than we wanted them. That's a good position to be in.

The final term sheet arrived two weeks later, and this time, the numbers got our attention in a completely different way.

I stared at the figure on my computer screen, reading it over and over again to make sure I wasn't seeing things. Robert was sitting across from me in our Hell's Kitchen office, and I could see his face change as he processed the same number.

"That's..." he started, then stopped.

"Life-changing," I finished.

It was more than life-changing. It was generational wealth. The kind of money that meant I could stop worrying about college tuition for three kids. The kind that meant Robert and I could travel, could take time to figure out what came next, could be present for our teenagers in ways we hadn't been able to when we were building the business.

But the money wasn't the only factor, and honestly, it wasn't even the deciding factor.

The Bright Horizons team had been incredibly thoughtful throughout the negotiation process. David and Morgan weren't just corporate suits trying to strip-mine our business for profit. They seemed to genuinely understand what we'd built and why it mattered.

"We've done several acquisitions of smaller, family-owned centers," David had told us during one of our final meetings. "In many cases, we've even kept the original names because we know how important it is not to disrupt the culture and community that already exists."

"You wouldn't be able to keep the Smarter Toddler name," I said, "since Robert and I plan to open other centers in the future."

"We completely understand that," Morgan had replied immediately. "But everything else that makes this place special–the arts programming, the baby yoga, the dance classes, the whole philosophy–that would absolutely stay."

They'd even worked with us on the transition plan. Robert had spent years curating the artwork throughout both locations, and most of it was personal and really expensive. We knew they weren't going to take on that liability, so we agreed that we'd take down all the art and they'd paint the walls in their signature colors. It felt like a reasonable compromise.

"We want to retain and nurture your best teachers," David assured us. "We know they're the heart of what you've created here."

That was huge for me. My staff wasn't just a workforce–they were part of the Smarter Toddler family. Knowing that Bright Horizons wanted to keep them, to invest in them, made the whole transaction feel less like abandonment and more like evolution.

Most importantly, Robert and I were still confident about our future. The non-compete clause had a time limit, and once that passed, we could do it all again. I was never afraid to compete with them, but apparently, they felt differently. They had to use their corporate might to make sure they didn't have to compete with us, at least not for a while.

"Look," Robert said one evening as we sat in our living room, the term sheet spread out on the coffee table between us. "We built something incredible once. We can do it again."

"You really think so?"

"I know so. But this time, we'll have the financial freedom to do it exactly the way we want, without the pressure of those early days when we didn't know anything and did it anyway or lying awake at night worried about a broken boiler."

He was right. The money would give us options we'd never had before. It would let us be strategic instead of reactive, creative instead of constantly crisis-managing.

But there was something else, something I hadn't fully admitted to myself until that moment.

"Robert," I said quietly, "I think I'm ready to let someone else carry this for a while."

He looked at me, understanding immediately what I meant.

Twelve years of being the person everyone turned to when something went wrong. Twelve years of missing school plays and soccer games because the health inspector showed up unexpectedly or a teacher called in sick. I loved what we'd built, but I was exhausted by the weight of carrying it all.

"The kids are growing up so fast," I continued. "Alexi's leaving for college in the fall. I don't want to miss what's left of their childhoods because I'm dealing with licensing renewals and broken dishwashers."

Robert reached over and took my hand. "So we do this. We take the deal, we take some time to be a family, and then we figure out what comes next."

"What if they change everything? What if it's not the same?"

"Then we'll know we made the right choice to start fresh somewhere else when the time comes."

The decision crystallized in that moment. It wasn't just about the money, though the money was incredible. It wasn't just about being tired, though I was bone-deep exhausted. It was about trusting that we could build something beautiful once, which meant we could do it again. In the meantime, we could give our kids the gift of having parents who were present, who weren't constantly pulled in seventeen different directions by the demands of running two schools.

"Okay," I said, and felt something shift inside me as I said it. "Let's do this."

We closed the deal in October 2014 for $7.2 million.

They tell you that selling your business is the dream. That it's the goal, the finish line, the exit strategy that proves you made it.

And yes, there's power in that moment.

But there's also something no one really talks about.

When you sell your business, you don't just walk away with a check. You walk away with a piece of yourself missing.

Because even if the deal is good, even if it was your choice, even if you were ready, you're still letting go of something you built from scratch. You're handing over something that once lived in your bones.

There's no denying the emotional high. That feeling of, *I can't believe we're really doing this.* From the moment you settle on a final number and move through the discovery and due diligence phase, you live on a fine line between exhaustion from all the years of hard work that got you here and the knowledge that soon this won't be yours anymore. It's a strange mix of relief and sadness.

All of this was happening behind the scenes of daily operations. I had to be careful about who I talked to, because any leak could blow the deal. There was a chance people wouldn't take the news well.

Robert and I spent hours talking about how to handle the announcement. We knew our staff deserved to hear it from us directly, in a way that honored what we'd all built together.

"Should we do it at the end of the day?" I asked Robert as we planned the meeting. "Or maybe over dinner, somewhere more relaxed?"

"I think here," he said. "In the space we created together. It feels more honest."

We decided to gather everyone at the Hell's Kitchen location after the children had gone home. I bought wine and cheese, trying to create an atmosphere that felt like appreciation rather than termination. But as I watched our teachers file into the main courtyard, settling into the tiny chairs where they usually sat for circle time with the children, my heart pounded.

"You all know how much this place means to Robert and me," I began, my voice steadier than I felt. "And you know how much each of you means to us. That's why this conversation is so hard."

I could see faces changing around the room. Laura, our education director, went very still. Maria, who'd been with us from the beginning, leaned forward with a worried expression.

"Bright Horizons has made us an offer to purchase both locations," I continued. "And after a lot of thought and discussion, we've decided to accept."

Nothing prepared me for the reactions. The silence that followed was deafening.

Maria spoke up, her voice shaking. "But we left corporate daycare to be here. We left places like Bright Horizons because of what you were building."

"I know," I said. My voice cracked. "I know, that's what makes this so complicated."

Laura was next to speak. There were tears in her eyes. "What happens to us? What happens to the children?"

"They've promised to keep all of you," I said quickly. "They want to maintain the programming, the philosophy, everything that makes this place special."

But I could see the skepticism on their faces. These were women who had worked in corporate childcare before. They knew the promises that got made and the realities that followed.

"When?" asked Lisa, one of our newer teachers.

"October," I said. "We'll have time to transition everything properly."

The meeting lasted two hours. There were tears, there were hard questions, and there was a sense of betrayal that hung in the air despite our best efforts to explain our reasoning. As people started to leave, Laura pulled me aside.

"I understand why you're doing this," she said quietly. "I really do. But it's going to change everything, isn't it?"

"I hope not," I told her, but even as I said it, I knew we were both thinking the same thing: of course it would change everything.

The family announcement was even harder. We decided to send a letter first, then host a meeting for anyone who wanted to discuss the transition.

The letter was carefully crafted, emphasizing continuity and Bright Horizons' commitment to maintaining our programming. But I knew that for many families, no amount of careful wording would soften the blow.

The phone started ringing within hours of the letter going out.

Jennifer, whose daughter, Emma, had been with us since she was three months old, called first.

"Kettia," she said, and I could hear she was crying. "I need you to understand something. We don't have family here in New York. You and your teachers, you ARE Emma's family. You're the people who celebrated her first steps, who helped her through her biting phase, who know exactly how she likes her sandwich cut. And now you're telling me you're handing her over to some corporation?"

I felt like I'd been punched in the stomach. "Jenn, I promise you, they're committed to keeping everything the same."

"But it won't be the same," she said. "How could it be? The thing that made this place home was YOU. Your vision, your heart, your attention to every detail. You can't transfer that in a business deal."

She was right, and we both knew it.

The family meeting was held on a Thursday evening in our Hell's Kitchen space. About forty parents showed up, filling the space with an energy that felt equal parts grief and anger.

"I chose this place specifically because you weren't a corporate chain," said David, father of twins in our toddler program. "I chose you because you knew my boys' names, because you understood that they needed different approaches, because this felt like a community, not a business."

"Will the teachers stay?" asked another parent.

"Will the programming stay the same?" asked another.

"Will you still be involved?"

The questions came fast. I tried to answer them honestly, but I could feel the trust eroding with each response. These families had invested in US, not just in a childcare center. They'd built relationships, created community, trusted us with their most precious possessions. And now we were telling them that all of that was being transferred to a company they'd specifically chosen not to use. When I think about it, I'm not sure how I reconciled choosing a company that represented everything our families had specifically avoided. Maybe it was because their promises felt genuine at that moment. Maybe it was because I believed our culture was strong enough to survive any corporate influence. Or maybe it was because I was tired enough to believe that someone else could maintain what we'd built while giving us the freedom to be present for our own family.

What I didn't fully understand then was that the very reasons our families loved us—the personal attention, the non-corporate feel, the intimate community—were inherently incompatible with corporate ownership, no matter how well-intentioned.

It was after that family meeting that I fully accepted this was really the end. Walking through the empty classroom afterward, seeing the artwork on the walls that Robert had so carefully curated, knowing that in a few months it would all be painted over with Bright Horizons' corporate-approved signature primary colors of yellows, blues and reds that looked nothing like the warm, earthy tones Robert had so carefully chosen. I felt the finality hit me.

We weren't just selling a business. We were dismantling a community. The personal relationships, the inside jokes, the way I knew the preschoolers' favorite book and every teacher's coffee order, the culture we'd built where families became friends and teachers became extended family—all of that was about to be corporate-ized.

"What are we losing?" Robert asked me that night as we sat in our living room, both of us emotionally drained.

"Everything that couldn't be written into a contract," I said. "The intangible stuff. The heart of it."

But even knowing that, even feeling the weight of what we were giving up, I still believed we were making the right choice for our family. I imagined a future where I could attend Alexi's college tours without checking my phone every five minutes. Where Robert and I could travel to places we'd only dreamed about. Where I could be fully present for Sophie's theater performances and Chloe's soccer games without part of my mind always being on staffing issues or licensing renewals.

I regretted that I couldn't figure out a way to grow personally without giving up professional control. I regretted that the families who'd trusted us had to experience this betrayal of that trust, even though it wasn't intentional. I regretted that my staff felt abandoned after we'd asked them to believe in something different.

Most of all, I regretted the timing. If I'd been more present for my own family from the beginning, maybe I wouldn't have felt so desperate to choose between my business success and my role as a mother. Maybe I could have found a way to have both without sacrificing either.

Looking back, here is my advice:

Feel all the feelings. Process them, whatever form they take. Joy. Sadness. Guilt. Regret. All of it. But most importantly, celebrate yourself. I didn't.

Because no matter what comes next—selling your business, especially one you built from the ground up—is a massive, rare, and humbling achievement.

Celebrate your wins. You deserve it. But celebration doesn't mean an absence of pain. There's an unspoken grief that comes with letting go of something you built with your heart and soul, something you and your partner poured everything into. Amidst the complexity, acknowledge how far you've come and honor the journey that led you here.

Success isn't always clean. Sometimes the biggest victories come wrapped in loss. Sometimes doing the right thing for your family means disappointing people who counted on you. Sometimes growth requires letting go of something beautiful to make room for something different.

That's the part you don't read about in those glossy business books or learn about in grad school when it comes to selling your company. It's not just a business transaction. It's an identity shift, a relationship change, a grief process, and a celebration all wrapped into one impossible, necessary moment.

And you have to find a way to hold all of that at once.

CHAPTER 6

The 100-Foot Fight

I took a break.

My version of a break didn't look like spa days or retail therapy. We didn't rush out to buy a new car or upgrade our lifestyle. We just breathed a little. For the first time in over a decade, I exhaled.

The break looked like finally having time to be present for my family in ways I'd been putting off for years. College touring with Alexi became my new full-time job, and honestly, it was a relief to have something concrete to focus on that wasn't about profit margins or staff schedules.

Robert and I divided up the college tour duties like we were planning a military operation.

"I'll take the Midwest and South," he said one morning over coffee, spreading out a map on our kitchen table. "Washington University, Emory, maybe Vanderbilt."

"That leaves me with the Northeast corridor," I replied, already mentally mapping out the drive from Boston to Philadelphia. "UPenn, Swarthmore, Boston University."

"You sure you want to drive all that?" Robert asked, knowing how much I hated long car rides.

"Are you kidding? Alexi and I in the car for hours with no interruptions? That's quality time I haven't had in years."

Unfortunately our road trip ended with Alexi sleeping with his headphones on while I drove. But we were spending time together so I took it as a win.

The point is that I was present during those tours. There was no interrupted conversation. No business calls. No emergencies. Just us, driving through New England, taking in the scenery and analyzing the schools we visited.

"Mom, what if I don't get into any of these schools?" Alexi asked during one of our drives between campuses, staring out the window at the Pennsylvania countryside.

"Then you'll go somewhere else amazing," I said. "But honestly? I'm not worried about you getting in. I just can't believe you're leaving."

He laughed. "You're not getting sentimental on me, are you?"

"Maybe a little."

But it wasn't just Alexi keeping us busy. Sophie was transitioning from middle school to high school, and she had her heart set on a performing arts program where she could major in music. Sophie had been playing piano since she was four, and watching her develop that passion over the years had been one of my greatest joys as a mother.

The audition process for performing arts high schools in NYC is brutal. We're talking about thousands of kids from all five boroughs competing for maybe 300 spots across the handful of decent programs in the city. The statistics are depressing: less than a 10% acceptance rate at most schools.

"Should I play Chopin's "Raindrop" prelude or should I switch to the one I played at the last recital, Debussy's Clair De Lune?" Sophie asked after practice, slumping onto the couch.

"They're both good," I said. "Play the one you're most comfortable with."

Robert glanced up from his laptop. "I agree; they both sound good. Plus, you're already a professional at overthinking everything. That's gotta count for something."

"Very funny, Dad." Sophie rolled her eyes but cracked a smile.

"I'm serious," I added. "You're talented. Any of those schools would be lucky to have you."

"You have to say that because you're my mom. But you're not the one that has to audition in front of all these people."

"No, but we've been listening to you practice the same piece for weeks on end," Robert said. "Trust me, you've got it."

Sophie grabbed a throw pillow and chucked it at him. "Thanks for the vote of confidence, I think."

The audition prep consumed our evenings. Sophie practiced for hours, and I sat nearby, pretending to read while actually listening to her play the same pieces over and over. There's something about hearing your child master something difficult that makes all the chaos worthwhile.

On top of college touring and high school auditions, both Chloe and Sophie were deep into their training at Alvin Ailey. What started as adorable four and five-year-olds in beginner classes had evolved into a serious commitment. Their schedules had ramped up to two to three weekdays plus Saturdays, which felt absurd considering my girls had no intention of going pro. But they found their tribe–dance friends who were completely separate from their school world–and they weren't complaining about the grueling schedule yet. My rule was simple: I'd keep driving them until they said stop. Because when your kids find something they love, something that challenges them and gives them confidence, you make it work, even if it means your weeks revolve around a studio schedule.

"We're basically running a chauffeur service," Robert said one Thursday evening as we passed each other in the hallway with him heading out to pick up Chloe, and me rushing to get Sophie to her piano lesson.

"I know," I called back. "At least there's no surprise equipment fees this week."

"Yet," Robert replied. "Give it time. But hey, at least you're not dealing with a DOH inspection right now."

"Oh my God, why would you even say that?!"

He was right. For the first time in forever, our dinner conversations weren't dominated by business talk. We were just being parents, dealing with normal parent stuff.

The real gift of that year was our Christmas trip to Panama. Even though we normally closed the schools for the Christmas holiday week, I always went in to prepare for the new year back-to-school rush. January had become just as important as September. Now, being able to move at a relaxed pace felt good, but strange. My nervous system had been conditioned to be alert, and it was hard to truly let go.

"My phone has been silent for three days," I told Robert as we sat on the beach, watching the girls build sandcastles like they were still little kids and Alexi chilling with a book.

"How does that feel?" he asked.

"Weird. Good weird. Like maybe the world can actually function without me micromanaging everything."

"Shocking revelation," he laughed. "Maybe we should do this more often."

"We most definitely should."

For once, my phone was strangely and mercifully quiet. No emergency calls about licensing issues or staff conflicts. No parents calling to complain about pickup procedures. Just the sound of waves and my children laughing.

But of course, all good things must come to an end. And by the spring of 2015, I was starting to feel that familiar itch again. The urge to build something. To create. To prove that the sale of Smarter Toddler wasn't the end of my story—it was just the end of chapter one. That year taught me something I'd forgotten: that taking a break isn't lazy or indulgent. It's necessary. It's the pause that lets you remember why you started in the first place.

***

Robert and I spent hours at our kitchen table during those early months of 2015, spreadsheets scattered between us as we explored different investment opportunities. We could have lived comfortably off a percentage of our windfall, paid all of our expenses, and still have plenty left over. On paper, it was the dream scenario. Financial freedom at a relatively young age.

But something about it felt hollow.

"We could put everything in index funds," Robert said one evening, scrolling through portfolio options on his laptop.

"Conservative approach, steady returns. We'd never have to work again."

I looked up from the investment prospectus I'd been reading. "But do you want to never work again?"

He was quiet for a moment. "No," he said finally. "I don't think I do."

The truth was, we were both too young to retire. I was in my early forties, Robert in his mid-forties. The idea of spending the next thirty years managing an investment portfolio felt incredibly passive, almost suffocating. We'd always been builders, creators, people who thrived on the energy of making something from nothing.

"What if we moved somewhere with a lower cost of living?" I suggested. "We could retire to Florida or North Carolina, buy a house on the water..."

Robert made a face. "And what exactly would we do all day? Can you honestly picture us doing that?"

I couldn't. The thought of leaving New York, of walking away from the energy and possibility of the city, felt like giving up. This was where we'd built our life, where our daughters were finishing high school, where we belonged.

"So what do we actually want?" I asked.

That question hung in the air for weeks. We talked about it during our walks around the neighborhood, over dinner when the kids were busy with homework, during long Sunday morning conversations over coffee.

"I keep thinking about legacy," Robert said one morning. "Not just financial legacy, but something we can be proud of. Something that outlasts us."

I nodded. "We're experienced now," I replied "Older. Wiser. We know what we didn't know twelve years ago."

"We know what mistakes not to make," he agreed.

That's when it clicked for me. The sale of Smarter Toddler hadn't been a failure or an ending. It had been an education. We'd learned how to build a successful business, how to navigate growth, how to manage staff and families and all the complexities that come with creating something meaningful. But we'd also learned our limits, our blind spots, the things we'd do differently if we had another chance.

"What if we did it again?" he said quietly.

I looked at him. "You mean..."

"I mean, what if we took everything we learned and built something even better? What if we created the legacy we always wanted to create, but this time with the wisdom of experience?"

The more we talked about it, the more excited we became. We weren't the same people who'd started Smarter Toddler in 2002. We were parents of teenagers now, business owners who'd successfully sold a company, people who understood both the rewards and the costs of entrepreneurship.

"We could do it right this time," Robert said. "From the beginning."

"Better systems. Better boundaries. Better everything," I replied.

"And this time, we'd know it's not just about building a business. It's about building something sustainable, something that serves our family as much as it serves our community." said Robert.

I felt that familiar spark of excitement, the same feeling I'd had sitting in our tiny apartment twenty years earlier, dreaming about what we could create. But this time, it was tempered with wisdom, grounded in experience.

We weren't going back into business because we had to. We were going back because we wanted to. Because we had something to prove, not to anyone else, but to ourselves. We could take everything we'd learned, everything we'd gained, and build something even more meaningful than what we'd created before.

This wouldn't just be another childcare center. This would be our legacy.

By summer 2015, our conversations had moved from theoretical to practical. We started seriously exploring spaces, and somehow word got out that we were considering a comeback. That's when my phone started buzzing with opportunities.

Realtors started reaching out to me, and the calls kept coming. Spaces were being offered to me left and right—ironic, considering how hard it had been to get that first lease years earlier.

It was like the moment word got out that I sold the centers, every broker in the city had my number. My phone buzzed constantly with new listings, "perfect opportunities," and spaces that were supposedly "exactly what you're looking for."

Robert would shake his head every time my phone rang. "Another one?"

"Yep. This one's in Tribeca. Says it's 'turnkey ready for childcare.'"

"Uh-huh. And the last three?"

"Also turnkey ready."

We'd laugh, but honestly, it was overwhelming. After years of begging landlords to even consider us, suddenly everyone wanted to work with us. Success has a funny way of opening doors that were previously slammed shut.

One location stood out: a corner space in the Financial District that used to house a Duane Reade. Prime spot. Great visibility. Solid bones.

The 100-Foot Fight

I remember the first time Robert and I walked through it together. The space was massive, bigger than anything we'd had before. Floor-to-ceiling windows flooded the rooms with natural light. The layout was perfect for what we wanted to do.

"This could work," Robert said, running his hand along the windowsill. "Really work."

"The foot traffic alone," I added, watching the stream of people walking by outside. "All these working parents rushing to catch the subway."

"And the visibility. No one's going to miss us here."

The landlord was eager to make a deal. The previous tenant had left suddenly, and they needed someone reliable to take over the lease quickly. We had the track record now. We had credibility.

Before George retired, he had introduced me to his protégé, Bob. He brought us across the East River to another great property, this one in North Williamsburg. It was a spacious ground floor commercial space in a stunning brand-new luxury development, with views of the water and just steps from the ferry. The kind of space you dream about.

The Williamsburg space was completely different. Sleek, modern, part of a high-end residential complex filled with young families who could afford premium childcare. The ferry had just started running regularly, making it accessible to parents commuting to work in Manhattan.

"This is beautiful," Robert said as we stood looking out at the Manhattan skyline across the water. "Look at this view."

"It's definitely beautiful. But it's also expensive. Really expensive."

"The demographic can support it though. Look at this building. These aren't people pinching pennies on childcare."

I was always the practical one. "Two locations means double everything. Double the staff, double the licensing headaches, double the risk."

"But think about the impact," Robert said, his eyes lighting up the way they always did when he was envisioning something big. "Two different neighborhoods, two different communities. We could really make a difference."

We spent weeks going back and forth. Late-night conversations over dinner. Pro-and-con lists that covered entire legal pads. Spreadsheets that projected every possible scenario.

"What if we just start with one?" I suggested, during one of these marathon planning sessions. "Get it running smoothly, then expand?"

"But which one?" Robert countered. "FiDi has this amazing energy, all those working families. And Williamsburg! Imagine what we could create in that space with those views."

"Exactly. We're trying to choose between two completely different strategies."

The more we talked about it, the more Robert became convinced we shouldn't have to choose. Both locations offered something unique. Both filled a different need in the market.

"What if we don't choose?" Robert said one evening, looking up from the sketches he'd been drawing of potential classroom layouts.

"What do you mean?"

"What if we do both? Open them at the same time, make a real statement. Show everyone we're back and we're serious."

I was quiet for a long moment, running the numbers in my head. "That's either brilliant or completely insane."

"Maybe both?"

"Definitely both. But..." I paused, already mentally calculating cash flow projections. "If we're going to do it, we need to do it right. Proper planning, proper funding, proper everything."

"So you're saying yes?"

"I'm saying let's run the numbers one more time. But yeah. I think I'm saying yes."

And just like that, we signed both leases.

The 100-Foot Fight

The plan was to open both locations roughly at the same time in the fall of 2016. Looking back now, that sounds wild. Two simultaneous launches. Two brand new neighborhoods. Two major markets.

But at that moment? It felt right. It felt like the natural next step for people who had already proven they could build something from nothing.

I felt ready. I had built it before. I could build it again.

What I didn't know was that the FiDi location was going to take me into the lion's den. Right into Bright Horizons' crosshairs.

I know some people will read this and think: How stupid were you? Why would you open a center near Bright Horizons knowing you had a non-compete?

And to those people, I say: I measured it.

I wasn't reckless. I wasn't naive. I did my homework, or at least I thought I did.

The non-compete clause was clear: I couldn't open within a certain distance of any existing Bright Horizons location. So I did what any reasonable person would do. I got out my measuring tools and went to work.

I walked the route from the FiDi location to the nearest Bright Horizons center. Not once, but multiple times. I traced different paths, trying every possible route between the two locations. I even brought Robert with me one weekend to double-check the calculations on my watch. He used his phone.

"Are you getting the same thing I am getting?" I asked him as we stood outside the Bright Horizons location, looking toward where our space would be.

"Definitely. There's no way this violates the clause."

I ran the route. Literally ran it, timing myself and tracking the distance with my trusty Garmin GPS watch. Block by block, turn by turn, I mapped out every possible path between the two locations. I was confident I was in the clear, well within the parameters as they were written in the contract.

The distance I calculated put us safely outside the restricted zone. It wasn't even close, according to my measurements. I had documentation. I had numbers. I had what I thought was proof.

What I didn't know was that there's a whole other way to measure distance.

I had never heard the phrase "as the crow flies."

I had no idea that legal distance could be measured differently than walking or driving distance. In my mind, distance was distance. If you couldn't walk from Point A to Point B in under the restricted amount, you were fine.

But "as the crow flies" means measuring in a straight line, completely ignoring streets, buildings, or any obstacles in between. It's the shortest possible distance between two points, regardless of whether a human being could actually travel that way.

Picture this: if you drew a straight line on a map from our John Street location to the Bright Horizons center, cutting right through buildings and city blocks, that line was shorter than the walking route I had so carefully measured.

The one thing I didn't do to measure the distance accurately? I didn't hire a professional surveyor. And that person would've told me about the damn crows.

I didn't even know professional surveyors existed for this kind of thing. I know that sounds naive now, but it's the honest answer. I thought measuring distance was measuring distance—you walk from Point A to Point B, you time it, you track it with your GPS, and that's your answer.

If I had known there were people whose entire job was to measure distances legally and professionally, of course I would have hired one. But I didn't know what I didn't know. I was operating with the knowledge I had, doing what seemed like thorough due diligence with the tools I understood.

It's like not knowing you need a specific type of lawyer for a specific type of case, or not knowing there's a specialist for something you thought was straightforward. You can't hire expertise you don't know exists.

The 100-Foot Fight

I thought I was being thorough. I thought my GPS watch and careful route planning were enough. I thought the fact that you'd have to walk several extra blocks to get from one location to the other meant we were safe. I was wrong.

By the time Bright Horizons came for me, it was too late. The contracts were signed. The buildout was nearly complete. And I was about to learn a very expensive lesson about the difference between common sense and legal reality.

They came at me like a wrecking ball.

The first sign of trouble was the email I received on the Amtrak on my way home from running the Boston Marathon. Several emails back and forth between attorneys didn't seem to put the issue to rest. Then came the formal legal document delivered to my office on a Tuesday morning. The kind of envelope that makes your stomach drop before you even open it.

That was the cease and desist.

By the time that legal envelope arrived, we'd been investing in FiDi for nearly a year with no income to show for it. The buildout alone had cost us over half a million dollars, and that was just one location. We were simultaneously developing Williamsburg, which meant we were burning through our reserves on two fronts: rent, staff salaries, licensing fees, and construction costs multiplied by two. Every month without revenue felt like watching our nest egg shrink, but we were confident we were just weeks away from opening and finally seeing a return on our investment.

I remember staring at the letterhead, reading the same paragraph over and over, trying to make sense of what I was seeing. The language was cold, clinical, and absolutely devastating.

"Immediate cessation of all activities..."

"Violation of contractual obligations..."

"Legal action will be pursued..."

At this point, the buildout at John Street was complete. We were in the final phase of licensing, just under two months away from opening. The classrooms were ready, painted in the warm earth tones and rich chocolate browns we'd spent weeks selecting, with accent walls in soft pink and sage green hues that created the perfect balance of energy and calm.

The materials had been ordered and delivered. Staff had been hired, people who had left other jobs to come work for us. Parents were already enrolled, families who believed in what we were creating. It was all happening.

And then, just like that, it wasn't.

I called Robert immediately. "We have a problem. A big problem."

"What kind of problem?"

"The legal kind. Bright Horizons is saying we're in violation of the non-compete."

There was a long pause. "But we measured. We were careful."

"Apparently not careful enough."

The next few days were a blur of phone calls to lawyers, frantic research sessions, and sleepless nights trying to figure out how we'd gotten it so wrong. The answer came back quickly: "as the crow flies" measurement put us just inside their restricted zone.

I alternated between shock, outrage, and numbness.

Because if we were forced to shut down, we were done. Cooked. There was no coming back from this. Williamsburg might still open, sure. But there was no world in which it could cover or recoup what we had already poured into FiDi.

Now throw legal costs into the mix and it was a recipe for disaster.

The cease and desist was just the beginning. What came next was worse.

I was overwhelmed. I was furious.

I was angry at myself for missing that one step. For not hiring that one person. For not anticipating this move.

But more than anything, I was disturbed by how they came at me.

This wasn't some corporate oversight or routine enforcement. The energy of it felt different. The force behind it was personal. The coldness was calculated. It felt punitive.

The legal papers weren't just asking us to stop. They weren't just trying to block the opening.

They were demanding damages. One million dollars, or what they called "being made whole."

When my lawyer called to discuss their demands, I nearly dropped the phone.

"A million dollars? For what?" I said.

"They're claiming lost revenue, competitive harm, breach of contract penalties. They want compensation for what they say you've cost them."

"But we haven't even opened yet. We haven't taken a single customer from them."

"That's not how they see it."

When I told them I didn't have that kind of money on hand, the response came back through lawyers, but the message was clear:

"What about the sale money?"

"What about what we paid you?"

It felt like they were asking for their money back.

Like they couldn't believe I had the nerve to take their check, cash it, and then rise again.

Like I got away with something I never should have. Like success wasn't supposed to happen to someone like me, not on my terms.

The implications were ugly.

There was something deeply unsettling about the way it all unfolded. The way they used the contract. The way they wielded their power. The way the tone shifted from corporate professionalism to quiet retribution.

This wasn't a routine business dispute. This felt personal, like punishment for having the audacity to succeed after they thought they'd bought me out of the game.

It wasn't just about a clause. It was about control. It was about sending a message.

And the message was clear: Stay in your place.

*****

This was supposed to be a time of celebration.

We were gearing up for a major launch party scheduled for late May 2016, timed perfectly with our planned opening. It was a grand opening meant to announce our return to the childcare world after our year-long break. I had been planning it for months, envisioning the perfect way to celebrate. The

The 100-Foot Fight

guest list was ambitious but heartfelt—everyone who had supported us through the journey.

My two big brothers, who are always so proud of me, had booked flights in from Texas. My mom and sisters were flying in from different cities. My family never missed my big moments, and this felt like the biggest one yet. Friends who had been with me since the beginning, longtime supporters who had watched Smarter Toddler grow from a crazy idea into a real business, even families from the early days who had become like extended family were all planning to attend.

The vendor relationships we'd built over the years meant everything to me. The woman who supplied our organic snacks, the guy who helped us source our beautiful wooden toys, the local musician who had been doing classes since we opened the first location–they were all planning to come celebrate with us.

It was going to be beautiful. A new chapter. A real moment of triumph.

I had hired a photographer to capture everything. Robert was planning an event for the books. He had been discussing ideas for weeks, talking about how he wanted to transform the space for the party. There would be live music, the kind of organic, joyful atmosphere that had always defined our brand.

The invitations had been sent. The catering was booked. I'd even bought a new outfit, something that felt worthy of the occasion–professional but celebratory, the kind of look that said "I'm back and I'm ready." The cease and desist arrived on a Monday morning, just three weeks before our planned celebration. By Thursday, I had made the devastating call to cancel everything.

I told everyone we were under a time crunch, that we'd do something later in the year. A quiet postponement that sounded reasonable and responsible. People were understanding, of course. They knew how complicated opening a new location could be.

But the truth? I was in a tailspin.

I couldn't face walking into that room with champagne glasses raised, knowing I was barely holding it together. I couldn't smile for photos when I didn't know if we'd even be allowed to open our doors. I couldn't give a speech about our bright future when lawyers were circling like vultures.

The thought of my brothers flying all that way, of my mom getting dressed up and excited, only to have to pretend everything was fine while my world was falling apart, I couldn't do it.

Robert found me sitting at the kitchen table the night I made the decision, staring at the guest list.

"You sure about this?" he asked.

"What choice do I have?" I said, defeated. How do I stand up there and talk about our grand reopening when we might be shut down before we even start?"

"We could tell people what's happening. They'd understand."

"Would they? Or would they just feel sorry for us? I can't have a pity party disguised as a launch party."

The hardest calls were to my family. My brothers were disappointed but supportive. "We'll be there for the real celebration," one of them said. "Whenever that happens."

My mom was worried. "Are you okay? This doesn't sound like you."

"I'm fine, Mom. Just need to focus on getting the business side sorted first."

But I wasn't fine. I was drowning, and I didn't know how to ask for help without admitting just how bad things had gotten.

The space that was supposed to be filled with laughter and celebration sat empty that evening. Robert and I walked through it together, looking at the beautiful classrooms that might never see their first students.

"We'll have our party," he said. "Just not today."

"Promise?"

"Promise."

I looked around at everything we'd built—again. For the first time I wondered if that promise was one we'd actually be able to keep.

The 100-Foot Fight

I was suddenly living in legal limbo. I didn't know whether or not to tell my brand-new staff that their jobs might disappear before we even opened. These were people who had left other roles, people who believed in me. Who believed in the vision. This was going to hurt them, too.

I kept going back and forth on it. Every morning I woke up thinking, "Today I'll tell them." And every evening I went home having said nothing.

There was Lisa, our lead teacher, who had left a corporate daycare specifically to work for us. She'd been so excited during her interview, talking about how she wanted to be part of something more personal, more meaningful.

There was James, our facilities coordinator, who had already started ordering supplies and setting up systems. He was methodical, detail-oriented, exactly what we needed. He'd even brought in family photos to put on his desk.

There was Shirley, our administrative coordinator, fresh out of college and eager to prove herself. She'd been staying late, making sure every licensing requirement was perfectly documented.

How do you look people in the eye and pretend everything is normal when you know their entire future is hanging by a thread?

But I also couldn't pretend nothing was happening. Something was going down, and it was bad. I was running out of the office every other day, either to my attorney's office or to court.

"Where are you going now?" Shirley would ask when she saw me grabbing my bag and rushing toward the door.

"Just a quick meeting," I'd say. "I'll be back later."

But "later" kept getting later, and "quick meetings" were turning into all-day affairs.

The staff started to notice. Of course they did. You can't run a tight ship for years and then suddenly become flaky without people picking up on it.

I was referred to a new law firm by my original attorney, who was honest enough to admit this was beyond his expertise. These were sharp, seasoned litigators who specialized in exactly this kind of corporate warfare. They didn't miss a beat, and while they were expensive—with a capital everything—they made me feel like they cared. Like they really wanted to help me find a legal solution that wouldn't just protect me, but restore me.

And I needed that. Because I was running on fumes.

The daily routine became surreal. I spent mornings at the center, trying to maintain normalcy with staff and touring parents who were excited about our opening. Then I slipped out for legal meetings where we'd strategize about damage control and settlement options. Then back to the center to pretend everything was on track.

The emotional whiplash was exhausting. One minute I'd be discussing classroom setup and curriculum plans. The next minute I'd be reviewing legal briefs about breach of contract and monetary damages.

"You seem distracted lately," Lisa mentioned one afternoon. "Everything okay?"

"Just a lot of moving pieces right now," I said. "Opening a new location is always chaotic."

But it wasn't chaos. It was something much worse. It was watching everything you've worked for hang in the balance while trying to keep everyone else's faith intact.

The first meeting with the new legal team was both encouraging and terrifying. Encouraging because they seemed confident we had options. Terrifying because they laid out exactly what we were up against.

"This isn't just about the non-compete," the lead attorney explained. "They're using this as leverage. They want to send a message about what happens when someone tries to compete with them."

"So what are our options?"

"We fight it, which will be expensive and time-consuming. We negotiate, which means paying them something. Or we walk away, which means losing everything you've invested."

Walking away wasn't an option. Fighting seemed impossible given our financial situation. That left negotiation, which felt like paying ransom to get back something that should have been mine in the first place.

******

I remember Mother's Day that year.

For the past few years, my family had started this sweet little tradition of taking me to the Rainbow Room for Mother's Day brunch. It's a feast for the eyes—classic New York glamour, with crystal chandeliers and skyline views that make you feel like you're in an old Hollywood movie. The kind of place where you automatically sit up straighter and speak a little softer.

It's also where we celebrated our engagement years earlier, so it held layers of meaning. Sentiment. Joy. A kind of full-circle magic that made it feel like our special place.

But that year? I felt like a dead woman walking.

The reservation had been made months in advance, back when I thought we'd be celebrating our grand reopening by now. Back when Mother's Day 2016 was supposed to mark a triumphant return to the childcare world.

Instead, I was sitting at a beautifully set table, surrounded by my family, trying not to think about the court date scheduled for the following Tuesday.

"Mom, you have to try this," Chloe said, pointing to something elaborate on her plate. "It's like a mini quiche but fancier."

"Looks delicious, sweetheart," I managed, forcing a smile.

Alexi was in a good mood, telling stories about college campus visits and making everyone laugh. Sophie was excited because she'd just gotten callbacks from two different performing arts programs. Robert was being his usual charming self, making jokes with the waitstaff and taking pictures of everything.

I tried to put on a brave face for the kids. Smiled for the photos. Laughed at the right moments. But inside, I was drowning.

Every bite of food felt like cardboard. The champagne in my mimosa might as well have been flat soda. I kept finding myself staring out at the Manhattan skyline, wondering if this time next year we'd be able to afford to come back here.

"I know it's hard but for just for a moment try and forget everything outside of this room," Robert said, leaning over to squeeze my hand. "It's going to be okay."

"I know it is. Just taking it all in," I said. "I am just feeling a bit sentimental I guess."

But I wasn't being sentimental. I was conjuring worst-case scenarios in my head—most of them ending with us losing the business we had just poured our entire life savings into.

We were so proud of not having investors this time. No loans. No equity partners. We had done this on our own, used the money from the sale to fund our comeback. It felt like vindication, like proof that we could build something sustainable without giving up control.

But that also meant that if it collapsed, it would collapse on us and no one else.

"Should we order dessert?" Robert asked, clearly trying to keep the mood light.

"I'm pretty full," Sophie said.

"Me too," echoed Chloe.

"Mom?" Alexi looked at me expectantly.

I realized I'd been moving food around my plate for the past twenty minutes without actually eating much of anything. "Whatever you all want is fine with me."

The kids started debating dessert options, their voices blending into a background hum while I watched families at other tables. Happy mothers opening gifts, taking selfies, enjoying what was supposed to be a celebration of motherhood.

I had a court date coming up that week. It would decide whether we could get a stay on the cease and desist or if the nightmare would continue in full force. Tuesday felt both forever away and terrifyingly close.

"Let's get a group photo," Robert suggested, signaling for our waiter.

I put on my smile and gathered my family close. In the picture, I looked happy. Relaxed. Like a woman celebrating Mother's Day with her beautiful family in one of New York's most iconic restaurants.

But inside? I was terrified.

Terrified that the business we'd risked everything to rebuild might be taken away before we even got to open the doors.

I wasn't going to ruin the day for my family. They deserved their Mother's Day tradition, their champagne brunch, their laughter and celebration.

As we gathered our things to leave, all I could think about was Tuesday. And whether the woman sitting at this table next Mother's Day would be celebrating or still trying to pick up the pieces.

*****

The court didn't rule in our favor.

I sat in that courtroom on Tuesday morning, wearing my most professional suit, trying to project confidence I didn't feel. My lawyer had prepared me for different scenarios, but deep down, I think we both hoped the judge would see reason. I hoped the judge would recognize that forcing us to shut down was disproportionate to whatever technical violation we'd committed.

The judge was matter-of-fact, almost clinical in his delivery. No drama, no emotion, just cold, legal reality.

"The court finds that the plaintiff has demonstrated a likelihood of success on the merits of their claim..."

I stopped hearing the rest. The words blended together into legal white noise while the weight of what he was saying sank in.

We were not allowed to open.

Just like that. Months of planning, building, hiring, preparing–all of it stopped by a few sentences from a man in a black robe who probably forgot about our case the moment he moved on to the next one.

I sat there trying to process what this meant. For the staff who'd already left other jobs. For the families who'd enrolled their children. For Robert and me, who'd invested everything we had.

My lawyer leaned over and whispered, "We'll appeal, but for now, we need to focus on negotiation."

Walking out of that courthouse felt like a death march. The late spring morning that had seemed promising a few hours earlier now felt cold and gray. People were rushing past on the sidewalk, heading to jobs and meetings and normal Tuesday morning activities, while my world had just collapsed.

I called Robert from the courthouse steps. This was our usual division of labor—I handled the legal and business crises, he was my emotional anchor and sounding board. We didn't always do everything together but we were a team.

"How bad?" he asked immediately.

"Bad. We can't open."

"At all?"

"Not unless we can work something out with them directly."

There was a long pause. "Okay. So what's next?"

That's what I loved about Robert. Even in crisis, he was already thinking about solutions instead of dwelling on the problem.

The only chance we had left was to negotiate directly with Bright Horizons. To literally appeal to their better angels—to ask them to let us open, to not destroy everything we had worked for, and in return, we would agree to pay damages. They wanted to be "made whole."

Whatever the hell that means.

The 100-Foot Fight

The settlement conversations were humiliating. Sitting across from their lawyers, listening to them calculate exactly how much my mistake was worth to them. They had spreadsheets. Projections. Charts showing their projected lost revenue from our theoretical competition.

"Our client is willing to consider allowing you to operate," their lead attorney said, "in exchange for compensation that reflects the competitive harm you've caused."

"We haven't caused any harm," my lawyer responded. "They haven't even opened yet."

"The harm is in the potential. The market disruption. The breach of trust."

The numbers they threw around were staggering. Not just the million they'd originally demanded, but interest, legal fees, ongoing monitoring costs. They wanted to turn my mistake into a profit center.

We didn't have the money. So now came the exact scenario we were trying so hard to avoid: scrambling for loans.

And not the helpful, flexible kind that banks offer to established businesses with good credit and solid projections. These were aggressive. Predatory. Some of them had repayment terms that kicked in before the business even opened its doors.

The loan officers I met with during that time had a particular look in their eyes—like sharks who'd smelled blood in the water. They knew I was desperate. They knew I didn't have options.

"Given the legal complications," one of them explained, "we'd need to structure this as a high-risk investment with corresponding interest rates."

"How high are we talking?"

"Eighteen percent, plus origination fees."

"Eighteen percent?" I echoed in disbelief.

"You're free to shop around, but given your current legal exposure, I doubt you'll find better terms."

We were proud not to have investors or debt this time around. We'd planned to prove that our concept was strong enough to succeed on its own merits, with our own money.

But now? The numbers didn't add up. The market had shifted. While our concept was still solid, we had to learn the rhythm and flow of a new demographic—and that takes time. Time we no longer had the luxury of taking.

By this point, we had competitors—competitors who had clearly studied our playbook and were now mimicking the very things that once made us stand out.

When we first opened Smarter Toddler back in 2003, we were pioneers. Live music classes for infants? Revolutionary. Organic, locally-sourced snacks? Unheard of in childcare.

Curated environments that looked more like boutique hotels than traditional daycares? We were the only ones doing it.

But success breeds imitation, and fifteen years later, everyone had caught on.

I remember walking through Tribeca one afternoon and passing a new childcare center that could have been our twin. The same aesthetic, the same marketing language, even similar class offerings. Their website talked about "mindful early childhood education" and "cultivating creativity through curated experiences."

"They're using our exact words," I told Robert that evening, scrolling through their promotional materials on my laptop.

"Imitation is the sincerest form of flattery?" he offered weakly.

"Imitation is the sincerest form of competition stealing your market share."

Live music classes were everywhere now. Every upscale childcare center in Manhattan had a musician on staff. Organic food wasn't a luxury anymore—it was an expectation. Yoga for infants, sensory play environments, nature-based learning—all the innovations we'd introduced were now standard offerings across the city.

The bigger operators had resources we'd never had. Marketing budgets that could flood social media with targeted ads. Corporate partnerships that gave them access to better rates on everything from insurance to supplies. Professional PR teams that could get them featured in parenting magazines and mommy blogs.

We were used to word-of-mouth marketing. To waitlists that stretched for miles because parents heard about us from other parents. To organic growth based on reputation and results.

But the market was saturated now. Parents had choices, and those choices all looked remarkably similar to what we offered.

"We need to differentiate ourselves," I said during one of our strategy sessions.

"How do you differentiate from people who are copying everything you do?" Robert asked.

"We do it better. We remind people who did it first."

But doing it better required marketing dollars we didn't have. Especially not with legal fees and settlement payments eating into our operating budget before we'd even opened.

The regulations were tougher too. Licensing took longer. What was already a bureaucratic maze became a full-blown administrative circus. New safety requirements meant costly modifications to spaces we'd already built out. Updated staff certification requirements meant higher payroll costs.

The cost of doing business had doubled in every way—time, money, stress.

Insurance premiums had skyrocketed. Real estate prices had gone through the roof. The same commercial spaces that were affordable in 2008 were now commanding Manhattan residential prices.

Even our core demographic had changed. The parents who'd embraced us in the early days were early adopters, people willing to try something new and different. But as the market matured, parents became more discerning, more demanding, and frankly, more entitled.

"I saw on your website that you offer music classes," one prospective parent said during a tour. "But I notice ABC Learning Center down the street offers violin lessons. What makes your program better?"

These were conversations we'd never had to have before. We used to be the only game in town for parents who wanted something special for their children. Now we were just one option among many, all of us fighting for the same affluent, educated families who wanted the best for their kids.

The irony wasn't lost on me. We'd succeeded so well at creating a new category of premium childcare that we'd attracted dozens of competitors who could do it cheaper, faster, and with better financing.

"Maybe we should have kept some of our secrets to ourselves," Robert joked one evening as we reviewed yet another competitor's marketing materials.

"Too late for that now," I said. "We just have to be better than everyone else."

"No pressure," Robert joked.

But the pressure was real. With every day that passed while we fought legal battles instead of serving families, our competitors were getting stronger, and our position was getting weaker.

CHAPTER 7

Keeping the Doors Open

We finally opened the doors.

But it felt bittersweet.

The day we'd been working toward for months arrived not with celebration, but with exhaustion and relief. After all the legal battles, the settlement negotiations, and the scrambling for financing, we were finally allowed to welcome our first families.

The settlement with Bright Horizons came at a steep price: one and a half a million dollars, to be paid over four years with a lump sum due every December. It was devastating to our cash flow before we'd even opened our doors.

The moment we reached that agreement, the legal stay went into effect immediately. I could finally move forward with opening.

The entire time we'd been fighting in court, I'd never stopped working toward our September opening. I refused to accept that we wouldn't open. While lawyers were arguing about cease and desist orders, I was still pushing through the licensing process, still doing tours for prospective families, still managing the day-to-day operations with full intent to open on schedule.

My staff thought I was either incredibly optimistic or completely delusional, but I had to hold that space for what I wanted to see happen. No one was going to do that for me.

The licensing came through down to the wire—just one week before our planned September opening. It wasn't luck; it was months of working our asses off to keep every piece moving while simultaneously fighting for our right to exist.

I remember standing in the doorway that first morning, watching parents drop off their children, trying to summon the excitement I should have felt. This was supposed to be a triumph. Instead, it felt like we'd limped across a finish line that kept moving further away.

"We did it," Robert said, coming up beside me as we watched a toddler happily exploring our sensory play area.

"Yeah," I replied. "We did."

But even as I said it, I could feel the weight of everything hanging over us. The lawsuit was settled but not forgotten. The debt we'd taken on to pay the settlement loomed over every financial decision.

I had a lawsuit hanging over my head in the form of ongoing compliance monitoring. Bright Horizons had negotiated the right to verify that we weren't violating any other terms of our original agreement. It felt like having a parole officer for your business—someone watching, waiting for you to make another mistake.

The threat of being shut down at any moment if I missed a single payment created a constant undercurrent of anxiety. Every month when the settlement payment was due, I held my breath until the check cleared.

I worked nonstop. There was no choice. There were too many people depending on me. The margins were so tight that I couldn't afford to delegate anything that I could do myself. Life became a blur of invoices, loan repayments, staff meetings, and barely enough oxygen to breathe.

The days started before sunrise and ended well after sunset. I arrived at the center before the first families showed up, and I left after the cleaning crew finished for the night. Weekends were spent catching up on paperwork, reviewing budgets, and trying to figure out how to make the numbers work.

"You're burning yourself out," Robert warned one evening as I sat at the kitchen table with spreadsheets scattered around me.

"What choice do I have? We can't afford to hire someone to do this."

"We can't afford for you to collapse either."

The personal toll was immediate and brutal.

My son was in college, calling home with stories about dorm life and new friends while I was too distracted to fully engage.

I'd find myself half-listening to his updates while mentally calculating whether we'd make payroll that week.

"Mom, are you listening?" Alexi would ask during our phone calls.

"Of course, sweetheart. Tell me about your economics professor again."

Meanwhile, my mind was somewhere else worrying about cash flow, settlement payments, or whether we'd have enough enrollment to cover our expenses.

My daughters were full-on teenagers now, and they were acting like it. Chloe was pushing boundaries in ways that required actual parenting, not just the distracted "mm-hmm" responses I'd been giving. Sophie was stressed about high school auditions and needed support I was struggling to provide.

I wanted to relaunch Smarter Toddler so I could spend more time with my children before they left home. Instead, I was doing the exact opposite. Working around the clock. Missing meals together. Showing up exhausted to parent-teacher conferences. Giving them what was left of me, not the best of me.

"Can we have one dinner without talking about the business?" Chloe asked one evening after I'd spent most of the meal on my phone dealing with a staffing crisis.

"You're right. I'm sorry. Phone goes away right now."

But even with the phone put away, my mind was still at the center. Still calculating, worrying, planning, trying to solve problems that felt bigger than I was.

I'd been carrying everyone and everything for so long that I'd forgotten how to put anything down. My children needed the "strong mom." My staff needed the "capable boss." My marriage needed the "woman who could handle it all." But somewhere in all that handling, I lost the part of me that knew how to be held.

The irony wasn't lost on me. I was running a business dedicated to nurturing children, creating spaces where little ones could feel safe and loved, while I myself had no idea what it felt like to receive that kind of care. I could give tenderness to a thousand toddlers, but I couldn't ask for it myself.

This wasn't an accident. This was learned. This was inherited. This was the way love had been modeled for me from the very beginning.

Strength kept me alive. It also kept me far from myself. To understand why, you have to understand where that strength came from.

*****

I didn't grow up with soft love. Not because I wasn't loved, but because in my culture, and in my home, love didn't come soft. It came structured. It came with discipline, responsibility, expectations. Love meant food on the table, a roof over your head, straightened beds, and straightened backs. It meant surviving. Getting good grades. Holding your emotions in check. Anything else? That was luxury.

My mother is a strong woman. A survivor in every sense of the word. But she didn't do softness. Not because she didn't want to, but because no one ever gave her permission to. I don't think she even saw it as an option. She didn't have the safety to explore it. Like many daughters of women who survived the unthinkable, I've had to unlearn strength as a default setting.

To understand me, you have to understand my mother. You have to understand what she survived, what she carried, and how that shaped the love she was able to give.

My mother came of age in Haiti in the 1960s, during a time when being a woman meant enduring in silence. She was raised to be useful, not comfortable. To work, not to rest. To carry burdens, not to put them down.

But what I've come to understand is that what we sometimes call strength is really just untreated trauma in a beautiful dress. My mother carried hers quietly, stoically, like so many women of her generation.

I only recently learned that in 1963—when she had her first child, my oldest brother—she underwent a cesarean section without anesthesia. A C-section. No anesthesia. Just the raw brutality of survival.

That kind of pain leaves an imprint. On the body, on the mind, and, though we don't always acknowledge it, on the lineage. That kind of experience teaches you that suffering is normal. That pain is part of the price. That comfort is not a right, it's a privilege you may never be afforded.

And that's how so many women like my mother live. Not because they're martyrs. Not because they want to be heroic. But because no one told them they deserved anything different.

This became her normal. Enduring became her language of love. She loved us by making sure we never experienced what she had experienced. She loved us by being harder than the world would be, so that when the world tried to break us, we'd already be strong enough to withstand it.

When I was sick as a child, she didn't coddle me. She made me soup and sent me to school anyway. When I cried about playground bullies, she didn't comfort me. She taught me how to stand up for myself. When I wanted comfort after a bad day, she gave me chores to do instead, something productive to focus on.

This wasn't cruelty. This was her version of armor. This was a woman who had been cut open without anesthesia preparing her children for a world that would not be gentle with them.

Years later, my mother developed a growth on her back. We, her children, including three who are medical doctors, urged her to get it checked. To have it removed. But she refused. She insisted it wasn't worth the trouble. She didn't want to make a fuss. She didn't trust the medical system. She waited.

Until one night, the growth burst. She ended up in the hospital. They sedated her. Gave her anesthesia. Removed it cleanly. Quickly. Gently.

And afterward, she couldn't stop talking about it.

She kept saying, "I didn't feel anything." "It was so quick." "I should have done this years ago."

Imagine that. A woman who birthed a child through surgery without anesthesia was stunned by the idea that medical care could be gentle. That she could be made comfortable. That relief was possible.

That conversation broke my heart and opened my eyes. That's the kind of stock I come from. Women who normalize pain because they don't know comfort is an option. Women who delay care because they've been taught that their comfort doesn't matter.

People always tell me I'm strong. But I ask, at what cost? How much of that strength is mine, and how much of it is unprocessed inheritance? What part of my hustle, my resilience, my ability to push through comes from watching my mother normalize pain and delay care? What part of me resists softness because somewhere deep down, I learned that comfort was optional and strength was mandatory?

I didn't get soft love from my mother. Not because she didn't love me, but because she didn't know softness herself. She never had the safety to explore it. And so, like many daughters of women who survived the unthinkable, I've had to unlearn strength as a default setting. I've had to teach myself that being cared for is not a weakness. That anesthesia is not indulgent. That healing should never be treated as a luxury.

I didn't realize until much later that I had internalized that version of love so deeply, I started replicating it. In my own marriage. In how I mothered. In my business. I showed love through acts of service, through fixing and doing and showing up, but I didn't know how to say, "Can you just hold me for a second? Can you just sit with me? Can I not be strong today?"

Because I wasn't raised with soft love, I leaned heavily into my masculine energy. The doing. The leading. The holding it all together. I was good at it. So good, in fact, that I started getting typecast into that role. The strong one. The boss. The fixer. The one with the answers. The one who didn't cry. The one who didn't need help. The one who could take it.

And I could. But I didn't always want to.

At my core, I'm not some hard-shelled matriarch. I'm not cold. I'm not unreachable. I'm soft in so many ways, but I didn't know how to raise my hand and say, "Hey, I didn't sign up for this role. I'm tired." It felt like a betrayal. Like weakness. Like if I said it out loud, everything I built might collapse.

But here's the thing: being typecast doesn't just happen in the movies. It happens in life. You play the role long enough, people stop asking if you want something else. They just keep handing you the same script. And sometimes you convince yourself it's the only part you know how to play.

Even in friendships and relationships, I found myself stuck in that pattern. People came to me when they needed strength, advice, a plan. Rarely did they come to pour into me. Rarely did they ask if I was okay. And honestly? I didn't blame them. I taught them that I was the one who had it all under control.

People kept handing me the same script. I kept performing. Softness was the role I had to write for myself.

If armor is inherited, softness must be learned. So I started practicing, mile by mile.

CHAPTER 8

Run the Mile You're In

The bright light on my phone read 5:47 a.m. and the Bridle Path was calling my name.

I laced up my Brooks, stepped out into the crisp morning air, and felt my body automatically turn toward Central Park. My feet knew the way: Mariner's Gate, up the little hill, cross into the East side of the park while trying not to get run down by the bikers, onto the soft dirt and gravel that hundreds of runners call home. Four point two miles of forgiving terrain that wouldn't destroy your knees the way concrete would.

Left foot, right foot, breathe.

The path was nearly empty except for a few other early morning runners and the occasional dog walker. I didn't run with music. Never had. Which meant it was just me, my footsteps, and the relentless chatter in my head.

Inhale for three, exhale for three.

By the time I hit the first mile marker, my body had found its rhythm, but my mind was already racing ahead to the day's problems. The licensing renewal that was overdue. The teacher who'd called in sick again. The settlement payment to Bright

Horizons that was due next month. Always next month, like a shadow that followed me everywhere.

Keep moving. Just keep moving.

This was my church, my therapy, my escape. Four to five days a week, I'd trace this same route, sometimes adding the reservoir loop to stretch it to six miles when I needed more time to think. Or when I needed more time to *not* think.

The funny thing about running without music is that you can't hide from yourself. No beat to get lost in, no lyrics to distract you from whatever's eating at you. Just the steady percussion of your feet hitting the ground and whatever's churning in your head.

A runner passed me going the opposite direction. Middle-aged guy in expensive gear, breathing hard, looking miserable. Probably thinking about his mortgage or his marriage or whatever crisis was chasing him out here before dawn. We gave each other that subtle nod runners share. The acknowledgment that we're all out here fighting something.

Today, like most days, I was solving problems. First my own: how can I stretch my revenue to cover an extra week of a 3-payroll month, whether I should hire that new teacher or wait, or if there was any way to renegotiate the terms of that contract that was bleeding me dry. Then, when my own problems felt too heavy, I'd move on to fixing the planet. World hunger. Healthcare. The fact that quality childcare was still treated like a luxury instead of a necessity.

Mile two. My breathing had settled into that sweet spot where my body was working but not fighting.

Run the mile you're in.

The mantra came to me somewhere around the reservoir, the way it always did. It wasn't new. I'd been carrying this phrase for years, ever since training with a coach for my second marathon. But lately, it had become more than a running technique. It had become survival.

Don't think about mile twenty-five when you're only at mile two. Just be here. Just this step. Just this breath.

I passed the spot where the path curves near the Shakespeare Garden. A memory flashed: bringing the kids here when they were little, Sophie wanting to hunt for fairies in the rosemary bushes while Alexi read every single plaque about the plants mentioned in the plays. Chloe had been more interested in the hot dog vendor outside the park. Simpler times, when my biggest worry was remembering to pack enough snacks.

Now Sophie was a junior in high school, stressed about college applications. Alexi was already in college, calling home less and less. Chloe was deep in her teenage attitude phase. And here I was, still trying to hold everything together, still running the same path, still carrying everyone else's problems on my back.

Focus. Breathe. Just this mile.

By mile three, the endorphins were starting to kick in. For a brief window, the weight I carried everywhere else felt lighter. Not gone. Never gone. But manageable. Like maybe I could handle whatever was waiting for me back in the real world.

My phone buzzed in my armband. Text message. Probably my assistant with another crisis that couldn't wait until normal business hours. I ignored it. Whatever it was could wait six miles. The world wouldn't end if I wasn't immediately available to fix it.

One foot in front of the other. That's all you have to do.

The path curved ahead of me, disappearing into a canopy of trees. I couldn't see where it ended, couldn't see what was around the next bend. But I knew if I just kept moving, kept putting one foot in front of the other, I'd eventually get where I needed to go.

Even if I had no idea where that was anymore.

My shoulders had been creeping toward my ears again. I forced them down, rolled my neck, tried to release the tension I carried like armor. It would be back before I reached the office. Hell, it would probably be back before I finished this run. But for now, for these precious few miles, I could let it go.

Run the mile you're in.

The only mile that mattered was the one under my feet right now.

When I got on that treadmill just to lose some baby weight after giving birth to Sophie all those years ago, if someone had told me I would turn into this person who would eventually complete 13 marathons, I would have laughed in their face. But running was the surprise I never expected.

What I learned through running is that the human body is incredible. Once it figures out what you're up to, it'll almost always adapt. So it's true: when you're going through hell, keep going. Your body will catch up to your determination.

My relationship with running evolved over time. What started as exercise became my solution to whatever was ailing me. When the business was crushing me, when the lawsuit felt overwhelming, when I couldn't sleep because my mind wouldn't stop racing through worst-case scenarios, I'd lace up my shoes and hit the road.

Running became my reset button. My therapy. My moving meditation.

It was the only place where I could practice what Coach John taught me: focus on what's right in front of you. This step. This breath. This mile.

Everything else could wait.

*****

I was crumbling under the weight of it all.

But I kept moving.

I stayed positive in front of my staff. I smiled. I showed up. I reassured parents. I kept the vision alive. I disappeared from my social life, stopped responding to texts, skipped the birthday parties, the brunches. I put my head down and worked.

I was in full-on survival mode. Always bracing for impact. My jaw was constantly clenched. My shoulders lived somewhere up around my ears. I'd catch myself holding my breath during meetings, like I was waiting for the next blow to land.

I started having these headaches that were like a hangover with none of the fun. Dull, persistent things that lived right behind my eyes. I'd pop Advil like candy, but they barely touched it. My neck felt like concrete. I'd roll it during phone calls, trying to work out knots that just kept getting tighter.

Always trying to stay ahead of the next impending crisis.

So I kept running. The only thing I was doing just for me.

I didn't run to train for another race. I couldn't even imagine racing again. Boston had been my last race the year before, and honestly, I didn't know if I'd ever line up at a starting line again.

But I ran anyway. Because it was the only thing keeping me sane.

And in those runs, my mantra became a lifeline.

Run the mile you're in.

That became my only focus. Not tomorrow. Not next week. Not what happened yesterday. Just this moment. This minute. This mile. That's all I had.

In my experience training for and finishing 13 marathons, (and for the record, my favorite marathon isn't Boston, though that was the dream. It's the one that got me there. The qualifier. That's where preparation met luck. My training plus great weather plus cooperative gastrointestinal conditions. Everything aligned, and I ran the race of my life), I've learned that the race is never just about your body. It's about your headspace. You can't start at mile 1 and immediately start thinking about mile 25. That's too much for the brain to process. You can't forecast the pain, the weather, the mental exhaustion. You'll never survive.

You have to bite-size it. One mile at a time.

How does it feel right now, in this mile? Check in. Breathe. Deal with this. Then move on to the next. And the next.

And if you just keep putting one foot in front of the other, eventually, mile by mile, breath by breath, you get to mile 26.

One way or another.

Over the years, I have coached myself, ran with groups, ran solo, and sometimes had a coach. I trained with a coach to qualify for Boston and then to actually run Boston. Training was intense because I took it seriously. I would run on vacation. Long runs were done early on Saturdays, sometimes starting as early as 5 a.m. so I could be back home by 8 a.m. to spend the rest of the weekend with my family.

That "run the mile you're in" mantra came from Coach John who trained me for the San Francisco Marathon. We'd do hill workouts on the 102nd Transverse to prepare for the brutal hills of San Francisco, and I'd sometimes have 10 to 12x 200-meter hill sprints ahead of me. He'd be on his bike with the timer, and I'd start out fine. But halfway through my reps, as I'd start to crest the steepest part of the hill, I would inevitably slow down.

The first few times, he yelled, "This is where you recommit! I need you to recommit!"

Between catching my breath, I gasped something like, "I can't believe I have six more of these."

"Is that what you're thinking about when you slow down? Worrying about the next rep?" he said.

"Yeah, and also how I'm possibly going to die on this hill."

"I want you to do me a favor," he said. "For the next few reps, only run the rep you're in. And for the race, you're going to do the same thing. You can't think about mile 24 when you're at mile 7. You are only to run the mile you're in."

I never forgot that. And I realized it was applicable to my life.

This philosophy started changing how I handled everything. Instead of lying awake calculating how I'd pay rent for the next six months, I focused on making it through this week's payment. When a parent complained about our policies, instead of spiraling into worst-case scenarios about losing enrollment, I dealt with that one conversation. That one problem.

When my lawyer called with updates about the case, I stopped myself from jumping to the settlement amount, the timeline, what this meant for my future. I listened to what he was actually saying. I asked about the next step. Just the next step.

It sounds simple, but it was revolutionary for someone whose brain default was to solve everything at once.

The morning a health inspector showed up unannounced, my old self would have panicked about licensing violations, potential fines, what parents would think if word got out. Instead, I walked her through our protocols one room at a time. I answered her questions. I showed her our documentation. I stayed present for that inspection instead of living in my head about all the ways it could go wrong.

But while I kept running, I also kept everything else inside.

I found it nearly impossible to talk to anyone about what was really going on. Part of it was shame.

I was embarrassed. I felt stupid for allowing myself to fall into this situation. I couldn't believe that I, of all people, had misread that clause. Not missed it. Misread it. I'd seen the non-compete. I'd measured the distance. I thought I was being careful. But I measured walking distance, not "as the crow flies." I didn't know there was a difference. I didn't know I needed a professional surveyor to measure legal distance. I thought my GPS watch and careful route planning were enough.

I was wrong. And that mistake was costing me everything.

The other part? Judgment.

People who've never started a business, who've never risked anything, are real quick to remind you how risky it is to open one. "Oh wow, I don't know how you do it." They say it like a compliment, but the subtext is clear: You're kind of crazy. You should've known better.

And when things go wrong? Some of those same people who once hailed you as successful suddenly vanish. Or worse, they turn on you.

I had a friend, someone I'd known for years, who said to me during one of our regular coffee dates, "Well, maybe this is a sign that you should have just stayed small. You had a good thing going with the first business. Why did you need more?"

That just reinforced all the reasons I didn't open up to anyone.

I wasn't ready for opinions like that. I didn't need advice from people who'd never put themselves on the line. I didn't need negativity from people who thought dreaming big was somehow greedy. I needed relief. I needed understanding. And I didn't know where to find that.

So I stayed quiet.

My sister Martine would call from Baltimore, wanting to catch up, and I found myself editing everything. She asked about the business, and I gave her the sanitized version. "Things are good. Busy, you know how it is." When she pushed for details about why I sounded tired, I'd blame it on the kids' schedules or say I was fighting a cold.

When I did meet up with the running group, I stopped going to post-run coffee sessions. These were women I'd been training with for years, people who knew my marathon times better than my own family. But sitting around discussing weekend plans and vacation destinations felt frivolous and self-indulgent. So, I'd finish my run and disappear before anyone could ask how things were going.

My neighbor Julia, Flynn's mom from the early Smarter Toddler days, texted about getting the kids together for dinner. I made excuses. "So busy with work stuff right now, maybe next month." Next month became next season. Next season became radio silence.

Even my relationship with Robert started to shift. He knew the basics, of course. You can't hide a lawsuit from your spouse and business partner. But I found myself managing his stress about the situation on top of my own. When he started spiraling about worst-case scenarios, I switched into reassurance mode. "We'll figure it out. It's going to be okay." I became the one holding us both together, which meant I had nowhere to fall apart.

The most painful one was my mom. She'd call with her usual check-ins, wanting to know how the grandkids were doing, when she could visit next. She was so proud of what I'd built. She'd tell her friends about her daughter who owned schools in Manhattan. How was I going to tell her I had fucked up?

So I told her what I told everyone else: everything was fine.

The isolation became its own kind of prison. I was surrounded by people who cared about me, but I couldn't let any of them in. The shame felt too heavy. The judgment felt too risky. And the fear that talking about it might somehow make it more real kept me locked in my own head.

It was just me, my problems, and those early morning runs where I could finally stop pretending everything was okay.

Even my kids, teenagers now, knew something was off. I couldn't burden them with this. I wanted them to be focused on school dances and graduation, not legal fees and lawsuits. I didn't want them worrying about problems they had no power to solve.

But they weren't asking anyway.

Teenagers are incredibly self-absorbed. That's not a criticism, it's just biology. Their brains are wired to focus on their own world, their own problems, their own drama. And my kids were no different.

Alexi was deep into his senior year, stressed about college applications and SAT scores. Chloe was navigating sophomore year social politics and complaining about teachers. Sophie was dealing with middle school friend drama and wanting to quit piano lessons.

They loved me, but they weren't checking in on my emotional state. Why would they? As far as they knew, Mom had everything handled. Mom always had everything handled.

My parenting strategy became about maintaining the illusion that everything was normal. Dinner still happened at 6:30 p.m.. Homework still got checked. Permission slips still got signed. I showed up to soccer games and school plays with the same energy I'd always brought, even when my phone was buzzing with messages from my lawyer.

The beauty of teenagers is that they're so consumed with their own lives, they don't notice when you're falling apart. As long as their immediate needs were met, they were fine. Food in the fridge, spending money when they needed it, someone to drive them to friend's houses. That was enough.

Robert stepped up more during this time with the logistics. He handled grocery runs, wrangled the kids to their activities, and still handled his side of Smarter Toddler business. But the emotional bandwidth still fell to me. When Chloe needed to vent about some teacher she hated, she came to me. When Sophie wanted help with a project, she found me. When Alexi needed to discuss college options, I was the one he sought out.

Not because Robert wasn't available, but because that's just how our family operated. I was mission control for everyone's emotional needs.

The kids never saw me cry. They never saw me panic. And they never asked if I was okay. Because in their teenage minds, parents don't have problems. Parents just exist to solve their problems.

I thought I was protecting them. But I was also protecting myself from having to explain something I could barely understand.

I was carrying all of this, and it was beginning to wear on my body. I started having pain that would wake me up at night, usually around 2 or 3 a.m.. Sharp. Persistent. Unexplained.

Doctors ran every test imaginable. The first thing they found was "you have a raging UTI." Okay, antibiotics for the UTI.

But little did I know this would be the beginning of a medical mystery that would take close to 10 years to solve.

The pain became chronic, but they stopped suspecting UTI and started testing for every imaginable scary thing. I kept getting referred from one specialist to another. At some point, I landed in the very posh offices of a Park Avenue surgeon who diagnosed me with a tortuous colon.

When you Google tortuous colon, here's what pops up:

"A tortuous colon is an abnormally long colon (large intestine) that has many twists and loops in order to fit inside the body. It is also known as a redundant colon. If the obstruction is caused by a twisting of the sigmoid area of the large intestine, a doctor may try to straighten out the twisting segment with lighted instruments (such as a proctoscope or sigmoidoscope) or a barium enema. But surgery is sometimes needed to fix twisting of the intestine."

Scary much?

Of course, he wanted to cut me open right away. And then he added, almost casually, that there was no guarantee the surgery would even work or relieve the pain.

I said no thank you, and walked out of his office.

I had no interest in being this man's modern-day Henrietta Lacks.

The most conservative doctor I saw diagnosed a tiny ovarian cyst. Too small, he said, to explain the level of pain I was in.

But I was desperate for something. A reason for the pain, some kind of fix.

So when they suggested surgery to remove it, I said yes.

Here's the part that sounds crazy: A small part of me saw that surgery as a break.

Two days in bed. Two days where no one could ask me for anything. Two days where I could justify feeling sorry for myself without guilt. No meetings. No deadlines. Just silence. Just rest.

Do you know how low you have to be for surgery to feel like relief?

It wasn't my best moment.

But it was real.

I had the surgery, but like I suspected, it didn't solve the strange stomach pains. The late-night wakeups. The constant hum of anxiety running in the background of my life.

Those two days in bed were supposed to be my sanctuary. My forced break from the chaos. But even drugged up on pain medication, even with doctor's orders to rest, my brain wouldn't shut off.

I'd lie there staring at the ceiling, mentally going through my to-do list. Who was covering my meetings? Had my assistant remembered to call the parents about the field trip permission slips? Was the licensing renewal paperwork filed on time?

My phone sat on the nightstand, buzzing periodically with texts and emails. I'd told everyone I was having minor surgery and would be unreachable for a few days, but the business doesn't pause for anyone's recovery. Not even the owner's.

Robert brought me soup and told me to rest, but rest felt impossible. My body was exhausted, healing, trying to recover from being cut open. But my mind was still running at full speed, still trying to solve problems from bed.

Even when I did drift off, I woke up in a panic, thinking I missed something important. Some deadline, crisis or emergency that required my immediate attention.

The irony wasn't lost on me. I'd been so desperate for a break that I convinced myself surgery was a vacation. But even with legitimate medical reasons to step away, I couldn't actually step away.

That's when I realized how broken my relationship with rest had become. I didn't know how to stop. Even when my body was literally forcing me to stop.

Doctors ran more tests after the surgery. They came up with everything but the truth:

"You're fine." "Maybe it's stress." "Maybe it's in your head."

For a moment, I wondered if maybe I was just broken.

But what I didn't realize then was that my body was trying to tell me something. I was holding all my stress, my fear, my tension in. And it had to go somewhere.

The body keeps the score, right?

Mine was keeping receipts. For every moment I pretended I was okay. For every panic I swallowed down. For every time I pushed through when I should have paused.

I was carrying the weight of trying to hold everything together while everything around me threatened to fall apart.

Something had to change. I just didn't have the luxury of time, or so I believed, to figure out what that "something" was.

I used to say I wasn't a napper.

Even when I had a rare pocket of time to myself, I couldn't rest. I told people, "I'm just not a nap person."

But I eventually understood there's no such thing as someone who can't nap. There's only someone whose nervous system doesn't feel safe enough to rest.

That realization came to me years later, when I started napping again. Often, and easily. I had to stop and ask myself: What's different? What changed?

It wasn't my body. It was my mind. It was my safety.

That was the revelation. I wasn't broken physically. I was unraveling mentally. I didn't need more specialists. I didn't need more pills. I needed space. Stillness. Grace.

Hindsight is always 20/20. But if I'd known then what I know now, I might've spared myself the endless parade of tests and pill pushers.

What I needed most was to finally let my body exhale.

*****

I used to think balance meant keeping all the balls in the air. Work. Marriage. Kids. Home. Self-care (maybe). But what no one tells you is that sometimes, no matter how well you juggle, a ball will drop. And what might surprise you is who picks it up.

One morning, when my daughter Chloe was in eighth grade, she was getting ready for her first overnight field trip to visit the Liberty Bell. The usual excitement was in the air. Packing, checking bags, outfit laid out. I was proud of her. Independent. Responsible. Everything was good.

But what caught me off guard was what she did before she left.

Without being asked, she quietly packed a full lunch for her younger sister; sandwich, snacks, juice box, all the trimmings, for that day and the next. She tucked a little note in there, too, just like I used to do when I had the mental bandwidth to remember things like that. When I asked her what she was doing, she said gently, "I just didn't want her to go without lunch...just in case."

Just in case.

Because she knew me. She knew I was trying my best, but sometimes my best wasn't enough.

The night before, I celebrated a huge win at work. One of my teachers had been facing a terrifying situation at home with an abusive partner, and with the help of a lawyer friend, I secured safe housing and legal support for her. It had taken weeks of coordination and sensitivity. That night, when I got the call that it was done and she was safe, I cried tears of relief. I felt like I had really done something important.

I was someone's lifeline. I helped a woman feel safe again. I was on it.

And yet, in that same breath, I forgot to pack my own child's lunch.

Before those two sentences about not caring, a wave of emotions hit me. Guilt crashed over me first, followed immediately by shame. Here was my 12-year-old daughter stepping into a mothering role because she couldn't trust that I'd handle the basics. Then came the pride, because she was so thoughtful and mature. Then more guilt for being proud that my child was compensating for my shortcomings.

And it wasn't that I didn't care. I cared so much it hurt. But the truth is, I had run out of capacity. That's the paradox of balance: you might be holding up someone else's world while your own feels like it's slipping out from under you.

Chloe's quiet act of thoughtfulness brought me to tears. It warmed my heart and simultaneously broke it in half. I was so proud of her and so ashamed of myself. I felt like I had won "worst mom of the year" on the very day I had done something objectively heroic.

I realized this myth of balance we chase isn't just unrealistic, it's cruel. It makes us believe that if we just try hard enough, plan better, wake up earlier, want it more, we'll get it right on all fronts.

But sometimes, even when you're doing your best, you still drop the ball. And when your 12-year-old is the one picking it up, it humbles you.

That doesn't mean you failed. It means you're human. And it means they're learning something too, about empathy, about care, about showing up for each other.

People love to ask working mothers how they "do it all."

For a long time, I played along. I smiled, nodded, gave some version of, "You know, it's a juggle." But the truth is, I wasn't balancing. I was barely staying afloat.

Because here's what no one tells you: Balance implies there's a version of this that feels even. That all the parts of your life, career, marriage, motherhood, self, can exist in harmony, if only you get the formula right.

But life isn't a formula. In reality, every day is going to be different. Some day's work demands more. On some days the kids need more. Some days you need more. The idea that you can distribute your energy equally across all areas every single day is not just impossible, it's maddening.

Sometimes something has to bleed. And sometimes that something is you.

I thought balance meant multitasking with a smile. It meant showing up for everyone, on time, prepared, emotionally available, while still holding myself to an impossible standard of performance. I'd be on a conference call while stirring dinner, reviewing homework while responding to parent emails, planning weekend activities while mentally running through Monday's staff schedule.

At work, I was leading. At home, I was nurturing. In the courtroom, I was fighting. On the inside, I was unraveling.

But from the outside? I made it look effortless. That was the trick. The illusion of balance is a performance we're taught to perfect.

And honestly: I was good at it. So good that most people didn't know how close I was to breaking.

There's a passage in Michael Singer's *The Untethered Soul* that says:

"You will get to a point in your growth where you understand that if you protect yourself, you will never be free."

That stayed with me. Because what I was protecting wasn't just my image, it was the entire infrastructure I had built.

I didn't feel safe enough to pause. To nap. To take a break. To feel.

Because I thought if I stopped for even a second, everything would fall apart.

But I didn't realize the toll that "holding it all together" was taking on my nervous system, my body, my spirit.

That's not balance. That's survival.

Later, when I started reading the work of Pema Chodron, something else landed. In *When Things Fall Apart*, she writes: "To be fully alive, fully human, and completely awake is to be continually thrown out of the nest."

That's what motherhood felt like. That's what entrepreneurship felt like. That's what being Black and female in business felt like.

I was being thrown out of the nest every day. And I still had to get dinner on the table.

The pressure is truly unfair for so many women. Looking back now, I realize what I was chasing wasn't balance, it was perfection. I thought if I got everything just right, I'd feel peace.

But peace doesn't come from getting it right. It comes from letting go. Letting go of the belief that you owe everyone everything. Letting go of the myth that your strength is in how much you carry. Letting go of the guilt for being human. Now, I believe in rhythm, not balance. Some seasons, I show up more for work. Some seasons, I'm more available to my kids. Some seasons, I tend to myself. It's not perfect. It's honest.

Balance asks you to split yourself evenly. Rhythm asks you to listen. To adapt. To breathe.

To trust that some days you'll be the one picking up the ball, and some days, if you're lucky, someone who loves you will pick it up for you.

CHAPTER 9

Doing Business While Black

The business began to cannibalize itself. We were making money, but we could never quite catch up. The loans we took out to pay Bright Horizons weren't in the original budget. Those payments undermined our operations from day one.

Every month felt like robbing Peter to pay Paul. The settlement payment came first, always first, because missing it meant immediate shutdown. Then payroll, because losing staff meant losing families. Then utilities, insurance, supplies. Rent often came last, which was a dangerous game in New York City real estate.

The biggest burden? Rent at FiDi, $60,000 a month.

Sixty thousand dollars. Every single month. It was more than some people made in a year, and we had to come up with it regardless of enrollment, regardless of unexpected expenses, regardless of anything else going wrong.

I had spreadsheets tracking every penny. Color-coded budgets that showed exactly how much we needed to bring in just to break even. The margins were so thin that a single family leaving could throw off our entire monthly calculation.

"We're making good money," Robert said one evening, looking at our revenue numbers.

"We're making gross revenue," I corrected. "Net is a different story."

"How different?"

I showed him the real numbers. After settlement payments, loan service, rent, payroll, insurance, supplies, licensing fees and everything else, we were barely scraping by.

"So what do we do?"

"We grow. Fast. Or we figure out how to cut costs without cutting quality."

But growing fast required marketing investment we didn't have. And cutting costs meant either reducing staff or compromising on the experience that made us special. Neither felt like viable options.

I fell behind by one month on the FiDi rent. It happened fast. A family emergency required unexpected travel. Three families moved out of the city in the same week. A major repair ate into our contingency fund. Suddenly, the $60,000 wasn't there.

"I can get it next month," I told myself. "With the new enrollments, I'll catch up."

But next month brought its own surprises. A staff member needed emergency surgery. The health department required an unexpected upgrade to the fire alarm system. Another loan payment was due.

And just like that, the eviction notice came. Swift. Brutal. Impersonal.

"Notice to Quit and Surrender Possession" in bold letters across the top. Legal language that basically said: pay up or get out.

I stared at that paper for a long time, reading the same sentences over and over. "You are hereby required to quit and surrender possession of the above-described premises to the landlord..."

This wasn't a friendly reminder or a grace period conversation. This was checkmate.

I tried everything to keep it at bay. I called the landlord's office multiple times, leaving increasingly desperate voicemails. I wrote formal letters explaining our situation and proposing payment plans. I even showed up in person, hoping to humanize what had become a purely transactional relationship.

Finally, someone agreed to speak with me. They gave me seven days. Seven days to come up with both the arrears and the upcoming rent.

$120,000. In seven days.

I had nothing left. The business account was depleted. Our personal savings had been emptied months ago to cover previous shortfalls. Credit cards were maxed out. There was literally nowhere left to turn.

Three days before the deadline, I was sitting at this little bar near the office, too exhausted to think, too paralyzed to move. I wasn't drinking. Just sitting. Staring at nothing, trying to figure out how to pull off a miracle I didn't believe in.

The bartender, a sweet guy who'd seen me there before during my more desperate moments, brought me a plate of fries without being asked.

"On the house," he said. "If not alcohol, carbs usually help with most things."

I almost cried at that small kindness. When you're drowning, even the smallest gestures feel enormous.

There was a stairwell off the side of the bar, leading up to the apartment building connected above. I walked up those stairs, sat down, and pulled out my phone. It was time to make the call I'd been avoiding.

I called the landlord's representative, a tough woman named Patricia. Tough might be generous. Maybe she was just doing her job. But she didn't have much warmth, and our previous interactions had been purely business.

I took a deep breath and dialed her direct number, the one she'd given me "for emergencies only." This definitely qualified.

"Patricia, this is Kettia from the John Street location. I know it's late, but I wanted to talk to you about the payment situation."

"What about it?" Her voice was clipped, professional but not encouraging.

"I don't have the rent. I'm not going to have it in three days either."

Silence on the other end. I could hear papers shuffling, probably my file being pulled up on her computer.

"We already gave you an extension once," she said finally.

"I know, and I appreciate that. But I'm asking if we could work out a payment plan. Something that would give me a chance to catch up without losing everything."

"A payment plan." Her tone suggested this was the most ridiculous thing she'd heard all week.

"Yes. I can make partial payments, with a schedule to catch up over the next few months. The business is solid, Patricia. We're just dealing with some unexpected circumstances."

That's when she started yelling.

Literally yelling.

"I should have known not to give you an extension! You people always think the rules don't apply to you! I know your capacity! What are you doing with all the money you're taking in?!"

Her voice was so loud I had to hold the phone away from my ear. People walking up and down the stairwell stared at me.

"You don't belong there! That space is too expensive for your little operation! I told ownership this was going to happen!"

I felt like I'd been slapped. The venom in her voice, the contempt, the way she said "you people" like it explained everything wrong with the situation.

I broke. I'm not a crier, especially not in business situations. I'd learned early that tears were seen as weakness, manipulation, proof that women couldn't handle the pressure. But sitting on those stairs, listening to her tear me apart, I couldn't stop the tears from coming.

I was mortified, but I couldn't stop them.

"Patricia, please," I said through the tears. "I'm not trying to take advantage of your business. I have families depending on us. Teachers I am responsible for. Everything we've worked for is at stake here."

I told her what would happen if we lost the space. The ripple effect through dozens of families who'd chosen us for their children. The staff members who'd believed in our vision. My own family, who'd invested everything we had.

I wasn't trying to manipulate her. I was just being honest about what was at stake.

She got quiet. I could hear her breathing, processing what I'd just said.

Then she softened, just a little bit.

"Look," she said, her voice calmer but still wary. "I've heard every sob story in the book. But you sound different."

"I am different. This isn't a game for me. This is everything."

Another pause. A long one.

"I'll give you one last chance. One payment plan. But you miss even one payment, even by a day, and you're out the next morning. No extensions, no excuses, no more phone calls."

"I understand."

"I hope you do. Because I won't have this conversation again."

Then she hung up.

As I stood up to leave, someone yelled from the top of the stairs: "Hey! If you're gonna use the stairs as your office, keep it down next time."

New York gonna be New York.

But I had my payment plan. I had a chance to save everything, one month at a time.

The question was whether I could actually pull it off.

*****

They tell you not to play the race card. They tell you to keep it professional. To focus on the work. To stay above it.

But when the rules change the second you walk into the room, when the deal feels different because of who you are, when the punishment doesn't match the "mistake," you realize something very quickly: This isn't just business. This is doing business while Black.

I know some might say, "You made a mistake. You violated the clause. You paid the price. It's just business."

But is it? Just business?

First of all, if you're not Black, and even if you are the biggest ally who's ever ally'ed, you will never fully understand this conversation. And if you're not a Black woman? You'll understand even less.

Over the years, I've brushed off so many incidents, I could write a whole book on the microaggressions alone. For example, there was the white parent who walked into our 89th Street location and assumed my white receptionist was the owner, even though I was sitting in my office, the one clearly marked as the director's. They didn't even blink.

Or the parent who said, "Oh, you're not like a real Black person. Look at this place!"

Then there was the wannabe investor, back when I only had one location, who offered me a deal where I'd walk away with $200,000. His pitch? "$200,000 is a lot of money for you, isn't it? I bet you've never seen that kind of money."

Imagine that. Offering to buy me out of my own vision like he was doing me a favor. Get outta here!

But sometimes, the sting comes from your own.

I remember a Black family came in for a tour. Afterward, the mother approached me and said, "Oh, you're Kettia? I thought you were Asian."

And just like that, she withdrew her application. Yep. Sometimes it's your own.

Then there was the young woman, an "investor" who came in as part of a group, probably putting in less than $20,000, who eyed the Gucci shoes I was wearing and asked: "So I see you like designer clothes. How are you able to afford any of that if you need an investor? How do I know my investment will be used properly and not on personal items?"

Mind you, I was wearing a plain black turtleneck and slacks, nothing flashy, just one small logo on my shoes. She scanned me head to toe like I was about to rob her blind.

It took everything in me not to go full Angry Black Woman on her.

Instead, I said, "You won't."

And I walked her right out the door.

There were other incidents. More aggressive. More hateful.

But I brushed them off my shoulders like a surprising flake on a black suit. Because what choice did I have?

Would this story have played out differently if I weren't Black? 100%.

I still hear my father's voice in my head: "Don't give in to that mindset. Don't say 'the man this' or 'the man that.' You work hard. That's all that matters."

And I believed that. For a long time, I really believed that.

There's that famous scene in *Scandal* where Papa Pope tells Olivia, "You have to be twice as good to get half of what they get."

What no one tells you is what happens when you are. When you are that good. When you do deliver at that level.

Sometimes, they come after you even harder.

Your excellence becomes a threat. Your success, an affront. It's like you took something they believe was never meant for you, and their need to knock you down becomes primal.

So no, this was never just about a contract. This was about control. About correction. About putting someone "back in her place."

You can't show up to these fights with a knife. You need a grenade. You need a plan. You need a *knowing*. And you need to tell the truth, even if it makes people uncomfortable.

The kind of knowing I'm referring to is the deep understanding that the rules are different for us, and we have to operate accordingly.

In other words, assume nothing is guaranteed, even when contracts are signed and deals are shaken on. Be sure to document everything—conversations, emails, even promises made in meetings. Keep records like your business depends on it, because it does.

Hire the best legal counsel you can afford from day one, not after the trouble starts. Budget for legal fees the same way you budget for rent, because legal protection is not a luxury for Black business owners—it's a necessity.

The same goes for relationships. Build them before you need them. Connect with allies in your industry, find mentors who've walked this path, advisors who understand the unique challenges you'll face. Join organizations, attend conferences, and make yourself visible in spaces where decisions get made.

Always have multiple exit strategies. Don't put all of your eggs in one basket, one location, one revenue stream. Diversify for growth, but also for survival.

Trust your instincts when something feels wrong, even if you can't prove it yet. When the energy shifts, when the tone changes, when promises start feeling empty, listen closely to that voice in your gut that's kept Black women alive for generations.

Most importantly, tapping into the knowing means you understand that your excellence is both your weapon and your target. Those who see your success as a threat will come for you not despite your success, but because of it. So prepare accordingly.

Build your business like you're going to war, because in many ways, you are. But ensure you build it with joy, with vision, with the unshakeable belief that you belong in every room you enter.

There's a cost to taking up space when that space wasn't built for you. And when you take it anyway, with grace, with excellence, with vision, they don't always clap. Sometimes they come for your crown and even knowing that, I'd still do it all over again. Because even when the game is rigged, playing small was never an option.

I was born in Haiti and raised by parents who believed in two things above all else: education and discipline. Not just as tools, but as armor.

In our house, feelings were optional. Excellence was not.

My parents didn't talk much about emotions, but they talked endlessly about hard work. They didn't raise me to be careful. They raised me to be excellent.

That belief shaped me more than anything else: the idea that success is earned through relentless effort, and that I belong in any room I work hard enough to enter.

For many Caribbean-Americans, that belief is cultural. It isn't arrogance. It's inheritance.

The collective pressure to maintain a certain standard was real. In our community, there were only a few acceptable paths: doctor, lawyer, engineer, or failure. You didn't argue. You didn't backtalk. You did your homework and you rose.

Which is why I need to talk about the difference between being Black in America and being Caribbean in America. Because they are not the same thing.

African-Americans are descendants of those who were enslaved in this country. Their legacy, America's original sin, is one of systemic brutality followed by centuries of intentional disenfranchisement. You don't have to look far to find its echoes in housing, education, healthcare, or business.

Caribbean-Americans, meanwhile, come from nations that were colonized but also liberated. Our histories carry trauma, yes, but also revolution. Toussaint Louverture. Marcus

Garvey. Jamaica. Trinidad. Haiti. The cultural narrative is simple and fierce: we rose up, we broke free, we survived.

That pride runs deep.

We may arrive in America as immigrants, but we arrive with the psychological imprint of a people who overthrew something. And that changes the way you walk through the world.

It doesn't mean we're not subject to racism. We are. But it means we weren't raised under the shadow of being taught we don't belong.

That's what I've come to understand. Many African-Americans are socialized into otherness from a very young age. Many Caribbean immigrants are socialized into excellence and told that otherness is just noise.

That difference isn't small. It shapes how we're parented, how we take risks, and how we experience success.

In many Caribbean households, your job is to make your family proud.

You're not raised to expect racism. You're raised to outwork it.

That mindset has its own cost. It often dismisses the psychological toll of navigating white spaces. It can lead to burnout, denial, and an internalized pressure that crushes you from the inside out.

But it also arms you with a kind of audacity that shows up when it counts.

When I started my first business, I didn't think twice. I didn't have a model or a mentor or a trust fund. But I had been told my entire life that education and effort would be enough. And I believed that.

So I acted accordingly.

When other people might have second-guessed themselves or spent months researching why it wouldn't work, I just started. When I saw an opportunity in early childhood education, I didn't worry about whether I had the right background. I figured I'd learn as I went.

That confidence to take risks, to believe I could figure it out, to assume I belonged in spaces where I might be the only person who looked like me, came directly from my Haitian upbringing.

My father didn't leave Haiti and work two jobs for nearly two decades so his daughter could play it safe. He did it so she could take big swings and believe she deserved whatever she was brave enough to build.

That mindset gave me the courage to walk into rooms and say, "I'm here to build something."

But confidence doesn't exempt you from racism. Excellence doesn't shield you from being punished for your ambition.

That's what I learned when I was sued over a hundred-foot technicality. That's what I learned when I was asked if I could be trusted with investor money because of the shoes I was wearing. That's what I learned when I watched something I created with love get copied and monetized by people who thought it was too good for me to own.

Yes, I was raised to believe I could do anything. But the world wasn't always ready to believe it with me.

There's power in where you come from. But no matter what country raised you, America will try to remind you who it thinks you are. When that happens, you'd better know for yourself, or it will decide for you.

That realization shifted my entire perspective on success. I began to understand that success isn't just about effort or confidence. It's about navigating systems that weren't designed for you to win.

The audacity my parents gave me was real and valuable. It got me in the door. It gave me courage to start. It sustained me through uncertainty.

But it also made me naive about the obstacles I'd face. I thought if I just worked hard enough, if I was excellent enough, if I was professional enough, that would be sufficient.

I didn't understand that sometimes you get punished not for failing but for succeeding too visibly. Not for doing something wrong, but for doing something right outside of someone else's blueprint.

That's the part Caribbean households don't prepare you for. They teach you to be excellent, but not what to do when your excellence threatens people who expected you to stay in your place.

Learning that lesson was painful. But it made me stronger in a different way.

It taught me that my power doesn't come only from confidence or hard work. It comes from understanding the game being played and choosing how to navigate it without losing myself in the process.

Now when I walk into rooms, I still carry that Caribbean audacity. But I also carry the wisdom that comes from knowing the playing field isn't level, and that real success requires not only effort, but strategy.

CHAPTER 10

Parallel Lives

As for my marriage?

The cracks were starting to show.

We were business partners, yes, but we had become little more than business partners. Smarter Toddler was all we talked about. Enrollment numbers. Cash flow projections. Settlement payment schedules. Staff issues. Licensing requirements.

The thing is, no relationship exists in a vacuum, and two things can be true at once. I could love Robert and be grateful for his solution-oriented approach most days—and I was. He was always there when I needed him, steady and supportive in his way. But that gratitude wasn't enough to bridge the distance that was growing between us.

I was so consumed by everything that was happening, so overwhelmed by the constant crisis management, that I didn't have the space or emotional energy to also be the loving, attentive wife I used to be. In that space where intimacy should have lived, distance crept in instead.

Is it all my fault? Of course not. Robert had his own way of dealing with stress, his own patterns of withdrawal. But I can take responsibility for my role in it. I was the one always in crisis mode, always needing to discuss the next emergency, always mentally calculating whether we'd make it through another month.

When you're drowning, you don't have much left to give to anyone else, even the person throwing you the life preserver.

Our conversations had become entirely transactional. "Did you call the insurance company?" "What time is the vendor meeting?" "Can you cover pickup today because I have to meet with the accountant?"

The kids had to reinstate their old "no business talk" rule at dinner, but this time it felt different. Before, our conversations had been about growth and possibility. Now everything was about damage control and survival. The business conversations had shifted from exciting updates about new families and creative programming to endless discussions about cash flow and legal compliance. Even our kids could feel the difference in energy.

"Mom, you're doing it again," Chloe said one evening when I started calculating settlement payment dates out loud while cutting a piece of bread.

"Doing what?"

"The thing where you talk about Smarter Toddler bills while we're trying to eat."

The problem was, we didn't know how to talk about anything else anymore. The business had consumed so much of our mental and emotional energy that we'd forgotten how to just be husband and wife.

Robert worked most nights now, doing maintenance, patching drywall, installing lights. He was either setting up or taking down some elaborate seasonal installation. Chinese New Year, Halloween, Valentine's Day, he went all out. He transformed the space inside and out, and parents and teachers were always in awe of his creativity.

But it meant our schedules rarely overlapped. I'd be leaving as he was arriving. He'd be finishing up his projects around midnight, sometimes later, while I was already asleep, exhausted from the day's crises.

"When's the last time we had a conversation that wasn't about work?" I asked him one rare evening when we found ourselves both home at the same time.

He thought about it for a long moment. "I honestly can't remember."

"That's not good."

"No, it's not."

We were like roommates managing a complicated household together. Efficient, polite, but missing the connection that had brought us together in the first place.

The space still radiated beauty. On the outside, we looked like we hadn't missed a step. Parents and visitors commented on how seamlessly we worked together, how lucky we were to share this passion project.

But on the inside?

We were just trying to survive from one day to the next.

The intimacy had been replaced by logistics. Romance had been sacrificed for responsibility. We were so focused on keeping the business alive that we'd forgotten to tend to the relationship that had created it.

"We need to fix this," I said one night as we passed each other in the hallway again, ships in the night of our own making.

"I know," Robert replied. "But how? There's always something urgent that needs attention."

"Maybe that's the problem. Everything feels urgent when you're constantly in crisis mode."

"So what do we do?"

I didn't have an answer. Because the truth was, I didn't know how to stop being in crisis mode. It had become our normal, and normal is a hard thing to change when you're just trying to keep your head above water.

Robert moved into the guest room before we ever admitted we were in trouble.

It wasn't a fight. It wasn't some dramatic turning point. It was quiet. Too quiet.

When he first suggested sleeping in the guest room, it felt more practical than anything else. He was putting in really late nights at the school, installing his elaborate seasonal displays, doing maintenance, handling the endless stream of tasks that kept our operation running. I was working days, handling enrollment, managing staff, dealing with the legal aftermath that still hung over everything we did.

Our schedules had become completely misaligned. I woke up at 5 a.m. to run with my running group, and I needed that sleep. When he came to bed at 1 or 2 a.m., exhausted and wired from work, it woke me up. Then I'd lie there staring at the ceiling, my mind racing through the next day's problems while he finally got the rest he needed.

"Maybe I should sleep in the guest room," he said one night after I'd been tossing and turning for an hour after he came home.

"If you think it would help," I replied, already half-asleep.

It seemed like a reasonable solution to a logistical problem. Couples with different schedules do this all the time, right? It didn't mean anything was wrong. It just meant we were being practical.

Except practical became permanent. Permanent became distant. And distant became something I didn't recognize until it was too late.

We went from being partners in everything to being ships passing in the night. Literally. I'd leave notes about business decisions on the kitchen counter. He'd text me about vendor meetings and supply orders.

The kids didn't notice, at least not then. They were self-involved in the way most teenagers are, dealing with their own problems that felt world-shattering to them—social drama, school pressure, friends, extracurriculars. Alexi was navigating his first year of college. Sophie was deep into her performing arts high school auditions. Chloe was managing her own teenage universe of friendships and activities.

And honestly, even though Robert and I had stopped being intimate partners, we were still supportive and familiar in the day-to-day ways that matter to kids. We still ate dinner together most nights, still enjoyed a glass of wine and relaxed together afterward. We never fought in the traditional sense of raised voices and slammed doors.

To our kids, we were just Mom and Dad—maybe busier than usual, maybe talking about work more than they liked, but nothing that set off alarm bells. They'd seen plenty of their friends' divorced parents, the drama and tension that comes with real marital conflict. We didn't fit that bill at all.

We looked like a couple that was simply consumed by running a business together, not a couple whose marriage was quietly unraveling. The crisis was so internal, so subtle, that even we didn't fully recognize it was happening until it was too late.

The intimacy didn't disappear all at once. It eroded slowly, so gradually that neither of us noticed until it was gone. Date nights became a thing of the past. When was the last time we'd gone out together, just the two of us? I honestly couldn't remember.

The business consumed everything. Every conversation, every thought, every moment of free time was dedicated to keeping our dream alive. We told ourselves this was temporary, that once we got through the financial crisis, once we stabilized, once we caught up, we'd reconnect.

But "once" kept getting pushed further into the future.

Robert and I never actually had that conversation. We stopped communicating about us. We stopped dreaming about our future together and put our relationship on autopilot. I was assuming we'd naturally find our way back to each other once the crisis passed, but that assumption was mine alone.

We weren't talking about what we needed from each other, what we were missing, or how we planned to rebuild what we'd lost. I was operating on hope and assumption while our connection quietly dissolved.

And in that space, in that growing distance between us, something happened that I never saw coming. Something that would shake the foundation of everything I thought I knew about us, about him, about the life we'd built together.

I wasn't snooping. I need to say that. I wasn't going through his things. I was looking for a file—one of the graphics we were using for an ad campaign. His computer was open, and there was a Word doc up on the screen. At first glance, it looked like a project outline or maybe a schedule for an event. But when I looked closer, I realized it wasn't business-related at all.

It was an itinerary.

7 p.m. dinner.
9 p.m. show.
Car service confirmed.

And I immediately knew two things:

> We didn't have plans.
> Robert didn't plan shit.

That was always my job. Birthdays, anniversaries, family trips, doctors' appointments, you name it! Even our weekly takeout routine–if it got scheduled, it was because I made it happen.

So, what was he doing planning a whole evening, complete with transportation, when we hadn't had a proper night out in weeks, maybe months? It hit me sideways.

The longer I looked at the file, the more something inside me started to twist. It wasn't just suspicion. It was something deeper. Like my body knew what my mind wasn't ready to admit.

I confronted him.

He didn't deny it. He didn't stutter or lie or try to gaslight me. He admitted it right away. That somehow made it worse.

I blew up. I said things I meant and things I didn't. I shook. But deep down, I was also in shock. In denial. Even though he said the words, even though he admitted it, I still couldn't wrap my head around the idea that my husband, my *person*, had betrayed me. We were supposed to be untouchable. We had built so much together. We were raising kids, building businesses, living this big, messy, shared life. I couldn't even fathom him being attracted to someone else, let alone stepping out on me.

It didn't make sense. My brain wouldn't compute it. My body rejected the information like a bad case of food poisoning.

"Robert," I said, my voice shaking as I stood in our kitchen, still holding the printed itinerary. "What is this?"

He looked at the paper, then at my face, and I watched something crumble in his expression. "Kettia, I..."

"Don't. Just tell me what this is."

He was quiet for a long moment. Then: "It's exactly what you think it is."

"Say it."

"I've been seeing someone."

The words hit me like a physical blow. I had to grab the counter to steady myself.

"How long?"

"Only a few weeks."

"A few weeks, like what is that? Two, three, eight weeks?" My voice grew louder. "How long has this really been going on, Robert? While I've been killing myself trying to save our business, you've been planning date nights with someone else?"

"It's not like that."

"It's not like what? It's not like you made dinner reservations? It's not like you arranged car service? It's not like you planned a whole evening that you never plan for your own wife?"

"You're right. You're completely right." His voice broke. "I'm so sorry, Kettia. It was stupid. It was the stupidest thing I've ever done."

"Stupid?" I was shaking now. "Stupid is forgetting to pay a bill. Stupid is missing an appointment. This is betrayal, Robert. This is twenty years down the drain."

"No, it's not. It doesn't have to be. It was a moment of weakness."

"A few months is not a moment! A few months is a choice. Over and over and over again."

He sat down heavily at our kitchen table, the same table where we'd planned our comeback, where we'd dreamed about our future. "I felt so lonely, Kettia. Like we were living parallel lives under the same roof but never actually in the same place."

"So you found someone else to be in the same place with?"

"It's not like that. I love you. I've always loved you. We just...we stopped connecting. We stopped seeing each other."

"I see you every day."

"You see your business partner. When's the last time you saw your husband?"

The question hung in the air between us, and I hated that I couldn't answer it immediately.

"That doesn't justify this," I said finally.

"You're right. Nothing justifies this. I know that. I'm not trying to make excuses. I'm just trying to explain how I let it happen."

"How could you let it happen? Like it was some accident? Like you tripped and fell into someone else's bed?"

"Kettia, please."

"Please what? Please forgive you? Please pretend this didn't happen? Please go back to normal like you didn't just blow up our entire life?"

I was crying now, angry tears that I couldn't stop. "We were supposed to be different, Robert. We were supposed to be the couple that made it. That got through anything together."

"We can still be that couple."

"No, we can't. Because that couple wouldn't have done this in the first place."

And the thing is, he wasn't wrong. About the loneliness. About the distance. But that didn't mean I could forgive him. Not then. Not yet.

What gutted me the most wasn't the betrayal itself. It was what it shattered.

Robert wasn't just my husband. He was my best friend. Best friends in the way that we could talk to each other about anything. Nothing was off limits. We were each other's favorite people to spend time with.

We could move from business strategy to astrology to what happened on *Lost* without missing a beat. There was always a new inside joke, some shared eye-roll over the absurdity of life.

His mom used to visit frequently from Bermuda, especially once we gave her those "grands" as she called her grandkids. She would always laugh at how much time we spent together. Not just as parents or co-founders, but just as two people who truly liked each other.

"I don't know how you two don't get tired of each other," she said once, curling up on our couch with tea. "I swear, you could talk from dusk till dawn and still have more to say."

"You two still act like you're dating," she'd say, shaking her head with a smile. "Most married couples can barely stand each other after twenty years, and here you are giggling like teenagers."

She wasn't wrong. We had this way of finding each other endlessly entertaining. Robert could make me laugh until my sides hurt just by doing impressions of our neighbors or reenacting something ridiculous that happened at work.

That's what made it so impossible to believe. That this man, my spy-game partner, my late night drinking buddy, my best friend, could be sitting across from someone else—having dinner, going to a show, mapping out a whole evening like it was nothing.

That kind of intimacy? That kind of play? That was ours.

And he gave a piece of it to someone else.

I thought we were the ones who *got* each other. The ones who never needed to explain the joke, who could communicate in a glance, who finished each other's sentences because we had been writing the same story for two decades.

I thought we were untouchable. Turns out, we were just very good at pretending.

Yes, the business consumed us. Especially the second time around. Yes, we stopped checking in the way we used to. But I didn't think it was bad enough to erase twenty years. I thought we had equity. I thought we had roots too deep to be pulled up by something like this.

Maybe I was approaching our marriage the same way I approached business—with the assumption that if you put in the work, if you build something solid, if you have a good foundation, it can withstand temporary neglect while you handle other priorities.

But marriages aren't businesses. You can't put a relationship on autopilot and expect it to maintain itself. You can't assume that past performance guarantees future results. You can't treat intimacy like a spreadsheet where good years balance out the bad ones.

Were there signs? Not really. Robert was always charming to everyone since I'd known him. He had this way of making people feel special, like they were the most interesting person in the room. I never felt threatened by it. Maybe I was naive, but I truly believed we were ordained. That we were somehow above the petty problems other couples went through. We'd been through everything together. From college in London to our move to Paris, and then New York. And then one random afternoon (pre-children) we decided to pack up and try life in Bermuda. Just like that. No big discussion. We just looked at each other and said, "Why not?"

We lived there for a year, but decided the weather wasn't for us. We moved back to New York like the whole thing was just an extended vacation. We were a team, two sides of the same coin. We moved to our own beat; we made decisions that seemed crazy to other people but always made sense to us.

So how could this happen?

I never imagined cheating was something we'd even have to talk about. That was for other couples. We were built differently. We had a bond I thought was unbreakable.

When we got married, we didn't have much money. We were both working low-paying jobs and couldn't really afford a fancy wedding, but we knew we just wanted to be together and didn't want to wait. So to keep things tight, we had a simple garden wedding at my older brother Sam's house in Long Island on my birthday, January 2nd, in the dead of a NYC winter.

Robert turned the space into a winter wonderland. Twinkling lights everywhere, white flowers, candles tucked into the snow that made everything glow. I honestly couldn't have asked for anything more. It was magical.

But he wasn't satisfied and always said when he made more money, we would renew our vows and I would have the fancy wedding with all the pomp and circumstance that I deserved.

"I'm going to give you the wedding you should have had," he said. "The one where money isn't an issue and we can do everything exactly how we want it."

I never cared, but he wrote it down like a little agreement in an old diary that I kept around for sentimental reasons. It was my planner from when I lived in Paris, and I liked to sometimes look through it and relive some of those crazy times.

I never cared to take him up on the fancy wedding when we finally made some money, but the one thing he insisted on was a "proper" wedding band.

On Valentine's Day of our fifteenth year, he surprised me with a Cartier band and matching earrings. I wore that ring like a badge of all we had built. All we had survived. All we had overcome.

So to sit there, in front of the man who gave me that ring, and hear him tell me he broke something I didn't even know was fragile, I couldn't process it.

I wasn't just losing a husband. I was losing my best friend. And that felt like more than I could bear.

*****

Motherhood is a full-time job. So is building a business. So is keeping a marriage afloat. So is pretending you're okay when your world is on fire.

I was doing all four at the same time.

The cost of pretending to be okay while juggling all of this was enormous. I was constantly code-switching between roles. In the morning, I was Mom, making sure everyone had lunch money and clean uniforms. By 9 a.m., I was CEO, handling staff issues and parent complaints. By noon, I was back to Mom mode for a school pickup, then Wife for a quick check-in with Robert, then back to Boss for an afternoon meeting.

Each role demanded a different version of me, and I never knew if I was getting it right. The exhaustion wasn't just physical. It was emotional. Mental. I was performing constantly, never quite sure if I was succeeding at any of it.

And even though my kids were loved, cared for, supported, I often wonder what version of me they actually got.

When I was pregnant with each of them, I had this vision of the kind of mother I'd be. I pictured myself as fully present, emotionally available, the kind of mom who would bake cookies after school and help with homework at the kitchen table. I imagined family dinners where we'd talk about our days, weekend adventures, bedtime stories that lasted as long as they wanted.

I wanted to be the mother who never missed a moment, who was always tuned in to their emotional needs, who created a home filled with laughter and warmth and unhurried time together.

The reality was different. Not worse, necessarily, but different.

I was present, but often distracted. I was available, but frequently interrupted by work calls. I did help with homework, but sometimes with one eye on my laptop screen. I was there for the big moments, the school plays and soccer games, but my mind was often somewhere else, running through the mental checklist of everything that needed handling at the centers.

I sometimes get a glimpse of the altered reality now that they're adults. When they bring up memories I don't even remember, I realize we were living in the same house through different lenses. Children may have short attention spans, but their memories are long.

My daughter Chloe, for instance, likes to remind me how I didn't pack lunch, or how I never baked. That my cupcakes were store-bought. Or how much they hated when the nanny made her go-to dinner of mac and cheese with chicken nuggets or hot dogs.

Did I ever feel defensive when she brought these things up? Absolutely. Part of me wanted to say, "Do you know what I was dealing with? Do you know how hard I was working to keep everything afloat?" But these conversations became opportunities to teach her about imperfection, about how doing your best doesn't always look like doing everything perfectly.

The memories they bring up are so specific, and sometimes I'm shocked I don't remember them. Alexi will mention the time I forgot to pick him up from soccer and he waited for two hours. Sophie recalls me missing her school concert because I had an emergency at one of the centers. Chloe remembers me taking work calls during her friend's birthday party.

These aren't the moments I held onto. I remember the big victories, the family vacations, the times everything went smoothly. They remember the small failures, the moments when work won over family time.

I would try to make up for the everyday shortcomings with elaborate Sunday dinners. These became my weekly redemption, my chance to be the mother I pictured in my head.

I'd spend hours planning the menu, shopping for ingredients, cooking dishes I'd learned from my mother and grandmother. Haitian griot with pikliz, American pot roast, sometimes fancy pasta dishes. I'd set the dining room table, light candles, put on music. The whole production.

Sometimes my parents would join us, sometimes Robert's family. The kids would complain about having to dress up for dinner, but they'd sit at the table and we'd actually talk. No phones, no distractions, just us.

But by then, their tastes had already formed around the nanny's simple meals, and what they really wanted was less about the elaborate food and more about the feeling of presence. They wanted me to sit still, to listen, to not be mentally planning the next week's schedule while they told me about their day.

That's what I missed sometimes, despite my best efforts.

Sure, I was able to schedule myself so I didn't miss recitals or school performances, but even when I was physically there, I wasn't always emotionally present. I was solving a licensing issue in my head. Or budgeting. Or wondering what fire was going to need putting out that night.

The irony is that I left my 9-to-5 to be more available to them. And I was, sort of. But I was also buried under the weight of building something bigger than myself.

I didn't always realize what that cost.

What I've learned is this: You can give your children everything and still sacrifice sacred moments you'll never get back.

I tried my best to keep my kids away from adult problems. I wanted them to enjoy their childhood and not carry the stress

I carried. But in hindsight, maybe I should have let them in more. Maybe they would've understood.

What if I had been more vulnerable with them? Not in an inappropriate way, but in a way that taught them that adults struggle too, that success comes with challenges, that it's okay to not have everything figured out all the time?

I think about what our relationship might have looked like if I'd let them see me worry sometimes. If I'd explained why I was stressed instead of just telling them everything was fine. If I'd asked for their help with small things, shown them that families support each other through difficult times.

Maybe those Sunday dinners would have felt different if I'd been honest about why they mattered so much to me. If I'd said, "I know I've been distracted this week, and I'm sorry. Let's just be together right now."

Maybe they would have learned that vulnerability isn't weakness. That asking for help is normal. That even strong people need support sometimes.

Instead, they learned to be independent, sometimes too independent. They learned not to burden others with their problems. They learned to figure things out on their own because that's what they watched me do.

I think we might have been closer if I'd shown them more of my humanity. If those elaborate Sunday dinners had included more honest conversation about the struggles I was facing, age-appropriately of course.

They often tell me now how different I am. How much I've changed. That I used to be more stressed. Shorter-tempered.

And they're right.

Kids are mirrors. And one day, they'll hold it up to you when you least expect it.

CHAPTER 11

The Cost of Showing Up

And through it all–I kept showing up.

I was sitting in my office at the Upper West Side location, reviewing enrollment applications, when the buzzer rang. Our 2 p.m. tour was right on time.

"I'll get it," I called out, pressing the door release from my desk. Allyson had stepped away from the reception area, probably to the bathroom or to grab something from the supply closet.

The woman who walked through our front door looked exactly like what I'd come to expect from Upper West Side moms: perfectly blown-out hair, a designer handbag, the kind of effortless polish that comes from having both money and time. She glanced around the space, taking in our carefully curated environment: the warm lighting, the children's artwork at eye level, the soft jazz playing in the background.

I stood up from my desk, smoothing my blazer, and waved hello with a welcoming smile. Just then, Allyson returned to her spot behind the reception desk, sliding gracefully into her chair like she belonged on the cover of a magazine rather than checking in toddlers.

Allyson was everything you'd picture when someone says "all-American girl next door." Tall, blonde, with that easy confidence that attractive people sometimes carry, the kind who were used to turning heads, especially among the dads who'd suddenly started volunteering for drop-off and pickup duties. She was from Wisconsin, had majored in philosophy at some party college, and married right after graduation. When her husband's job brought them to New York, she'd been looking for something meaningful to fill her days and genuinely loved working with children. The job was perfect for her.

What wasn't perfect was her wardrobe budget. Allyson showed up to work in designer pieces that belonged more in the "ladies who brunch" scene than behind a preschool reception desk. Today was no exception. She looked like she was heading to lunch at the Rainbow Room rather than managing naptime schedules.

The touring mom's eyes moved from me to Allyson, and I watched her face make a calculation that I'd seen countless times before.

She walked directly to Allyson's desk, extended her manicured hand, and said with confident certainty, "You must be Kettia."

I paused halfway out of my office, watching this familiar dance unfold.

The Cost of Showing Up

Allyson glanced between us, a flicker of confusion crossing her face. "Oh no," she said, pointing toward me with an uncomfortable laugh. "That's Kettia over there. I'm Allyson. I'm the receptionist."

The woman turned to look at me again, and I could see her mental computer trying to process this information. Her smile faltered slightly, like she was experiencing a brief system error. But instead of correcting course, she turned back to Allyson.

"Oh," she said, but continued addressing the receptionist as if I wasn't standing ten feet away. "Well, I'm here for the two o'clock tour. I'm Sarah Matthews. We spoke on the phone?"

Allyson shifted uncomfortably in her chair. "Actually, you'll want to speak with Kettia. She's our founder and director." She gestured toward me again, more insistently this time.

I took a breath and stepped forward, extending my own hand. "Ms. Matthews, I'm Kettia Ming. Welcome to Smarter Toddler."

Sarah finally looked directly at me, her composure cracking just enough to reveal her embarrassment. "Oh! I'm so sorry, I just...I assumed..." She didn't finish the sentence, but we all knew what she'd assumed.

"No problem at all," I said, keeping my voice warm and professional, though inside I was calculating: Is this worth the energy? Do I call it out or let it slide? Do I educate or just move forward?

I chose to move forward. "Shall we start the tour?"

But let me pause here and talk about what it actually means to do business while Black.

There's a certain tightrope we walk. Those of us who dare to build something beautiful in spaces where we were never expected to exist. There's the business itself: the real estate, the strategy, the staffing, the licensing. And then there's the landscape underneath it all. The invisible, shifting terrain of doing business in a world that is still wired to doubt us. To question us. To watch and wait for the first sign of failure.

See, the thing is, when you're Black, you're often assumed to be the employee. The assistant. The person who "helps." Even when you're the owner. Especially when you're the owner.

There is always a shadow trailing behind you. Waiting. Watching. For a misstep. A mistake. A missed payment. So it can point and say, "See?"

Because the unspoken narrative is this: You don't belong here. You got lucky. You don't deserve this level of excellence. And if you fall, well, of course you did. That's how the story is supposed to go.

What people don't understand is that just standing in certain rooms, as a Black woman, is an act of resistance. Owning something, building something, makes people uncomfortable. Not always overtly. Sometimes it's subtle. Sometimes it's buried in language like "too aggressive" or "not the right fit." Sometimes it's blatant, like getting yelled at on the phone by a landlord's rep. But it's always there.

And not just from outsiders. Sometimes from our own.

I'll never forget the day a Black investor-operator was introduced to me. He ran centers somewhere in Long Island, and he came for a visit, just to see the space, talk shop, maybe explore partnership possibilities.

He walked in and just froze. You could see it on his face. He looked around, at the warmth, the design, the detail, the artwork, the soft lighting, the music, and you could feel his brain recalibrating. His exact words were, "Wait. This is yours?"

He was floored.

And the part that got me? I had forgotten how people see this space. I had forgotten the feeling it gave people when they walked in. To me, it was just home. It was mine. It was normal.

But seeing it through his eyes woke something up in me. It reminded me that I had built something that wasn't just beautiful, it was bold. It was soft power. It was joy in the face of a world that doesn't always give us joy. It was art, soul, and safety wrapped into one.

And here I was, doubting myself. Shrinking. Apologizing for a misstep instead of honoring the mountain I had already climbed.

I thought of my dad.

My father was a dreamer wrapped in pragmatism, a man who believed so deeply in the promise of America that he was willing to tear his family apart temporarily to rebuild it stronger.

He left Haiti when I was only two years old, leaving behind his wife and children in search of something better than what our small island could offer. It wasn't a decision he made lightly. In Haiti, we had family, community, a place where we belonged. But my father saw further than the horizon. He saw possibility.

The plan was methodical, the way everything was with him. First, he'd establish himself in New York. Then bring my mother. Then the children, one by one, when he could afford it and when the paperwork allowed. My mother joined him first, and shortly after, she gave birth to my little sister Martine. That baby became our family's golden ticket, the American citizen who would help secure green cards and make it possible to send for the rest of us.

My two older brothers, Sam and Didi, came first. Then my sister Esther and I arrived together when we were fourteen and twelve. Five children in total, all of us eventually reunited under one roof on the Upper West Side, in a tiny railroad style

The Cost of Showing Up

1 ½ convertible bedroom apartment, all of us carrying the weight of our father's dreams and expectations.

For nearly ten years, my father worked two jobs to make this dream real. Days he drove a cab through the chaotic streets of Manhattan, navigating traffic and demanding passengers with the same steady determination he brought to everything else. Evenings and weekends, he worked security at The New York Historical Society, an American history museum on the Upper West Side.

I remember many Sunday afternoons when my mother would send Esther and me to bring him a hot lunch at the museum. We'd walk the few blocks from our apartment, carrying containers of rice and beans that were still warm, speaking only Creole to each other as we navigated the sidewalks.

His coworkers were fascinated by us. Here were these two little Black girls who couldn't speak English, walking through one of Manhattan's most prestigious neighborhoods like we owned the place, bringing lunch to their colleague who spoke in a mixture of heavily accented English and Creole words he'd throw in completely unperturbed by whether his listeners understood.

"How is it you don't speak English?" they asked us, speaking slowly and loudly as if volume could bridge the language gap. They couldn't understand the anomaly we represented: Black children on the Upper West Side, daughters of a man who was simply a low wage immigrant employee but lived in their neighborhood.

My father was a tall man with a medium build and a personality that filled every room he entered. Even after ten years in America, his English remained beautifully broken, a patchwork of Creole and English that he wore like a badge of honor rather than shame. He refused to shrink himself to fit other people's expectations of how an immigrant should sound or act.

When Esther and I finally arrived in New York at ages fourteen and twelve, my father laid down three non-negotiable rules that would govern our lives: Church, Education, Family, in that order. Follow these three principles, he told us, and you'd be golden. Everything else was negotiable.

Those principles shaped all five of us, though we each interpreted them differently. Sam, Didi, and Martine all became doctors, following the traditional path of education and achievement that made my father beam with pride. Esther became a chef and now owns a restaurant in Florida. And I built Smarter Toddler. Different paths, but all rooted in the same foundation of excellence and determination.

We've remained incredibly close throughout the years, maintaining my father's vision that family comes over everything. When one of us succeeds, we all succeed. When one of us struggles, we all show up. That bond he forged through sacrifice and intention has held us together across different states, different careers, different life choices.

My siblings all still go to church, honoring that first principle our father laid down. While I may have eschewed religion for religion's sake, my spiritual life has become richer since learning and practicing meditation. Spirituality has allowed me to come to terms with life on life's terms. It has allowed me to process difficult experiences and become stronger and wiser because I stayed conscious through the experience, coming to know myself in deep communion with a Higher Power. This spiritual foundation, different as it looks from my father's churchgoing faith, is still rooted in the reverence and respect for something greater than myself that he taught us.

But the most important thing he taught us was to dream big. My father didn't believe in systemic racism, at least not in the way it's discussed today. He truly believed that higher education and hard work would put us on the same playing field as anyone else." You can do and be whatever you want to be," he'd tell us over dinner, his voice carrying the weight of absolute conviction, "as long as you put in the work. Everything else is noise."

Looking back, I realize this was part of the difference between African-Americans and Black people from the islands and diaspora. My father hadn't grown up with the same generational understanding of American racism. He came here believing in meritocracy because in his mind, America was still the land of opportunity he'd dreamed about from Haiti. His optimism wasn't naive; it was strategic. He knew that if we believed the system was rigged against us, we might not even try.

That mindset became my foundation. When the world told me to shrink myself, I held onto his words. When landlords questioned my capacity or competitors tried to shut me down, I put in the work. I kept showing up. I kept pushing.

My father lived to see both the 89th Street and 55th Street locations of Smarter Toddler, and he was beyond proud. He'd walk through the spaces with the same awe he'd shown when we first moved to the Upper West Side, marveling at what his daughter had built. He understood that this was the fruition of everything he'd worked for, everything he'd sacrificed, everything he'd believed possible when he left Haiti all those years ago.

He passed away two years before the sale to Bright Horizons, which means he never had to see me fight that battle. In some ways, I'm grateful for that. He got to see his daughter succeed on the terms he'd taught her, in the country he'd chosen for us, believing until the end that hard work and excellence would always be enough.

Growing up in our household, I always felt protected, if not necessarily cuddled. My father's love was expressed through structure, through his unwavering belief that we could achieve anything, through the sacrifices he made to give us opportunities he never had. He didn't coddle us because he knew the world wouldn't coddle us either. Instead, he armed us with confidence, work ethic, and an unshakeable belief in our own worth.

*****

This was more than just a business fight. This was spiritual warfare.

I wasn't just trying to save a school. I was trying to save a part of myself.

It wasn't just about keeping the doors open. It was about the part of me that still believed I was capable of greatness. The part that thought my dreams, no matter how big, were worth fighting for. I was fighting for my right to take up space in a world that wasn't designed for me to succeed.

Every day, I was battling voices that whispered: "Who do you think you are?" "You got lucky once, but lightning doesn't strike twice." "Maybe you should have stayed small." "Maybe you should have been grateful for what you had instead of reaching for more."

These weren't just external voices, though those were loud enough. These were the insidious internal whispers that creep in when you're exhausted, when you're scared, when you're one missed payment away from losing everything you've built. The voices that sound suspiciously like every person who ever looked surprised when you walked into a room, every banker who questioned your projections, every competitor who assumed you'd fold under pressure.

The spiritual warfare was about refusing to let those voices win. It was about holding onto the vision of myself that my father had instilled: the woman who belonged in any room she entered, who had every right to dream beyond what others thought possible for someone who looked like her.

I was fighting for the part of me that still believed I deserved ease, not just struggle. That believed I could build without constantly having to prove my worthiness to exist in the space I'd created. That believed my success wasn't an accident or a fluke, but the natural result of vision, hard work, and excellence.

Most importantly, I was fighting for something bigger than myself. I was fighting for the next Black woman who would walk into an investor meeting with a business plan. For the next entrepreneur who would be told her dreams were too big, her vision too ambitious. For the next little girl who would need to see that it was possible to build something beautiful and refuse to apologize for taking up space while doing it.

The spiritual warfare was about remembering that my survival wasn't just about me. It was about the legacy I was creating, the blueprint I was laying down for the next woman who dared to dream. And that made every battle worth fighting, even when the path to victory wasn't always clear.

The Cost of Showing Up

I started to show up differently.

Not because the circumstances had changed, but because I had to change if I was going to make it through. I was still running on fumes, still one HVAC malfunction away from disaster, but I stopped letting that reality steal every waking moment of my life.

I started trying—really trying—to rediscover the joy in my business. The joy in this community I'd built. The smiles of the children, the rituals of the classroom, the laughter of the teachers, the shared mission of something bigger than myself. I had to remind myself, day by day, that this was still beautiful.

My favorite classroom ritual was our twice-weekly African drumming class. There's something about the sound of African drums that's healing, primal in the most beautiful way. You can't help but smile when you hear them, and some deep part of you awakens like "oh, I remember this." Watching eighteen-month-olds and four-year-olds sit in a circle, their tiny hands beating rhythms that seemed to come from their souls, their faces lit up with pure joy, reminding me why I'd fallen in love with this work in the first place.

Then there were those perfect mid-morning moments, after snack but before naptime, when all the classrooms were buzzing with purposeful activity. I'd walk past the infant room during their yoga class, watching babies barely able to sit up attempting downward dog with the most serious expressions, while their teacher guided them through gentle stretches in a voice soft as silk. Down the hall, the preschoolers worked on some complicated indoor wall plant project, hands deep in rich, dark dirt, their little faces pinched in concentration as they carefully transplanted seedlings, creating our living wall garden one plant at a time.

We were always lucky to have one or two male teachers at our school—unfortunately, too few men choose to work in preschools—and one of those special souls was Mr. Adam. He had this loud, booming voice that he used for all sorts of character imitations to the children's absolute delight. The thing that never failed to put a smile on my face was hearing him sing the Hello Song during circle time in the most spectacularly off-key voice I'd ever heard. I was never sure if he did it on purpose to entertain the kids or if he really was tone deaf, but either way, it became one of our most beloved traditions. The children giggled and tried to match his impossible pitch, creating this chorus of joyful noise that could be heard throughout the building.

Pickup time was always a scene, and watching it unfold became one of my greatest sources of satisfaction. Parents would hustle and bustle through our doors after long workdays, only to find themselves negotiating and bribing their children to leave. "Just five more minutes in the art room!" "But we're not finished with our castle!" "Can we take the puzzle home?" As painful as those negotiations might have been for tired parents, they always brought me joy. I had created a space where children didn't want to go home. Where learning felt like play, where every corner held possibility, where goodbye was the hardest part of the day.

And at the end of the day, wasn't that what it was all about?

The bills weren't going anywhere. We weren't even close to profit. We were making just enough to keep the lights on and the doors open. That was it.

My accountant, who was probably the only person who truly knew the ins and outs of every penny, tried his best to be encouraging. He'd say, "You'll get there." And maybe I would. But every week felt like a game of financial Jenga. One emergency, one busted pipe, one health code surprise, and we were in the red again.

The thought of taking on any more debt? Absolutely out of the question.

I worked for three straight years with no vacations, no long weekends, no real break. Because honestly? I was scared. Scared to leave the business in anyone else's hands. Scared that the minute I let go, even for a moment, it would all come crashing down. So I stayed. I showed up. I handled every fire, every late-night email, every problem.

And then, in early 2019, something broke—quietly, privately.

Robert and I separated.

After I found out about Robert's infidelity, we decided to go to counseling. Life went on, as it does, even when you're not sure how to move forward. We tried many different therapists, searching for the right fit, someone who could help us find our way back to each other. Some helped, most didn't.

What I discovered in the world of marriage counseling is that there's this innate societal pressure to convince you to stay married, short of physical abuse, and even then...The underlying assumption was always that saving the marriage was the goal, regardless of whether that marriage was actually worth saving.

To be fair, we weren't trying to separate when we started. We went into those sessions with good intentions. We both wanted it to work. We made promises in those sterile offices, sitting on uncomfortable couches, speaking to strangers about our most intimate failures.

"It won't happen again," Robert said, his voice carrying a conviction I wanted to believe.

"I'll be more attentive," I promised in return. "We'll make more time for us. We'll have more sex."

But what no one seemed willing to discuss was this: what if sometimes it's okay to accept that this is where you leave each other? What if it's possible to acknowledge that you've had a beautiful journey together, that you came together and created an incredible life and brought three amazing souls into the world, and now it's time to gracefully bow out? Not every journey is meant to go all the way to the end. Sometimes people are meant to only come with you so far.

Anyway, we stayed together as a family. We took care of our kids and experienced all the rituals. College drop-off first with Alexi, followed by Chloe two years later. And then there was one: Sophie. Sophie was seventeen and a high school senior when we finally decided to separate.

There was no big bang, no major argument, no dramatic breaking point. Just two people who had been going through the motions and got tired of pretending.

The conversation happened on a random Tuesday night in February 2019. We were sitting in our bedroom, watching some forgettable show on Netflix, both of us scrolling through our phones during commercial breaks. It was the kind of parallel existence we'd perfected—together but not really together.

"You know what's funny?" I said during a lull in whatever we were watching.

"What?"

"I was thinking about London. About Christmas."

Robert muted the TV and turned to look at me. We'd taken the family to London the Christmas before, on a whim. Alexi was doing a semester abroad in Egypt and could meet us there. Chloe was home from college in Boston. The plan was to spend the holidays and my birthday, also our anniversary, in the place where it all started.

We stayed at a great Airbnb, celebrated the holidays and my birthday as a family, took the girls around our old haunts and showed them our dorm. We even connected with Robert's best friend from college. It should have been magical.

"What about it?" Robert asked, though I could see in his expression that he knew where this was going.

"I think we were looking for something that just isn't there anymore," I said quietly. "Like maybe if we went back to where we fell in love, we could time travel back to being those dreamy-eyed nineteen-year-olds who were madly in love with life and with each other."

"But that didn't happen."

"No. Because you can't go back. The only way is forward."

We sat in silence for a moment, both of us understanding what we were really talking about.

"The thing is," Robert said finally, "we needed to fall in love with who we've become. With our future selves. But we didn't. Maybe because we needed to love ourselves separately first."

"And we don't," I said. It wasn't a question.

"No. We don't."

Another long pause. The TV flickered in the background, some laugh track filling the quiet between us.

"We're not getting any younger," I said eventually.

"No, we're not."

"And we deserve to be happy."

"We do."

"But we're not. Happy, I mean. We're married, but we're unhappily married. So why not just...separate?"

The word hung in the air between us. Separate. It sounded so clinical, so final, and yet somehow also like relief.

"Okay," Robert said simply.

"Okay?"

"Yeah. Okay."

We typically didn't fight like normal people—no screaming matches or thrown dishes or dramatic door-slamming. We never really raised our voices with each other. Even this conversation, this moment when we decided to end our 20+ year marriage, was quiet. Civil. Almost businesslike.

Maybe that was part of the problem. We'd been so careful not to hurt each other that we'd forgotten how to be real with each other.

"What do we tell Sophie?" I asked.

"The truth. That we love each other, that we love her, but that we're not happy together anymore."

"And the business?"

Robert looked at me for a long moment. "The business is for you and the kids, Kettia. It always has been. I just helped you build it. You take whatever you think you'll need and we'll figure out the rest."

After that conversation, I learned something no one talks about.

Divorce with older kids hurts just as much. Maybe even more. Teenagers live in this fragile in-between space—not quite children, not quite adults. They are old enough to understand the permanence of divorce, but not always mature enough to process it without taking it personally. They can grasp the logistics, the legal side, even the "we still care about each other" speech, but emotionally, they are still kids who want the security of knowing their parents' foundation is solid.

When that foundation cracks, they feel it in a very specific way. It is not just the loss of a family structure; it is a blow to their idea of stability right when their own identities are still forming. And unlike younger kids, who might adapt more easily to new routines, teenagers often have a stronger sense of how things "should" be. They replay the years in their heads, looking for signs they missed. They can feel blindsided, and that can turn quickly into anger or mistrust.

That is exactly what happened with my kids. They didn't see it coming. Because we didn't fight. We were still kind to each other. Friends, even and that was partly our fault. They didn't see the unraveling because we kept it away from them. We dealt with our pain in whispers, in late-night conversations, in quiet sadness. So when we told them, it felt—at least to them—like it came out of nowhere.

Their reactions hit me harder than I expected. I wanted to rush in and fix it, to explain in a way that would make it hurt less. But there is no way to make it hurt less. Seeing their pain made me second-guess everything, even though I knew the decision was right. In that moment, I was not just ending a marriage. I was shattering their picture of what home looked like.

I truly thought they'd be okay. Not happy, but okay. They were teenagers. They were independent. They knew we had been through a lot. But what I didn't expect was the shock and the anger.

I wasn't planning to tell Sophie or the other kids right away. Alexi and Chloe were away at college, focused on their studies, and I didn't want to mess with their concentration or put anything heavy on them. My plan was to wait, to figure out the logistics first, to have answers before creating questions.

But Robert decided to tell Sophie. And to make matters worse, he told her the truth. The whole truth.

The Cost of Showing Up

I came home from work that evening to find Sophie sitting at our dining table, her eyes red and puffy, looking like someone had just told her the world was ending.

"Mom," she said the moment I walked through the door, her voice shaking. "Dad told me about...about everything."

My heart sank. I would have never told her about the infidelity. That wasn't any of their business. It was grown-up business, the kind of pain that children shouldn't have to carry, even when those children are seventeen years old.

"Sophie, honey—"

"Is it true?" she interrupted. "Did he really...did he cheat on you?"

I sat down across from her, trying to find words that would somehow make this easier. "Yes. But that's not what matters right now. What matters is—"

"Of course it matters!" she exploded. "Everything matters! What's going to happen next? Where is he going to go? What about my graduation? Who's doing college drop-off with me in the fall? What about Christmas? What about everything?"

All legitimate questions. All questions I didn't have good answers for yet.

"We're going to figure it out," I said, reaching for her hand across the table. "All of it. Together."

"But why can't you just fix it?" she asked, and her voice broke on the word 'fix.' "You fix everything else, Mom. You always fix everything."

And that's when it hit me—the weight of being the family fixer, the one everyone turned to when things went wrong. The one who was supposed to have solutions for problems that couldn't be solved with phone calls and determination.

"I can't fix this one, sweetheart," I said quietly. "Some things can't be fixed."

When I called Alexi later that night, I could hear the shock in his voice even though he tried to sound measured and mature.

"Wait, what do you mean separated?" he said after I'd given him the basics. "Like, Dad moved out?"

"Not yet, but he will."

There was a long pause. "But...well, can you fix it? You gotta fix it, Mom. I don't get it. Why you guys? You're not supposed to be like other parents. What's gonna happen Mom?"

By the time I got on the phone with Chloe, I was mentally exhausted. But there was no more hiding. Her siblings had probably already told her, and knowing them, they probably weren't tactful about it because they had a ton of questions and were processing their own shock.

"Mom?" Chloe's voice was small when she answered. "Sophie texted. Is it true?"

"Yes, it's true."

"But why? You guys don't even fight. You still laugh together. You still...I don't understand."

"I know it's confusing, sweetheart."

"Well, will we still do family vacations?" she asked, and I could hear the little girl in her voice, the one who was trying to figure out what this meant for all the traditions that had anchored her life.

All very different responses, but all of them came down to the same question: Why? And somehow, even though Robert had confessed to cheating, even though he was the one who had broken our vows, I was the one getting blamed. I was the fixer who couldn't fix it. I was the mom who was supposed to hold everything together, and instead, I was letting the family fall apart.

It was really hard not to get angry in those moments. Part of me wanted to lash out, to explain exactly why their father was at fault, to defend myself against their accusations. Maybe I should have. But I knew they were hurt, and it wasn't their fault that they'd been thrown into the middle of something they never should have had to navigate.

"You guys just don't understand," I said to each of them, in different conversations, with different words but the same sentiment. "You felt blindsided because you know plenty of kids whose parents are divorced and can't attend the same school functions because they can't be in the same room together. We don't fit that profile. We were never the screaming, fighting couple. But that doesn't mean we were happy."

But trying to explain the difference between civil dysfunction and actual happiness to young adults who'd never seen us fight? It was like trying to explain color to someone who'd only ever seen black and white. They couldn't understand how two people who were kind to each other, who laughed together, who still functioned as a family unit, could decide to stop being married.

And honestly? Some days I wasn't sure I understood it either.

The next couple of months were a blur of logistics and emotions I wasn't prepared for. I started looking at apartments almost immediately because I didn't want to be in that big family apartment by myself, especially knowing that Sophie was due to leave for college that September. The thought of rattling around in all that space alone felt unbearable.

I also knew that Robert wouldn't start looking for a place and wouldn't make a move until I did. That was just our dynamic. I was always the one who initiated the practical steps, who moved things forward when they needed moving. We'd both agreed we couldn't stay in the family apartment. That space had served its purpose.

Walking through those four large bedrooms, taking in the ample living and dining space where we'd hosted countless family dinners and holiday celebrations, I felt a complicated mix of sadness and gratitude. The kids had their own wing, their own space to grow and become themselves. It had been the perfect family home, and in that moment, I felt nothing but deep gratitude and appreciation for the fact that this had been my children's experience growing up.

When I thought about the tiny railroad apartment only three blocks away on Columbus Avenue where my siblings and I had lived when we first came from Haiti—the same building where my mom and dad lived until he passed—I felt nothing but pride. The distance we'd traveled, literally and figuratively, from that cramped space to this spacious home on the Upper West Side represented everything my father had dreamed of when he left Haiti all those years ago. I frequently hosted my parents here, and they'd gotten to be close to their grandchildren, to see the fruits of the sacrifices they'd made.

But it was time to say goodbye to the space that had served my family so well and move into the next phase of my life.

I moved out in May 2019 into a smaller, much less palatial three-bedroom apartment about a mile north from the family home. It felt strange to be packing up twenty years of shared life, deciding what belonged to me and what belonged to us and what belonged to the version of us that no longer existed.

Then came June and Sophie's high school graduation, marking the longest I had not seen Robert since the day we met in college.

The morning of graduation, I stood in front of my bathroom mirror in my new apartment, getting ready for an event that should have been pure celebration but instead felt loaded with complexity. How do you navigate your daughter's milestone when you're still figuring out how to be divorced parents?

When I arrived at the school, I spotted Robert immediately. He was standing near the entrance wearing all white, looking cool on what was a scorching early summer day. We made eye contact across the crowd of families and gave each other that small acknowledgment wave that said, "We're doing this. We're going to be fine."

We were our usual civil selves throughout the ceremony. We sat together because we were going to be a unit for Sophie. We took lots of pictures, and to anyone watching, we probably looked like any other proud parents celebrating their daughter's achievement.

"She is something else," Robert said as we watched Sophie walk across the stage, tall with this confident regal air as if everyone was here to celebrate her.

"Yes she is," I agreed. "We did good with that one."

"We did good with all of them."

The Cost of Showing Up

It was the first real conversation we'd had in months, and it reminded me that whatever had broken between us as a couple, we were still connected as parents. That would never change.

Alexi and Chloe were in the middle of finals and couldn't make it home for graduation, so my sister Martine had come in from Baltimore with my two nieces to represent the extended family. Having them there felt like a bridge between my old life and my new one—familiar love and support as I navigated this strange territory of being a single parent at my daughter's graduation.

After the ceremony, we all went out to a celebratory dinner. Sophie sat between Robert and me, unconsciously trying to keep us connected, keep us functioning as the family unit she'd always known. The conversation flowed easily—talk of college plans, summer jobs, vacation possibilities. For a few hours, we felt like ourselves again. Different, but still fundamentally us.

As we walked back to our separate Ubers afterward, Robert caught my arm gently.

"Thank you," he said.

"For what?"

"For making this easy. For her. And for me."

I nodded. "We're always going to be her parents. That doesn't change."

"No," he said. "It doesn't."

And for the first time since we'd decided to separate, I felt like maybe we were going to be okay. Different, but okay.

*****

It felt like the shortest summer. One minute we were celebrating graduation and the next I was dorm shopping and in the throes of college move-in preparations. Sophie was headed to Temple University in Philadelphia.

I coordinated all the information with Robert via text: move-in times, parking instructions, what to bring. Between me and Sophie, he had all the information he needed and all he had to do was show up and drive the rental truck. I just wanted Sophie to have the same send-off her siblings had received. I didn't want her to feel left out or short-changed because her parents were now separated.

We'd done the whole family send-off when Alexi went to Emory in Atlanta. Then a newly licensed Alexi had driven the family to Chloe's drop-off at Emerson College in Boston. I wanted Sophie to have that same supportive send-off, surrounded by her family. Unfortunately, Alexi's semester started early so he couldn't be there, but we made it a fun day for Sophie anyway.

The four of us talked the whole drive from New York to Philadelphia. It felt like any other family road trip we'd taken over the years, complete with the girls' terrible music choices and Robert's running commentary on other drivers. Sophie was practically vibrating with excitement or nervousness, or maybe both. She never mentioned anything about the separation or asked any questions about what our family would look like going forward. Maybe she was too focused on her own transition, or maybe she was giving us all the gift of normalcy for one more day.

When you get to campus, it's a flurry of activities and organization: cleaning, unpacking, last-minute Target runs. There's not much time to reflect or think about anything beyond making sure your child has everything they need, that they're safe and settled and happy. You hug a few times, and then you hug again as if you'll never see them again. At some point, they turn and walk away and the door closes behind them, and you still stand there for a minute in case they forget something and come back out.

With Alexi's drop-off, it had been our first experience with this whole world. Back when Robert and I went to college, there wasn't all this pomp and circumstance. I went to college in a whole other country and I don't even remember my parents dropping me off at the airport! Alexi was super independent and figured out all the logistics on his own. Robert did all the handyman work needed to set him up, but Alexi didn't care about decorations or creating a Pinterest-worthy dorm room, so it was quick work.

With Chloe, she'd wanted the full Pottery Barn dorm experience, and that's exactly what she got. The process was longer and more involved, but we'd all buckled down and made it through.

With Sophie, we were now veterans. We could anticipate what she would need and what we knew the dorm wouldn't provide. The process was fairly painless, but it was deeply bittersweet when we said our final goodbyes.

Because here was the reason Smarter Toddler had started in the first place: this little girl who had come home from Ms. Elsie's daycare looking so defeated and resigned. The child whose spark I'd been determined to protect and nurture. And now she was walking into her college dorm to begin a whole new life, confident and excited and ready for independence.

I didn't cry, but there was a sadness I couldn't quite classify. Like, wow, this is truly the end of an era for me and for my family. As I watched her disappear behind that dorm room door, I realized that Smarter Toddler wasn't just my legacy: it was hers too. Everything I'd built, every battle I'd fought, every compromise I'd made had been wrapped up in the hope that one day she'd be proud of what I'd created, that it would somehow benefit her world.

Her leaving for college marked the end of the chapter that had started it all. And suddenly, I wasn't sure what the next chapter was supposed to look like.

A few months earlier—in May, around the time I'd moved into my new apartment—I signed up for a meditation retreat. The timing felt like divine intervention: it was scheduled for exactly one week after Sophie's drop-off. I remember feeling emotionally raw when the email crossed my desk, as if the universe knew just what I would need in that moment.

The retreat was being led by Light Watkins, a meditation teacher I'd been following for years. A friend had taken me to one of his talks a few years back, and I'd really connected with his approach. I'd even taken his course, three nights, about two hours each night, and had learned the basics of meditation. But like so many things in my life, I had good intentions about maintaining a practice but never got consistent. Between the kids' schedules and the business demands, there was always something more urgent that needed my attention.

I continued following Light's work over the years, and I'd always see these retreat announcements. Between running two schools and managing three kids' lives, I could never make the timing work. So when I saw the dates on this particular email and realized it would be exactly one week after I dropped off Sophie, when I'd be returning to my new, empty apartment as a newly single mother with no children at home, I jumped at the chance and signed up.

I needed something. Anything. A moment to be still, to think, to feel. To reconnect with the version of me that wasn't running on stress and survival mode. For the first time in years, I was going to do something just for myself.

I prepared everything with my team. I went over every detail, every contingency. I made sure the school could function without me for seven days. I turned on my out-of-office message and packed my bags.

And for the first time in years—I stepped away alone.

That retreat didn't fix everything. It didn't magically solve my financial problems or make the settlement payments to Bright Horizons disappear. It didn't repair my marriage or erase the years of stress that had worn us both down. It didn't eliminate my fear and doubt about what the future held or suddenly give me a clear roadmap for what came next.

But it gave me myself back.

For the first time in years, I would be able to sit still and reflect on the person I was before everything happened. Before the lawsuits and the debt and the constant crisis management. Before I became someone who lived in survival mode, always bracing for the next emergency.

The retreat would give me the tools to deal with where I was now instead of constantly fighting against it. It would teach me that I could acknowledge my problems without letting them consume every waking moment. I could carry my responsibilities without carrying them in my shoulders, my jaw, my sleepless nights.

Most importantly, it would give me permission to catch my breath and just be. To remember that I was more than the sum of my struggles. To dream a little about what my future could look like instead of just trying to survive each day.

I still had the same challenges waiting for me back in New York, but a different relationship with them. I wasn't going to let them define me anymore. I was going to move like water, flowing around obstacles instead of beating myself against them.

And it was that shift in perspective that changed everything.

What I Hope You Carry - *A letter to my children.*

> *I may not always know how to explain who I am to you, and maybe you sometimes feel like I failed you. But I am a product of my upbringing. Not to make excuses, but perhaps to help you understand if I fell short of the mom you wanted me to be.*
>
> *For most of my life, softness felt like a luxury I couldn't afford.*
>
> *I knew how to be strong. I learned that early. I learned how to take care of myself as an ESL student in elementary school when kids picked on me at recess or called me "Frenchie" for not speaking English, even though those kids were in ESL too. I learned how to navigate a foreign country as a college student and hustle to pay my own living expenses. I knew how to create something from scratch and make it beautiful.*

My resilience was forged by necessity. I didn't have the luxury of being vulnerable. I had to push through when things were crumbling around me.

But soft? Soft was seen as weakness. Soft could get you hurt. Soft didn't survive in boardrooms, in lawsuits, in investor meetings, spaces where the stakes were sky-high and the expectations even higher.

This lesson started early, at home. In my Haitian household, showing emotion was not encouraged. When I cried as a child, I was told to stop. When I was scared, I was told to be brave. When I wanted comfort, I was told to be strong. Love was shown through action, not words. Through making sure we had what we needed, not through hugs or "I love you."

My parents weren't cruel. They were preparing us for a world they knew would be hard on us. In their minds, softness was a luxury Black children, immigrant children, couldn't afford. The world would try to break us, so we had to be unbreakable first.

So I hardened myself. For the mission. For the kids. For survival.

And people praised me for it.

"She's a boss." "She's fierce."
"She's unstoppable."

But no one ever asked if I was tired.

The truth is, I was beyond tired. I was brittle. My strength had made me disconnected from joy, from the simple pleasure of just being present without an agenda. I didn't even realize how much I was missing softness until I stumbled back into it.

It crept in quietly. Through learning meditation. The way I exhaled once I realized how long I'd been holding my breath. The way my voice shook when I let it. The way I allowed myself to nap and felt no guilt.

That softness felt foreign at first. Like a language I once spoke but had forgotten how to pronounce.

But the more I softened, the more I started to feel like myself again. You noticed. You told me how much I'd grown. Not the high-functioning, over-performing, hyper-responsible version of me. Just me.

Did the softness help me reconnect with them? I think so. You started calling more. Sharing more. The conversations became less about logistics and more about life. You seemed less careful around me, less worried about adding to my stress.

One of the things I hate most is when people call me a strong Black woman. Or when they say, "You're so strong, you can handle it."

I know it's meant as a compliment. But it never lands that way.

It always feels like a setup. Like a way of saying, "We don't need to worry about you." Like permission to lean on me without ever checking to see if I'm about to collapse.

Everyone assumes I'll be okay. That I'll figure it out. That I've got it handled.

And I usually do. But that doesn't mean I want to.

So much of my strength was shaped by survival. But I don't want survival to be my brand anymore.

I want softness to have space in my life. I want joy to be unhurried. I want rest that doesn't have to be justified. I want to cry without apologizing.

If I seemed hard sometimes, if I wasn't the soft, nurturing mother you might have wanted, please understand that I was doing the best I could with what I knew. I was raised to believe that love looked like protection, like providing, like making sure you had everything you needed to succeed.

I didn't learn how to just sit with you in your feelings. I learned how to fix them. When you were sad, I wanted to solve it. When you were struggling, I wanted to remove the obstacle. I thought that was love.

What I didn't realize is that sometimes love looks like just being present. Like listening without trying to fix. Like letting you feel what you need to feel without rushing you through it.

Softness doesn't mean I'm falling apart. It means I'm finally safe enough to stop pretending I'm not tired.

If I could do it over, I would have let you see me cry sometimes. I would have let you know that adults don't have all the answers. I would have asked for help more often, so you could learn that it's okay to need people.

I would have shown you that strength and vulnerability can live in the same person. That being soft doesn't make you weak. That taking care of yourself isn't selfish.

I would have let you see me rest without guilt. I would have modeled that it's okay to say no, to set boundaries, to choose your own peace over other people's expectations.

But here's what I need you to know: Even though I might have seemed hard, even though I might have been distracted or stressed or unavailable in ways that hurt you, everything I did was because I loved you so fiercely it scared me sometimes.

I worked as hard as I did because I wanted to build something that would give you choices. I stayed strong because I thought that's what you needed from me. I pushed through because I believed that showing you how to persevere was the greatest gift I could give you.

I didn't know that what you might have needed most was just to see me be human.

When I was building the business, when I was fighting lawsuits, when I was trying to hold everything together, I thought I was protecting you by keeping you away from the stress. I thought I was being a good mother by making sure my problems never became your problems.

But maybe I was also protecting myself. Maybe it was easier to carry everything alone than to risk looking weak in front of the people whose respect I valued most.

I'm learning now that there's a different kind of strength. The kind that asks for help. The kind that admits when it's overwhelmed. The kind that chooses connection over perfection.

I'm learning that softness isn't passive. It's powerful. It's presence without pressure. It's listening without fixing. It's sitting in silence and still being seen.

For so long, I thought I had to earn love by being valuable, by being the one with solutions, by being indispensable. But soft love doesn't need a checklist. It just needs truth. Vulnerability. An open hand instead of a clenched fist.

In this next chapter of my life, I'm learning to love differently. I'm learning to receive. To lean. To admit when I need to be held. To stop over-functioning when I'm feeling empty.

And maybe most importantly, I'm learning to offer soft love to myself. To stop beating myself up for what I didn't know then. To stop criticizing the version of me that was just trying to stay afloat. To stop demanding perfection from a woman who carried more than most people ever will.

I don't want to pass down more emotional armor. I want to pass down the tools for softness. For spaciousness. For choosing joy that isn't tethered to achievement.

If any of you become parents someday, I want you to know that you don't have to choose between being strong and being tender. You can hold your children when they cry and also teach them how to be resilient. You can show them how to work hard and also how to rest. You can protect them and also let them see you struggle sometimes.

I want you to know that asking for help doesn't make you less capable. It makes you human. That crying doesn't make you weak.

The Cost of Showing Up

It makes you real. That taking care of your own needs isn't selfish. It's necessary.

I want you to give yourselves permission to feel whatever you're feeling without rushing to fix it or push through it. To sit with discomfort without immediately trying to solve it. To be gentle with yourselves when you make mistakes.

If I have a granddaughter someday, I want her to grow up knowing what soft love feels like from the beginning. I want her to know that she can be strong and tender. Fierce and vulnerable. That she doesn't have to choose. And that if she ever needs to say, "This role no longer fits," she'll know the language to say it and the freedom to walk away from the script.

To my son: I want you to know that soft love isn't just for women. That being gentle doesn't make you less of a man. That showing emotion isn't weakness. That taking care of people emotionally is just as important as providing for them financially.

I want all of you to know that the best parts of life can't be earned through performance or perfection. They come from connection. From presence. From the courage to be seen as you really are, not as who you think you should be.

Soft love, I'm learning, is a practice. And I'm just now giving myself permission to begin.

The mother you got was the one who knew how to fight for you, who knew how to build for you, who knew how to work for you. But the grandmother you might get someday? She's learning how to just be with you. And maybe that will be enough to heal some of what my strength might have accidentally broken.

CHAPTER 12

The Surrender Strategy

It was September 2019, exactly one week after dropping Sophie off at Temple University. I was spiritually starving, financially drowning, and emotionally exhausted from nearly three years of fighting to keep my business alive while my marriage fell apart. The settlement payments to Bright Horizons continued every December like clockwork, the rent on both locations devoured most of our revenue, and I was still operating in survival mode, one crisis away from collapse.

But for seven days, none of that would matter.

The retreat took place at Eremito, a "Contemporary Monastery" tucked deep in Italy's Umbrian hills. This wasn't a spa retreat or wellness resort. Eremito was an ascetic sanctuary designed for digital detox, a celebration of simple, uncluttered life. There was no internet, no business centers, no minibars, no televisions. Dinner was eaten in complete silence. There was only warm stone and bright stars, wind whispering around the trunks of ancient trees, and a river winding its way through verdant hills.

The flight to Italy felt like an escape from a life that had become unrecognizable. Somewhere over the Atlantic, as I watched the sun set through the airplane window, I realized I couldn't remember the last time I'd sat still for eight hours without checking email, returning calls, or solving some crisis. The forced stillness felt foreign and necessary. Then out of nowhere I started spiraling into anxiety and second-guessing everything.

Are you crazy? the voice in my head kept asking. *Who do you think you are, running off to some monastery in Italy when your business is barely hanging on?*

I shifted in my seat, trying to quiet the mental chatter, but it kept coming.

What if this is weird? What if the people are weird? What if you spent money you don't have on some new-age nonsense that won't actually help anything?

I stared out the airplane window at the endless expanse of ocean below, feeling completely out of my depth. Here I was, a practical businesswoman from New York, flying to Italy to meditate with strangers in a converted monastery. When I said it like that, it sounded absolutely insane.

You're supposed to be home figuring out how to save your business. You're supposed to be networking, hustling, finding solutions. Instead, you're running away to sit in silence with a bunch of people you've never met.

But then another voice, quieter but more persistent, would whisper back: *What do you have to lose?*

That was the truth that kept me in my seat instead of turning around at touchdown. What did I have to lose? I was already drowning. I was already at my breaking point. The traditional strategies weren't working. The hustle wasn't working. The constant crisis management wasn't working.

What if this is exactly what you need? That quieter voice suggested. *What if the answer isn't more pushing, but less? What if you need to stop trying so hard and start trusting?*

By the time we started our descent into Rome, I'd made peace with my decision. Maybe I was crazy. Maybe this was a waste of time and money I couldn't afford. But maybe, just maybe, this was exactly where I needed to be.

When my cab wound its way up the mountain roads toward Eremito, I caught my first glimpse of the building and gasped out loud. It looked like an ancient monastery that had been waiting for me in these hills for centuries, but there were these subtle modern touches that made it livable: the underfloor heating, the carefully designed lighting, the way every stone seemed placed with intention.

The anxiety that had plagued me during the flight began to dissolve. This place felt right in a way I couldn't explain. Sometimes you just know when you're exactly where you're supposed to be.

The entire structure was a masterpiece of design and restraint. Marcello, the owner, had spent years building this place to absolute perfection, and it showed in every detail. It felt like an ancient sacred space, but with just enough contemporary comfort to make you feel held rather than punished.

My room was tiny but exquisite: minimalist in the most gorgeous way possible. The sink and vanity were carved from local stone, beautiful in their simplicity. The space was small enough to feel cozy, like a monk's cell that had been designed by an artist who understood that beauty and austerity could coexist.

The views across the valleys and hills were stunning. From my window, I could see layers of green rolling into the distance, dotted with cypress trees and ancient farmhouses. The silence was so complete it felt almost tangible. No car horns. No sirens. No construction noise. Just wind and birdsong and the kind of peace I'd forgotten existed.

For someone who had spent years obsessing over paint colors and lighting and creating beautiful spaces for children, being in this environment felt like coming home to a part of myself I'd lost. Here, the aesthetic wasn't about impressing anyone or creating an experience for others. It was about stripping away everything unnecessary until only beauty and peace remained.

This was exactly what my soul had been craving without me even knowing it.

The bellman placed my bag on the simple wooden bench and smiled. "Dinner is at seven. The bell will call you."

After he left, I stood in the center of my small room and looked around. Stone walls. A narrow bed. A single window overlooking the hills. Everything I didn't know I needed.

I sat down heavily on the edge of the bed and felt my shoulders drop for the first time in months. "What am I doing here?" I whispered to the empty room.

But even as I asked the question, I knew the answer. I was exhausted. Not just physically. I was spiritually starving.

The last time I'd felt spiritually connected was on long runs, the kind of training runs that feel punishing but purposeful, hitting a goal or target that matters to no else but you and that's the best kind. But since Boston, I hadn't really been running. In fact, there wasn't a single race scheduled on my calendar for the first time in years. The thing that had always been my meditation, my church, my direct line to something greater than myself, I'd let it slip away when I needed it most.

For months, maybe years, I had been moving on autopilot, pouring from a cup that had been empty for so long I'd forgotten what "full" even felt like. I was running a school, managing a staff, keeping the bills paid, holding what was left of my family together, pretending in every room I entered that I was fine. My smiles were real enough to pass inspection, but underneath, I was fraying.

Every morning, I woke up and put on my armor: the competent businesswoman, the devoted mother, the gracious professional who could handle anything thrown her way. I greeted my staff with energy I didn't feel, reassured parents with confidence I didn't possess, solved problems with creativity I had to summon from reserves that ran deeper into deficit each day.

It wasn't just the work that wore me down. It was the constant performing like I was okay. Like I had it all under control. There's a particular kind of fatigue that comes from keeping your armor on 24/7. You start to forget where you end and the armor begins. You forget that you were ever more than the fixer, the leader, the one who absorbs everyone else's storms while never letting them see yours.

I'd been so busy being strong for everyone else that I'd lost touch with the part of me that was simply human. The part that needed rest, that craved silence, that deserved to be held instead of always doing the holding. I'd forgotten what it felt like to just be, without having to prove my worth through productivity or problem-solving.

Here in this room at Eremito, surrounded by centuries-old stone walls and that profound Italian countryside silence, I felt like I was meeting myself for the first time in years. The woman underneath all the roles and responsibilities and relentless forward motion. The woman who was tired. So very tired.

Eremito met me exactly where I was: exhausted, unsure, and just hoping for a reset.

The pace was slow. Intentional. We rose early. We moved from one class to the next—rounding sessions, meditations, quiet walks under the trees. Some days, our last session ended just before dinner. After our silent meal, we gathered for a short knowledge talk. And then we went to sleep in full darkness, no distractions, no phones glowing beside us. Just sleep.

Blissful, unbroken sleep. I couldn't remember the last time I had felt so rested.

There were small breakout groups where we could speak openly about why we were here, the challenges we were carrying, and what we hoped might shift once we went back to our regular lives. I'm typically pretty guarded, especially around strangers, so it speaks to how much of a safe space it must have felt like for me to open up to people I'd just met.

We sat in a circle of six, our yoga pillows arranged in the late afternoon light filtering through ancient stone windows. The problems in our small circle didn't discriminate and came in a garden variety: someone was going through a tough marriage, someone else's daughter had just passed away, another was struggling with alcoholism. But there was something about being total strangers in this ancient stone room overlooking rolling green mountains that took the weight off these heavy truths. We could share them without the baggage of history or judgment.

When it was my turn, I took a breath and said something I'd never said out loud before.

"I want to sell my business."

The words hung in the air for a moment. Not because someone was courting me or because I had a deal on the table, but because I was ready to move on. Saying it out loud in that room, surrounded by people who were also trying to find their own next chapter, made it feel less like giving up and more like choosing myself.

"I've been running these schools for almost twenty years," I continued, surprised by how easily the words were flowing. "And I'm tired. Not just tired of the work, but tired of carrying it all. The debt, the stress, the constant crisis management. I want my life back."

It felt strangely weird but also like relief. It was almost like, I didn't know that was what I wanted until I said it. But as soon as I articulated it, it all made sense to me. It was the first time I'd admitted it even to myself.

"But I'm apprehensive," I added. "I don't know how I'd find a buyer. I don't want to go chasing one and look desperate. I'm still carrying so much trauma from the last sale, from the lawsuit, the judgment, the debt. I'm still licking wounds. And honestly? I'm no longer sure of myself."

The woman across from me, dealing with her own marriage crisis, nodded knowingly. "Sometimes admitting what we want is the hardest part."

"Yeah," said the man struggling with alcoholism. "I spent years pretending I was fine before I could say out loud that I needed help."

There was something magical about that circle, about being able to name our truths without having to fix them or explain them or justify them. We were just witnesses for each other's honesty.

Our days at Eremito weren't asking much of us, so we could set aside the things we'd carried in and perhaps walk out with new armor better suited to pick them back up when we returned to the world.

On my first day there, I was so exhausted that when the organizers had me sharing a cab with Lisa, another participant who'd been on my flight, I had no interest in small talk during the two-hour drive. I just stared out the window, too depleted for conversation.

But by day three or four, when Lisa came up to me during one of our breaks, I seemed different.

"You look so different," she said, smiling. "You have this light now. You look happy."

"I feel different," I admitted. "Lighter somehow."

"Me too," she said. "I was thinking about that cab ride. I could barely make small talk either because I felt so tired and heavy. But look at us now."

She was right. Something was shifting, day by day. I was beginning to feel lighter, like I was putting down a heavy backpack I didn't realize I'd been carrying for years.

That backpack held everything—fear, debt, doubt, guilt, pressure, pride. And as I laid it down, I remembered what it felt like to simply be.

The day we left, The ride back down the winding mountain roads felt different this time. I noticed the way the morning light hit the hills, the way shadows moved across the valleys like gentle waves. I was not rushing. I was not rehearsing the next crisis in my head or mentally calculating which bills were due when I got back.

At the airport, I moved through security without the usual knot in my stomach. The TSA agent checking my passport smiled and said, "Hope you had a good trip."

"I did," I replied, and meant it. "Really good."

On the long flight home, I watched a movie without checking my phone or mentally drafting emails. When the flight attendant offered me wine, I said yes and sipped it slowly, looking out at the clouds below. For the first time in years, I believed I might be able to live differently.

I landed at JFK in the late afternoon. The air was thicker, louder, more impatient than the quiet green hills I had just left behind, but I still felt steady. That peace carried me all the way to baggage claim, even as a small thought flickered at the edges of my mind: life had a way of testing you the moment you thought you had found your footing.

It only took 48 hours.

Two days later, while I was at my desk catching up on emails, my phone rang. The caller ID showed my attorney's office.

"Kettia, we have a situation," he said without preamble. "One of your more aggressive creditors filed a lien on the business yesterday. They are threatening to bring in a marshal to seize property."

I felt my stomach drop, but something was different. Before Eremito, that kind of call would have sent me into a tailspin: panic, worst-case scenarios, sleepless nights spent calculating and recalculating numbers that never added up right. But something in me had shifted.

"Okay," I said, surprised at how calm my voice sounded. "What are our options?"

"Come in this afternoon and we will go over it," he said.

An hour later, I was sitting across from him in his downtown office as he spread papers across his desk like a battle plan.

"I have a strategy," he said. "It is unconventional, but it might be exactly what you need. We put the business into bankruptcy. Not to walk away, but to buy time. To reorganize. To take a breath.

And if you really want to sell, this could signal it. It could help draw out a buyer."

The word "bankruptcy" hit me like a punch. I had spent years clawing my way through financial messes, keeping the doors open, the staff paid, and my reputation intact. Bankruptcy felt like failure, like waving a white flag for everyone to see.

I thought about one of Light's talks at the retreat, where he spoke about moving like water. Water finds its way around anything: mountains, rocks, obstacles. It does not fight the obstacle; it flows around it, over it, through it. It adapts and keeps moving toward its destination.

That image shifted something in me. Bankruptcy was not me giving up. It was me flowing around the mountain instead of smashing myself against it.

When I told Robert, he did not hesitate.

"How do you feel about it?" he asked.

"Like it makes sense," I said. "It's strategic. I am going to use whatever tools are available to get this done."

"If it gives you breathing room and options, do it," he said.

His calm reinforced what I already knew: this was a business decision, nothing more, nothing less. And I was finally ready to play the game the way it was meant to be played.

The woman who had returned from that monastery was different. She wasn't carrying the same white-knuckled grip on every problem. She was learning to trust that there would be a way through, even when she couldn't see it yet. And she was willing to use every tool at her disposal to make it happen.

I was not operating from fear anymore. I was operating from trust.

And if you take nothing else from this part of my story, take this: fear makes you reactive, trust makes you strategic. When you are in fear, every decision feels like a fire drill. You grab whatever you can to put the flames out, often without thinking about what you might be sacrificing in the process.

Trust is different. Trust is not blind optimism or pretending everything is fine. It is the decision to believe that you will figure it out, even if you cannot see the full path yet. It gives you the space to pause, assess, and make choices that align with your bigger goals rather than just your immediate survival.

If you are facing your own version of a "creditor at the door" moment, ask yourself:

- What decision would I make if I knew I would be okay?
- Am I reacting to the fear of the moment, or am I protecting the future I want?

- What tools or strategies might be available to me that I have not considered because I am too busy trying to outrun the fear?

Operating from trust does not mean you ignore the problem. It means you take the wheel instead of letting the fear drive. That shift was the turning point for me, and it can be for you too.

And it worked.

The bankruptcy filing did exactly what my attorney said it would. It stopped the bleeding. The creditors who had been circling were forced to wait. That pause gave me room to think, to plan, and to let the right buyer find me instead of me running after them.

Here is what most entrepreneurs do not realize: bankruptcy creates a public record. That means potential buyers can see the filing. Serious players in your industry monitor those records the way some people check real estate listings. They are looking for opportunities, businesses that have value but are in distress, and they are ready to make a move when they spot one.

In my case, that was exactly what happened. The filing sent a quiet but clear signal: I was open to offers. Within weeks, a few came in. The first were predictable lowball attempts from people hoping to take advantage of the situation. The vultures. That is part of the game, and you have to know how to spot them.

Here's how you tell the difference:

- Vultures lead with price. Their offer is quick and far below market value. They often pressure you to sign fast, hoping you are desperate enough to take anything. They may not have the resources or commitment to actually close a deal.

- Serious buyers lead with questions. They want to understand your operations, your numbers, your strengths, and your challenges. They are willing to negotiate on terms, not just price, and they usually come with proof of funds or a track record of closing deals in your industry.

A vulture is looking for a fire sale. A serious buyer is looking for a fit.

When the call came from KinderCare, one of the biggest names in the childcare industry, I knew we were talking to a real contender. They knew the market, had the infrastructure, and most importantly, they had the ability to follow through. This was not just an offer—it was an opportunity to close this chapter on my terms.

From the first conversation with KinderCare, I knew this was not the time to play small. My attorney and I agreed that we would not rush the process. Serious buyers expect you to know your worth, and how you negotiate tells them exactly how you value your business.

KinderCare's team wanted to see everything: financial statements, enrollment numbers, staffing rosters, lease agreements, licensing records. They came in with a long list of due diligence requests, and I gave them what they needed, but I also made sure they understood the value they were getting. I highlighted the brand reputation I had built, the loyal staff who knew how to run the centers without me, and the prime locations in a competitive market.

Here is something I learned in the first sale that really helped me here. When you are selling your business, you are not just selling assets and numbers. You are selling the years of goodwill, the systems you put in place, and the customer trust you have earned. That is what drives real value.

Negotiations are a dance. They opened lower than I wanted, which was expected. My attorney and I countered, not just with a number but with a narrative. We showed them why my business was worth their investment, how it could fit into their portfolio, and where they could see immediate returns.

This was where the bankruptcy strategy worked in my favor again. Because the creditors had been paused, I was not negotiating from a place of panic. I could afford to walk away if the terms were not right, and the buyers sensed that. Buyers respect a seller who is willing to walk.

Weeks of back-and-forth followed. Every call, every email, every term sheet was a reminder that this was not just about getting out from under debt. It was about exiting with my head high and my work respected.

When KinderCare finally came back with the number and terms that aligned with my goals, I felt a quiet sense of victory. It was not loud or celebratory. It was the deep satisfaction of knowing I had navigated a storm and made it to shore on my own terms.

*****

There's this image we carry: Black woman, boss, wife, mother. Capable. Unshakable. Always getting it done. And maybe some of that is true. But the part that gets left out? The cost.

I've worn all those titles at the same time. And for a long while, I thought the only way to honor them was to carry everything, everyone, on my back. No dropped balls. No signs of fatigue. Just keep going.

But the truth? We don't get medals for doing it all alone. We just get tired. Burnt out. Isolated. And no one really talks about how hard it is to trust others when the stakes feel so high, or how scary it can feel to admit we need help.

When you're a Black woman in business, you're not just building for yourself. You're carrying your whole lineage. You're showing up for the ones who didn't have the chance. You're pushing through doors that weren't built for you in the first place.

That weight can be beautiful, but also exhausting.

I've found myself in rooms where I felt like I had to be flawless just to be seen. Where I had to prove I was worthy of the seat, even after I'd already earned it. And that pressure doesn't stay at the office door. It follows you home. Into the kitchen. Into bedtime routines. Into your marriage.

You become the person who makes everything run, but rarely pauses long enough to ask: What do I need?

Burnout doesn't show up all at once. It trickles in. It starts when you skip lunch for the third day in a row because emails won't stop. It settles in when your child tells you a story and you nod, but you weren't really listening because your brain is somewhere else. It shows up in the heavy sighs, the quiet resentment, the nights when you're so wired with anxiety that even rest feels impossible.

And the worst part? We don't say anything.

We keep performing. Keep smiling. Keep moving. Because asking for help feels like failure. Like we've dropped the ball on being "strong."

In so many of our communities, asking for help is laced with shame. We're taught to be independent. Self-sufficient. Resourceful. And if you can't do it all yourself? Well, maybe you're not cut out for it.

That message is everywhere, in business, in motherhood, even in our friendships. We assume we're the only one struggling, the only one barely holding it together.

And so we suffer in silence. We over-function. We try to control every little thing because we don't trust that anyone else will show up the way we do.

I remember during the height of my business stress, I wouldn't even delegate simple tasks to my assistant. I preferred to stay up until midnight handling things myself than risk someone else doing it "wrong."

When Robert offered to take over the kids' evening routine so I could focus on work, I found myself hovering, correcting, stepping in. Not because he was doing anything wrong, but because I convinced myself that if I wasn't managing every detail, something would fall through the cracks.

The irony is that by trying to control everything, I was actually making everything harder. I was burning myself out while training everyone around me that I didn't really trust them to help.

But here's what I've learned: you can be the backbone and still need a break.

Asking for help isn't about being weak. It's about being wise. It's about recognizing that you're human, and humans weren't designed to carry everything alone.

It means hiring someone not just to help, but to take something off your plate completely. It means accepting your partner's version of dinner even if it's not how you would've done it. It means letting your kids see you rest. Not because you're lazy, but because you're human.

It means building a team and letting them lead. It means not answering every email at midnight. It means saying "I need help" without apology.

And it means trusting yourself to know your limits, to pivot when needed, to choose peace over perfection.

We've been sold this idea that success means juggling everything flawlessly. But what if success looks more like ease? Like boundaries? Like joy?

What if it looks like walking away from the idea that you're the only one who can make everything work?

For me, real success started the day I stopped trying to do it all and started building systems of support, at work and at home. And that shift? It changed everything. Not overnight. But enough to breathe. Enough to begin healing.

I started small. I hired a bookkeeper to handle the finances I'd been managing myself for years. I let my assistant actually assist instead of micromanaging every task. I asked Robert to handle bedtime routines without me checking in every five minutes.

When the Magic Showed Up

The hardest part wasn't the logistics. It was the mental shift. Learning to trust that other people could handle things differently than me and that different didn't mean wrong.

I had to learn that asking for help doesn't diminish your value. It actually multiplies it. When you free yourself from the tasks that drain you, you create space for the things only you can do.

Here's what I want every woman reading this to understand: asking for help doesn't make you less of a mother. Delegating doesn't make you less of a leader. Resting doesn't make you less of a warrior.

It just makes you whole.

And whole is where your power lives.

Let's normalize hiring help. Let's normalize therapy. Let's normalize women, especially Black women, choosing rest without guilt. Let's normalize crying in the car if that's what today calls for, and then walking into that meeting like the queen you are.

Let's normalize letting someone else carry the weight for a bit.

Because we weren't meant to do this alone.

The strongest thing you can do is recognize when you need support and be brave enough to ask for it. The people who love you want to help. The people who work with you want to contribute. But they can't if you don't let them.

And if you're still struggling to ask, let me say this as plainly as I can: You don't have to earn the right to receive help. You don't have to prove you deserve support. You don't have to be at the breaking point to ask for what you need.

You're valuable not because of what you do, but because of who you are. And who you are deserves care, support, and rest.

CHAPTER 13

When the Magic Showed Up

I've always trusted hard work.

Building Smarter Toddler from a basement daycare to four Manhattan locations taught me that. I knew how to grind. How to show up at 5 a.m. to handle a broken boiler before the first families arrived. How to figure it out when the health department showed up unannounced or when a teacher quit mid-semester. Again and again, I'd found a way through.

I knew how to work 18-hour days during licensing inspections, sleep four hours, and still tour prospective families the next morning with energy and enthusiasm. I could solve payroll shortfalls, negotiate with landlords, and manage staff drama all before lunch.

But what I was lacking was faith.

Not the Sunday service, hymn-singing kind. I'd had plenty of that growing up. What I was missing was the deep, quiet trust that everything would work out even when I couldn't see how. The belief that I didn't have to carry every burden, solve every problem, or control every outcome through sheer force of will.

When the Magic Showed Up

I was searching for a way to stop white-knuckling my life. To believe that my effort was enough, that the universe wasn't waiting for me to hustle harder or prove my worth through exhaustion.

I grew up in the Seventh-day Adventist church. I heard plenty of sermons about faith. But that version of church rhetoric always left me cold.

It was the hypocrisy. Their actions didn't match their words. There was always a holier-than-thou energy coming from leadership and certain church members. Preaching against premarital sex but quickly marrying off a 19-year-old with no explanation, only for her to give birth six months later. We all know how long it takes a baby to cook.

Or the deacon's wife with the mystery bruises on her arms and neck, or the black eye buried under massive dark sunglasses worn indoors. The lack of compassion for those who dared to struggle out loud.

I grew up with a front-row seat to all the shenanigans, and it was hard to believe that this is what Christianity was about. That I had to follow these examples to be a good person, to inherit eternal life. It just didn't gel for me.

And then, somewhere in the middle of all the chaos from the lawsuit, just my life at the time, I picked up a book a friend had recommended. A close friend I admired deeply.

My friend Nadja recommended the book to me. She was someone who got shit done, who seemed to have strong spiritual beliefs that grounded her days. She moved with this kind of unshakable faith that she was "blessed and highly favored," her phrase. That certainty, that peace in the middle of uncertainty, was something I wanted to understand.

The book was *The Infinite Way* by Joel S. Goldsmith. It's small. You could read it in one sitting. I certainly did. But I kept coming back to one chapter.

Prayer.

This is what I read:

"Ye ask and receive not, because ye ask amiss," says the Apostle James. Have you ever thought of this when you've prayed for some time, and found no answer? "Ye ask amiss." There is the reason.

Prayer, when based on the belief that there is a need unfilled or a desire unsatisfied, is never in accord with true scientific prayer. A prayer to God to do something, send something, provide, or heal is equally without power.

Any belief that that which we are seeking is anywhere but within us, within our very own consciousness, is the barrier separating us in belief from our harmony.

That stopped me cold.

"Instead of seeking, asking, waiting... we turn our thoughts inward and listen for the still small voice which assures us that even before we asked, our Father knew and fulfilled the need."

I remember reading that chapter over and over again. Each time, something shifted in me. Something clicked.

I realized I had it all wrong.

Up until that point, my prayers had been a laundry list of demands. Please help me win this lawsuit. Please make the settlement payments manageable. Please don't let me lose the business. Please, please, please fix this mess I've gotten myself into.

I was praying like I was placing an order at a restaurant. Like God was some cosmic customer service department that would solve my problems if I just asked nicely enough or desperately enough.

But this was saying something completely different. That everything I needed was already within me. That instead of begging for solutions, I needed to get quiet enough to hear what was already there.

I didn't need to fight harder. I didn't need to ask louder.

I needed to go inward. I needed to flow.

That's how things were going to unfold. Not through force, but through faith.

This shift didn't happen overnight. But slowly, I started approaching problems differently.

Instead of lying awake at 3 a.m. calculating worst-case scenarios, I'd catch myself and ask: What if I trusted that a solution already exists? What if instead of trying to force an outcome, I got quiet enough to see what was actually possible?

When my lawyer would call with updates about the case, instead of immediately spiraling into panic mode, I'd take a breath before responding. I'd listen to what he was actually saying instead of what I was afraid he might say.

During staff meetings, instead of trying to control every detail and micromanage every decision, I started asking my team what they thought. What solutions did they see? What ideas did they have? And I was amazed by how much wisdom was sitting right there in the room, waiting for me to stop talking long enough to hear it.

I stopped chasing new business so desperately. Instead of frantically trying to fill every empty spot, I focused on serving the families we already had really well. And somehow, referrals started coming more naturally.

Even simple things changed. When parents complained about policies or question our procedures, instead of getting defensive and over-explaining, I paused. I listened. Sometimes they had a point. Sometimes they were just venting and needed to be heard.

The biggest shift was learning to sit with uncertainty instead of immediately trying to fix it. When I didn't know how we'd make next month's rent, instead of panicking and scrambling for quick solutions, I got still. I asked myself: What step can I actually take today? Just today.

And almost always, there was a step. Just one. But that was enough.

It started small. A parent who had been on the fence about withdrawing her child because of her changing financial situation decided to stay after I sat with her concerns and worked out a part-time schedule that fit her budget. Grateful for the support, she later referred two new families.

A teacher who I thought was about to quit came to me with a creative solution for the scheduling problem that had been stressing everyone out. The solution was so obvious I couldn't believe I hadn't seen it before. But I'd been too busy trying to control the situation to leave space for anyone else's ideas.

The insurance company that had been jerking us around on a claim suddenly had a different representative call me. This one was helpful, reasonable. The claim that had been stuck for months got resolved in a week.

A vendor who I owed money to called, and instead of my usual panic about how to handle the conversation, I was honest. "I want to pay you, and I will. Here's what I can do right now, and here's when I can do the rest." He agreed. No drama, no threats. Just a reasonable payment plan.

The really weird part was how opportunities started appearing. Not because I was chasing them, but because I was finally paying attention.

A business consultant reached out through a mutual friend, offering to help with restructuring our debt. She had experience with exactly our type of situation and was willing to work with our budget.

A reporter from a local parenting magazine wanted to do a story about innovative childcare approaches. The article brought in more inquiries than any advertising we'd ever paid for.

These weren't coincidences. Or maybe they were, but I was finally calm enough to notice them. When you're running around in crisis mode, frantically trying to force solutions, you miss the doors that are quietly opening around you.

The stillness made space for things to happen. Not the things I thought I needed, but the things that actually moved us forward.

Looking back, I realize that the retreat at Eremito made it possible for me to be open to The Infinite Way. I don't think I was ready for it before my trip. I wouldn't have understood it or been able to apply it. That book showed up because I was finally ready for it. Before the retreat, I would have been too closed off to understand these lessons.

There, in that little stone monastery in Umbria, I learned what it meant to surrender. To stop chasing and start listening. To stop fixing and start receiving.

And that's when the magic showed up.

*****

I signed the purchase agreement with KinderCare in early November 2019.

It felt surreal, like I was crossing a finish line I'd been chasing for years. I was ready. Ready to sell. Ready to release. Ready to begin the next chapter of my life. KinderCare was serious. Seasoned. Solid. The kind of buyer who knew the value of what I had built. This time, I was coming to the table clear-headed and calm. This was a decision rooted in alignment, not desperation.

The difference between this process and the Bright Horizons deal five years earlier wasn't about how I was treated. Bright Horizons had been careful, strategic. They wanted my centers badly and knew exactly what to say to get me to sell.

But I had been apprehensive about selling to them. Deep down, I always knew they would change everything. I sold anyway, but with some hesitation.

With KinderCare, the main difference was simple: I wanted to sell and was very ready to sell. There was no apprehension, no hesitation. Just negotiations.

Their team flew in from Portland for a full-day site visit. They asked thoughtful questions about our operations, our staff retention, what made families choose us. When they requested financial records, the process was straightforward. When we disagreed on valuation, we worked through it professionally.

Most importantly, I wasn't conflicted this time. I knew exactly what I wanted: to close this chapter and move on. Every conversation reflected that clarity.

That still didn't stop them from trying to pull a fast one though.

I was sitting at my kitchen table, contract spread out in front of me, pen in hand, ready to initial the final pages of the KinderCare agreement. It was late, maybe 10 p.m.. The kids were in their rooms, the apartment was quiet, and I was finally getting through the last of the legal documents.

Page after page of standard acquisition language. Asset transfers, liability assumptions, employee transitions. I was scanning more than reading at this point, eager to get through the stack and move closer to closing this chapter of my life.

Then I saw it.

Buried in the middle of a paragraph about intellectual property transfers: "Seller agrees that all trademarks, including but not limited to 'Smarter Toddler,' shall transfer to Buyer at closing."

I stopped. Read it again.

They wanted to own the name Smarter Toddler. Just like that. Casually thrown into the agreement like it was part of the furniture.

Never mind that the name was trademarked. Never mind that the trademark was registered to me and Robert, not the LLC they were purchasing. Never mind that I had spent years building equity in that brand, that parents across Manhattan knew and trusted that name.

They wanted it. And they expected it for free.

I felt my jaw clench. After everything I'd been through, after all the negotiations where they'd treated me with respect, here was the same old assumption: that everything valuable I'd created should just be handed over without question.

The audacity was breathtaking.

I picked up my phone and called my lawyer, even though it was past 10 p.m..

"Did you see this line about the trademark?" I asked when he answered.

"Which line?"

"Page forty-seven. They're claiming ownership of the Smarter Toddler name."

Silence on his end as he flipped through his copy. Then, "Yeah, I saw that. I figured we'd address it in revisions."

"Address it? They can't just take my trademark."

"Well, they're buying the business..."

"They're buying the LLC. The trademark is registered separately. It's been independently valued at over a million dollars."

More silence. Then, "Let me call their attorney in the morning."

I hung up, staring at the contract. This wasn't an oversight. This was a test. They were seeing how much they could get away with, how much I'd roll over and accept just to get the deal done. And my dumb ass lawyer was letting it happen. Sometimes I wondered who this man really worked for, me or them?

When my lawyer called the next day with their response, I wasn't surprised.

"They say it's unfair," he reported. "They assumed the name came with the business. They're claiming they wouldn't have made the offer if they'd known the trademark was separate."

"Unfair?" I laughed, but there was no humor in it. "What's unfair is expecting me to throw in a million-dollar asset for free."

"They didn't ask. They presumed."

And in that moment, I had one clear thought: I should be doing business in the headspace of entitled white men.

Because the confidence? The audacity? The expectation that everything is negotiable in their favor?

Mind-blowing. But also instructive.

When you build something from scratch, especially as a Black woman, you know every inch of what it took to get there. You know what it cost. You know what it's worth. And still, you're taught to feel like you're asking for too much when you ask to be paid for it.

But I knew better. I was the brand. Smarter Toddler wasn't just a name. It was a living, breathing identity that I had carefully crafted over years.

I remembered registering that trademark. I remembered filing the paperwork, knowing that someday, this brand would mean something. Robert and I chose that name with intention, something that sounded playful and sharp at the same time. Something that said, "Yes, we're early childhood education, but we're doing it differently."

The aesthetic. The curriculum. The vibe. All of it lived inside that name. And yet here they were, trying to throw it into the deal like an extra set of keys.

It was a revealing moment, not just about the deal, but about the ecosystem I was navigating. White corporate culture often operates on assumptions of ownership. Assumptions that they are the rightful inheritors of everything valuable. Assumptions that once they've entered the room, the rest of us should just hand over the goods.

And yet, here I was, Black, female, first-generation immigrant, telling them: No. Not this. Not for free.

Power doesn't always come from posturing. It comes from knowing what you built, meaning sometimes you just gotta check people. Because the truth is, if I had been anyone else, they probably would've gotten away with it. And they knew it. That's why they tried.

Would a white male founder have been asked to throw in a million-dollar brand asset for free? Would the same casual entitlement be applied to a tech founder, or a startup entrepreneur with a Stanford MBA and venture capital backing? Doubtful.

So yes, sometimes I think: maybe I should do business in the headspace of entitled white men. Because they never feel bad for asking. They never second-guess their worth. They never think twice about saying no to a bad deal.

But here's what I also know: I don't need to act like them to win. My power comes from knowing exactly what I built and what it's worth, and refusing to let that be erased, stolen, or discounted.

The negotiations stalled for two weeks over the trademark. Their team kept pushing, trying different angles. Maybe we could license it to them? Maybe we could include it for a nominal fee?

Each time, my answer was the same: No.

"Look," I finally told their lead negotiator during a conference call, "you want the name? Buy it. It's been independently appraised. You know what it's worth. But it's not part of this business sale, and it never was."

The silence on the call stretched long enough that I wondered if they'd hung up.

Finally, "We'll need to discuss this with our team."

Three days later, they came back with a decision. They would proceed with the sale without the trademark. I could keep the name Smarter Toddler.

They didn't get the trademark. They had to walk away without it.

And that was a win not just for me, but for every woman who's ever been told to be grateful for crumbs when she baked the whole damn cake.

The deal moved forward. But something had shifted in the dynamic. They knew now that I wasn't going to roll over for their convenience. That I knew exactly what I owned and what it was worth.

Know what you own. Know what you've built. And never give it away just because they expect you to.

We forged ahead with due diligence. Licensing transfers. Financial audits. All the tedious but necessary work that makes a clean deal take forever.

The timeline was clear: six months. The plan was to close in May or June 2020.

Of course no one could have predicted what happened next.

March 2020. The global pandemic.

And just like that, chaos was back.

In those first few weeks, businesses shuttered. Cities locked down. Schools went remote. Fear pulsed through every news headline. And in the childcare world?

It was catastrophic.

Overnight, the industry collapsed. Classrooms closed. Teachers were laid off. Parents, many of them now unemployed or working from home, pulled their kids out indefinitely. Some centers tried to pivot to online programming. Others just disappeared.

We were one of the few who kept the doors open. Why? Because we were in contract to sell. We needed to show continuity. Stability. Viability.

It didn't matter that we were hemorrhaging money. It didn't matter that half our enrollment vanished. We had to hold on.

We were now in a high-stakes game of just stay alive.

The truth is, childcare was always fragile. People just didn't see it until it broke.

The pandemic didn't create the cracks. It just exposed them.

Early childhood centers were already operating on razor-thin margins across the country. Most staff were underpaid. Licensing was overbearing everywhere. Real estate was expensive, especially in cities like New York. And while we were essential, we were never treated that way by policymakers or the broader economy.

When COVID hit, the entire country suddenly realized how crucial childcare is to the economy. Parents couldn't work without it. Businesses couldn't function. And yet there was no real safety net. No bailout. No cushion. Just a wave of closures and a whole lot of uncertainty.

We kept the doors open with a skeleton crew. A typical day started at 7 a.m. with staff arriving to take temperatures at the door. Every child, every staff member, every parent who entered had to be screened. Temperature checks, health questionnaires, constant hand sanitizing.

Between the two centers, we'd gone from serving 160 children to maybe 60 on a good day. But those 60 kids needed the same ratio of teachers, the same level of care, the same attention to safety protocols. Except now we were also wiping down every surface every hour, keeping children in pods that couldn't mix, and somehow explaining to toddlers why they couldn't hug their friends.

When the Magic Showed Up

The stress on my remaining staff was enormous. They were scared about their own health, worried about bringing something home to their families, but still showing up because these essential worker families needed them. I spent half my time reassuring teachers and the other half reassuring parents who were torn between needing childcare and fearing for their children's safety.

Every day brought new guidelines from the city, the state, the CDC. Mask requirements that changed weekly. Outdoor time restrictions. New cleaning protocols. I'd get emails at 8 p.m. with updated regulations that had to be implemented by 7 a.m. the next morning.

The financial math was brutal. We were paying full rent for both locations while operating at 40% capacity. Staff salaries, utilities, insurance, all the fixed costs remained the same while revenue plummeted. Every day we stayed open, we burned through more money.

But we had to keep going. We had to show KinderCare that we were viable, that this was a business worth buying, that we could weather the storm.

We cleaned, sanitized, reassured. We kept the teachers safe. We kept the children safe.

I wasn't particularly worried about the deal falling through. The contract had buffer language that protected both sides. KinderCare could only pull out for specific reasons like our inability to transfer licenses or other operational issues that would prevent them from running the business. COVID was considered force majeure, something neither party could control or predict.

Besides, companies like KinderCare had the financial resources to wait out a pandemic. They could afford to be patient. It was the smaller, independent centers that were suffering and closing permanently.

The real concern was how much money we'd burn through while keeping the doors open until closing.

Suddenly, every working parent in America was living the impossible math that childcare providers had been navigating for years.

I'll never forget the phone calls that started pouring in during those first few weeks of lockdown. Parents who had never used our services, calling desperately from all over the city.

"Please," one mother said, crying on the phone. "I'm a nurse at Mount Sinai. My husband is a paramedic. Our daycare closed yesterday and we have a three-year-old and a baby. I don't know what to do. I can't not show up to work right now."

Another call: "I'm trying to work from home with my law firm, but my five-year-old needs constant supervision and my toddler is climbing the walls. I haven't been able to complete a phone call in three days. My nanny quit because she's scared of getting sick. Do you have any openings?"

The desperation in these voices was heartbreaking. These were people who had previously taken childcare for granted, who maybe complained about the cost or the pickup procedures. Now they were understanding what essential workers had always known: without childcare, the entire system falls apart.

I watched families try to navigate impossible choices. Keep working while their children destroyed the house in the background of Zoom calls? Quit their jobs to supervise remote learning? Send their kids to stay with elderly grandparents who were most at risk?

One of our existing families, both parents doctors, were working back-to-back shifts at the hospital. Their eight-year-old was supposed to be doing remote learning, but was essentially raising his four-year-old sister during 12-hour stretches when both parents were gone. An eight-year-old making lunch, managing tantrums, trying to help with homework he didn't understand himself.

Another parent, a single mother who worked for the city, told me she was setting up her laptop in our lobby area so she could work while her daughter played in our small outdoor courtyard, which was the only safe outdoor space they could access.

The pressure cooker was real. Parents were trying to accomplish full-time work while homeschooling children they'd never homeschooled before, keeping up with constantly changing medical guidance, sanitizing everything they touched, and staying isolated from the support systems they'd relied on. Grandparents, friends, babysitters, all suddenly off-limits.

I watched marriages strain under the pressure. I saw parents having complete breakdowns on the sidewalk outside our building after failed attempts to work from home. I heard stories of children acting out because their entire world had been turned upside down, and parents who were too overwhelmed to know how to help them.

The irony wasn't lost on me. Here we were, childcare providers, finally being recognized as essential workers. But many of us were also being forced to close because there was no financial support to help us weather the storm. The very infrastructure everyone suddenly realized they needed was crumbling in real time.

I remember one particularly devastating call from a mother who worked in marketing for a tech company. She was trying to manage a major product launch from her one-bedroom apartment with twin toddlers.

"I'm hiding in my bathroom to take this call," she whispered. "It's the only place I can get five minutes of quiet. I put on a movie for them, but they keep fighting and screaming. My boss doesn't understand why my productivity has dropped. She keeps saying 'just get a babysitter' like babysitters are still a thing right now. I'm going to lose my job, and I can't afford to lose my job. But I also can't leave my two-year-olds alone to go to the office."

Another family reached out through a mutual friend. The father was an ER doctor working 16-hour shifts, the mother was a teacher trying to run virtual classes from home while managing their own kindergartener's remote learning plus their three-year-old.

"I'm teaching 25 kids on Zoom while my daughter is melting down in the background because she doesn't understand why she can't go to school," the mom told me. "My son keeps interrupting my classes asking for snacks or help with his own virtual lessons. Parents are emailing me complaining that they can hear my kids during instruction time. I'm failing at everything."

One of the most heartbreaking stories came from a family where both parents worked for the MTA. Essential workers who couldn't work from home. Their regular childcare had closed, their backup nanny was too scared to work, and their family lived in another state.

"We're leaving our seven-year-old in charge of our four-year-old for ten hours a day," the father admitted. "We check in every few hours, but we don't have a choice. If we don't work, people can't get to their jobs at hospitals and grocery stores. But I'm terrified something will happen to my kids while we're gone."

So many stories that could fill a whole book!

These weren't isolated cases. These were happening in every neighborhood, in every city, across the entire country. The invisible infrastructure that allowed society to function, that allowed parents to work and contribute to the economy, had disappeared overnight. And everyone was scrambling to figure out how to hold it all together with duct tape and prayer.

You'd think with all this desperate demand, business should have been booming for the centers that stayed open. But we were caught in a catch-22 that many small businesses faced during COVID.

While families were frantically calling for spots, we couldn't just start adding kids because we were losing staff. The government had started issuing stimulus checks, essentially paying people to stay home, and that's exactly what many did. Especially staff members who had elderly family members or underlying health conditions. They were terrified of bringing the virus home to vulnerable relatives.

So unlike many other industries that could pivot or benefit from increased demand, we were stuck. We had desperate families wanting our services and we had the physical space, but we didn't have enough healthy, willing staff to safely care for more children.

Like many other small businesses, we didn't benefit from any boom because we were chronically short-staffed at the exact moment when demand was highest.

I thought I was done with chaos. I thought the worst was behind me.

But now the whole world was living in the same kind of insecurity I had been carrying since opening my doors straddled with this insidious lawsuit.

Only difference? I had practice.

I knew how to keep moving when everything around me was uncertain. I knew how to run the mile I was in.

I applied for the coveted PPP loan and thank God, we got it.

The Paycheck Protection Program was supposed to be a lifeline for small businesses during the pandemic. Forgivable loans designed to help companies keep their staff employed when revenue disappeared. But getting approved wasn't guaranteed. Thousands of businesses were competing for limited funds, and the application process was a nightmare of constantly changing requirements and crashed government websites.

I spent days refreshing the SBA portal, trying to submit our application before the funding ran out. Banks were overwhelmed, understaffed, and many were prioritizing their largest clients first. Small businesses like mine were left scrambling.

When our approval came through, it felt like winning the lottery.

That loan helped us hold on longer than most. Without it, we wouldn't have made it through the first two months. It gave us just enough oxygen to stay open, to pay staff, to pretend, on the outside, that we were okay.

But inside? The truth was stark.

Overnight, our enrollment disappeared. You'd think with all the desperate demand we'd heard about, we'd be packed. But our clientele was a specific demographic: white-collar professionals who could afford second homes in the Hamptons, weekend houses upstate, beach properties where they could ride out the pandemic. When the city shut down, they grabbed their families and left town to work remotely from their other properties.

So we lost our existing families to their escape plans, but we couldn't replace them with the desperate families calling us because we were losing teachers to stimulus checks. We were caught in the worst possible position: no students and no staff.

We were operating at barely 40%. Our breakeven point? 60%. The numbers weren't numbering.

We were paying staff. Keeping payroll going. Keeping hope alive. But we couldn't keep up with the rent.

Between the two centers, we were falling behind by $100,000 a month.

The only reason we weren't being locked out was because of the pending sale. Our landlords were very aware that we were in contract to sell, and they were already salivating at the idea of having a corporate tenant like KinderCare on their roster. So they waited.

They were lenient, not because they believed in me. But because they knew they'd get paid. One way or another.

It was a strange kind of protection. The same deal that was forcing me to stay open and burn through cash was also the only thing keeping the landlords from evicting us. They could afford to be patient because they saw KinderCare's name on the contract.

"We understand the situation," my FiDi landlord told me during a phone call. "These are unprecedented times. We're willing to work with you because we know this sale is happening."

Translation: We'll let you dig yourself deeper into debt because we know the corporate buyer will make us whole.

And every month that passed? Every rent bill that went unpaid? That money was quietly subtracting from our profit.

We weren't just burning time. We were burning equity.

The math was brutal but simple. Every month of reduced enrollment meant more debt piling up. Every month we couldn't pay full rent meant less money we'd walk away with when the deal closed. The landlords would get paid from the sale proceeds, along with all the other creditors who'd been patiently waiting.

I was essentially working for free, using my own sale money to keep the business alive long enough to sell it.

By the time it was all said and done, we didn't close in May or June 2020 like we had hoped.

We didn't close in the fall.

We closed in January 2021 on Martin Luther King Jr. day.

After everything we had been through, we closed the deal.

But not with a windfall. Not with the profit we had projected.

We lost more than $900,000, out of what should have been ours from the sale.

That money? Gone. Paid out in rent arrears to keep the deal alive.

Money we had earned. Money that was supposed to help us start over. Money that disappeared month by month, while we fought to keep the dream afloat just long enough to hand it off.

I know for a fact the reason my business didn't thrive the second time is because it was snuffed out before we even opened.

It never had a chance.

The debt from the Bright Horizons settlement was like a weight around our neck from day one. We opened already behind, already bleeding money we didn't have. Every month we had to make those settlement payments meant less money for marketing, for improvements, for building the reserves that every business needs to weather tough times.

We weren't starting fresh. We were starting wounded.

I remember having a conversation with a Bright Horizons executive once, during the first sale. It was casual. Off the cuff. I mentioned something about maybe opening another center in the future, something light, forward-looking. And his response?

"Well, we don't want to compete with you."

Said with a smile. But it hit me like a brick.

That wasn't just a throwaway comment. That was a confession.

The fear of Black excellence in white corporate spaces is real. It rattles people. It disrupts the unspoken rules.

I believe, truly, that Bright Horizons saw our original deal as something that needed to be corrected. It wasn't that I broke a rule. It wasn't that I violated a clause.

It was that I rose too high outside their blueprint.

I wasn't punished for doing something wrong. I was punished for doing something right, too visibly, too successfully, too freely.

But even in that truth, I find power.

Because I didn't just build a business. I built a vision. A community. A standard.

And they couldn't unbuild that, no matter what they tried.

I had no regrets. We made it. By the skin of our teeth. But we made it.

There's a version of success that doesn't make headlines. It's not the ribbon-cutting, champagne-popping, press-release kind. It's the kind where you lose more than you thought you could survive losing, and still find the strength to stand up and say: I did that.

Sometimes success isn't what you take away. It's what you leave standing.

And even after the storm, after the lawsuits, the debts, the pandemic, the pain, we handed off something whole.

That's not failure. That's legacy.

*****

Legacy. It's one of those words that carries a lot of weight: expectation, pride, history. It sounds noble, almost poetic. But for first-generation entrepreneurs, especially Black women with Caribbean roots like mine, legacy isn't an abstract idea. It's personal. It's the dream you build with your own two hands, and it's the story you hope your children will one day tell.

My father's journey from Haiti to New York, working two jobs for nearly ten years to bring his family to America, wasn't just about survival. It was about building something that would last beyond his lifetime. That inheritance shaped how I approached everything, including Smarter Toddler. This wasn't just about running a successful daycare. This was about proving that his sacrifice had been worth it. That his daughter could not only succeed in the country he'd chosen for us, but could build something meaningful, something that mattered.

When we designed those spaces, we weren't just thinking about what would work functionally. We were thinking about creating beauty and excellence because we deserved both. The Haitian flag hanging in our multicultural display wasn't just decoration. It was representation. It was my way of saying that our culture, our story, our presence in this space was not only welcome but essential.

The way I insisted on live music, real art, authentic materials, that came from growing up understanding that just because we were immigrants didn't mean we had to accept second-best. My father taught us that education and excellence were our pathways to belonging anywhere we chose to go.

Even my approach to hiring reflected those values. I looked for teachers who understood that children from all backgrounds deserved to see themselves reflected in their environment, who knew that a Haitian child and a Danish child and a Japanese child could all thrive in the same loving, intentional space.

Creating the second iteration of Smarter Toddler wasn't just chasing financial freedom. I was building a foundation my children could look at and say, "My mother built that." A legacy they could inherit, not just in dollars, but in meaning. Proof of struggle. Proof of triumph.

So when the time came to sell it the second time? I was ready.

Remember this wasn't my first rodeo. Five years earlier, when Bright Horizons had come calling, I'd been giddy and flattered. Someone wanted what I'd built! But I'd also felt tremendous guilt about selling something I'd created from scratch, something that felt so personal, so tied to my identity as a mother and entrepreneur.

Now? I was in a completely different headspace. My children were about to fly the nest. My marriage had crumbled. I was carrying the business by sheer willpower, weighed down by debt from the Bright Horizons lawsuit that had nearly destroyed everything I'd worked for.

I wasn't selling because someone was courting me with flattery and promises. I was selling because I was exhausted. Because I needed to close this chapter and start fresh. This time, I had clarity about what I was walking away from and why.

Still, letting go of a business was more than signing paperwork. It's an unraveling. A reckoning. And for me, it was the start of a deeper question: What does legacy really mean?

Building Smarter Toddler as a first-generation Black woman entrepreneur meant I wasn't just creating a business plan. I was creating proof that my father's sacrifice had been worth it.

Every decision, from the art on the walls to the teachers I hired, was a declaration that we belonged in these spaces, that excellence was our birthright, not a privilege to be earned. I wasn't thinking about legacy in the academic sense. I was thinking about diapers and licensing and payroll and paint colors. But in hindsight, I was laying bricks in a house I hoped my children would someday live in, figuratively and maybe even literally.

I saw it as theirs. I was building it for them.

But my children didn't see it the same way I did. When I finally told them about the sale, their reaction was predictably self-absorbed. "Okay, sounds great Mom," Sophie said, barely looking up from her phone. She was deep in her studies at Frank Sinatra High School of Performing Arts, obsessing over her next performance and thinking about college.

Alexi was wrapped up in college life and spending the next semester abroad to perfect his Arabic. He was building his own vision of his future, and it didn't involve running daycare centers.

Chloe had discovered cinematography and film production at Dwight High School and was already planning her path at Emerson College. She was proud of what I'd built, but she was much more excited about the short film she was working on.

They were proud of me, absolutely. But they were teenagers, already building and obsessing over their own interests, their own dreams, their own futures. They weren't sitting around thinking about inheriting my business. They were thinking about their next test, their college applications, their weekend plans.

I was part of the vessel that got them there. I made the sacrifices I was happy to make. The late nights, the stress, the financial risks, all of it was so they could have the freedom to pursue whatever called to them. And they were doing exactly that.

It hit me that I'd been carrying a burden they'd never asked me to carry.

The clarity that followed was immediate.

Maybe what I was really giving them was something far more powerful than a business to inherit.

The courage to build something of their own. The confidence to pivot. The understanding that legacy doesn't have to look like a deed or a plaque or a signed lease.

Legacy is presence. Legacy is knowing you have a right to take up space. Legacy is watching your mother navigate fire and still find a way to bloom.

Once I let go of the idea that legacy had to be something tangible, something surprising came in its place: peace.

Not right away. But over time. Because I realized this wasn't the end of anything. It was just a shift. An evolution.

When the Magic Showed Up

I didn't lose my legacy when I sold my business.

I expanded it.

The truth is: legacy isn't fixed. It grows with you. It morphs. It moves. It bends around your becoming.

My children will inherit more than a balance sheet. They'll inherit a story. A mindset. A vision. They'll inherit my resilience, my creativity, my hustle, and hopefully, the wisdom to know when to hold on and when to let go.

Alexi will carry forward the understanding that languages and cultures matter, that diversity isn't just a buzzword but a lived experience that enriches everything it touches. He saw that in our classrooms every day.

Chloe will know that creativity and business can coexist, that you don't have to choose between art and entrepreneurship. She watched me create beautiful spaces that also generated revenue.

Sophie will understand that performance and authenticity aren't opposites. She saw me show up every day, putting on the show that leadership requires while still being genuine with the people who mattered.

They all learned that when a situation no longer serves you, you have the power to change it. That walking away from what's draining you isn't giving up. That sometimes the bravest thing you can do is choose your own peace over other people's expectations.

This is the legacy that endures.

The finality of it all hit me during our last Thanksgiving cultural potluck in 2019. I was standing in the courtyard, watching families from twelve different countries sharing dishes and stories. There was Kenji's grandmother teaching other kids how to use chopsticks. Maria's family explaining the significance of their Día de los Muertos altar. The Danish family sharing homemade kringle while their toddler played with children who spoke four different languages at home.

I looked around at the Koons sculpture hanging above us, the carefully curated art on every wall, and realized this wasn't just a daycare that happened to be beautiful. This was a cultural institution. A place where families who might never have crossed paths were creating community together.

That's when the weight of what I was about to sell really hit me. This wasn't just my business. It was their gathering place. Their village.

The Thanksgiving potluck tradition one of my favorite traditions that started way back when we were still in the apartment. I noticed early on that our school attracted a global community. Families came from everywhere: Denmark, New Zealand, France, Tibet, Japan, Australia.

The tradition began as a "getting to know you" event, but also because Thanksgiving is very much an American holiday. I had so many expat families, and this wasn't their holiday. It was a way to include them and make it theirs too.

We asked families to bring a dish from their culture and to share its story. Why it mattered. Where it came from. What it meant to them. Instead of just celebrating American gratitude, we were celebrating global community.

New York can be a lonely place, especially for those far from their families. I wanted to create a space where people felt connected. Where we could learn from one another. Where we could gather.

Over the years, the potlucks grew in size and geography. They became one of the most cherished traditions we had. We gathered in the courtyard, surrounded by art. Rothko and Chihuly hung above us, and tables overflowed with dishes from every corner of the world.

Those were the memories that made it hard to let go. Those were the things that lived in my heart, even when my head told me I am doing the right thing.

Because deep down, I knew what would happen to everything I'd created. KinderCare never made promises about preserving what we built. They were honest about their intentions from the start. But that honesty didn't make it easier to accept.

They wouldn't keep the teaching artists. They wouldn't understand the why behind the velvet sofas or the live jazz or the yoga in the infant room. Those details that made us special would disappear into corporate efficiency.

They think in numbers. Not in impact.

So, no, letting go wasn't easy. No matter how much money was on the table. I was walking into this sale with my eyes wide open, knowing that the culture I'd spent years building was about to be erased.

It felt like I was walking away from something sacred.

The only difference this time is that I wasn't being deceived by false promises. I knew exactly what I was giving up. And somehow, that made the sentiment even more bittersweet.

But what I've come to understand is that legacy isn't just about buildings or programs or even businesses. Legacy lives in the people whose lives you've touched.

The teacher who learned she could trust her instincts because I believed in her judgment. The parent who discovered they could advocate for their child because they watched me advocate for mine. The little girl who grew up thinking it was normal for women to own businesses because that's what she saw every day.

Margaret, with her Nelson Mandela doll, learned that kindness was a daily choice because her father reminded her every morning. But she also learned that beauty and learning could exist in the same space, that school could feel like home, that adults would listen when children spoke.

The Danish family learned American holiday traditions while teaching us about their own. The Japanese mother who was so far from her own family found community with strangers who became friends.

Kenji's grandmother, who taught other kids to use chopsticks, got to be the wise elder in a room full of young families who appreciated her presence instead of seeing her as just someone in the way.

All of those teachers who worked for me learned they could expect more from their jobs than just crowd control. They could be educators, artists, nurturers. They could have a voice in curriculum decisions and be trusted with children's emotional development.

That legacy doesn't disappear when you sell a business. It lives on in every interaction those people have moving forward. It shows up in how they parent their own children, how they approach their next jobs, how they see themselves in the world.

The impact isn't in the building or the name on the door. It's in the ripple effects of all those relationships, all those moments, all those lessons that will keep spreading long after the last day of operations.

CHAPTER 14

Closure

It was January 2021, still in the throes of COVID. Masks were still mandatory everywhere and people avoided "in person" like the plague. So the closing didn't happen in some law office conference room, the way I once imagined it would. It happened on Zoom, through email chains, DocuSign, and whatever other digital forms of communication were necessary.

I remember that day clearly. Vendors were still popping out of the woodwork. My copy machine company was chasing me down, asking if their contract would be renewed or if KinderCare would buy them out. The music class vendor and the ASL sign language vendor still didn't have contracts and wanted to know if they had a future under new ownership. Everyone wanted their piece of the pie, right up to the very end.

Bright Horizons was first in line to be paid because of the judgment. Then came the lawyers. Then the landlords. After that, the people we had taken loans from. Then the vendors. And then, way at the bottom, the owners. Which meant me.

That order isn't accidental. It's written into bankruptcy law. Creditors, vendors, and anyone with a legal claim against the business get paid first. Owners are last in line, what's called a "residual claimant." It sounds polite, almost clinical, but what it really means is if there's nothing left after everyone else takes their share, you get nothing. And most of the time, there is nothing left.

That's how I ended up watching everyone get paid—except me.

I wasn't sad. I was relieved. Since the day we opened those doors in 2016, I had been operating with the shackles of Bright Horizons' lawsuit—building a business under the constant threat of losing it. Even with that hanging over my head, I still made sure teachers were supported, parents felt confident, and children were thriving. The community trusted me and I carried that responsibility every single day.

And then came COVID. Almost overnight, the weight doubled. New rules from the city dropped every week. Parents demanded answers I didn't have. Staff called out sick. Every single problem still landed on my desk, as if the lawsuit wasn't already enough to manage. Carrying the business through 2020 had been sheer torture.

So when the signatures were done and the transfers confirmed, what I felt wasn't grief. It was peace.

I sat there staring at my laptop screen after everyone had logged off the Zoom. The silence in my apartment was deafening. Eighteen years of work, reduced to a series of wire transfers that didn't include my name.

Closure

No golden parachute. No safety net. I hadn't had a 9-to-5 in almost two decades. We were still deep in the pandemic. The world was uncertain. And so was I.

I felt lost. But also...strangely free.

I thought about that day in 2003 when I first started watching kids in my apartment. How excited I'd been to make $1000 a week. How that had grown into something I never imagined possible. Four locations in NYC. Families from around the world. Teachers who became like family. A reputation that meant something.

Now it was gone. Sold. Over.

I should have been devastated. By all rights, I should have been crying or raging or falling apart. Instead, there was a lightness in my spirit that I hadn't felt in years. While it looked bleak on paper, I was secretly thrilled by the possibilities. By the idea of starting fresh. Of creating my own path—without boards, leases, payrolls, lawsuits.

For the first time in years, I didn't owe anyone anything. I wasn't responsible for keeping doors open or making payroll or managing crises. The weight I'd been carrying for so long was finally off my shoulders.

I closed my laptop, stood up, and took a deep breath. No more inspectors. No more payroll panic. No more waiting for the other shoe to drop. My phone could ring and it didn't mean disaster. For the first time in years, the weight was gone.

I went to my kitchen, opened the fridge, and pulled out a very expensive bottle of champagne that had been sitting there forever—waiting for a moment.

This was the moment.

I popped it. I toasted. Not to what was lost. But to what was.

And then I immediately started dreaming about what's next.

The kids were all in college now. Alexi was studying abroad in Cairo when COVID hit and he decided to stay another year. Chloe and Sophie were back in their dorms. The children were busy building their own dreams, their own futures.

My marriage was over. The business was sold. I was starting completely fresh.

For the first time in decades, I had no one to answer to but myself.

I left Manhattan. Moved 30 minutes north to Westchester. Changed my scenery. I was ready to put my old life in the rearview mirror, literally and figuratively.

This was the first time I had moved on my own. And by that, I don't just mean signing the lease. I mean physically, logistically, emotionally. On my own.

Closure

I had always joked that I went from living in my father's house to my husband's, with a brief stint in between sharing an apartment with my best friend and college roommate. But I had never lived alone. Never navigated a move solo. Never had to figure out where the extra box of batteries went or worry about the moving guys ripping me off.

And as much as we like to believe we've come a long way, there's still something about being a woman alone that people try to take advantage of.

Which is exactly what happened. From quote day to move day, it was a mess. I was lowballed, up-charged, dismissed, and ignored. The moving company that had seemed so professional during the estimate suddenly had "additional fees" that weren't mentioned in the contract. The cable installation that was supposed to take two hours stretched into an all-day affair with three different technicians.

I remember finally making it through the day, surrounded by boxes, eating lukewarm takeout on a flattened cardboard box, and calling my best friend. I could feel the tears welling up before I even opened my mouth.

"This is hard," I told her. "I didn't realize how hard this was going to be."

She immediately went into protective mode. She doesn't usually see me like that. I'm the strong one, the capable one. The one who always figures it out. The one who helps others move.

But in that moment, I wasn't strong. I wasn't composed. I was exhausted. Not from lifting, but from letting go.

Because when I said it was hard, I didn't mean the physical labor. There were enough movers for that. I meant the emotional labor. The silent toll of doing this chapter change solo.

The freedom I gained from leaving a situation that was no longer working came with a cost. A piece of the puzzle was missing.

But there was something restorative about the quiet in my new place. After years of constant noise and chaos, the silence felt good. I could finally breathe without feeling like I was holding my breath. That's what it felt like, moving into my new place. No shared closet. No noise from upstairs. No husband. No kids, at least not full-time. That would change. But in those first few days, it was just me. My books. My memories. My thoughts.

It wasn't glamorous. There were no big announcements. No "new beginnings" captions on Instagram. Just boxes. Lots of boxes.

One of my first memories in that new space was sitting cross-legged on a box, wearing sweatpants and an oversized shirt, eating out of a takeout Chinese food box resting in my lap. I had just sold my business of 18 years. I'd never lived alone before. My kids were all living independently, and I was newly divorced.

Closure

And then I had an epiphany: I was going to need a car.

Because how was I going to buy groceries without one? How was I going to get anywhere in Westchester, where everything required driving?

I pulled out my phone, opened Carvana, and bought a car right then and there. COVID made it possible to do things like that. Point, click, purchase. It showed up a week later, like magic. That was the first moment I felt like I had control again.

This wasn't just a new address. It was a reclamation.

I moved out of the Upper West Side to Westchester not because I had some grand plan or five-year vision. I moved because I needed space. Literal and emotional.

For years, my life had been crammed into the margins. A corner of a shared desk. A few pages of a planner. A to-do list that never stopped running. Everything revolved around someone else's schedule. My kids, my staff, my clients, my emergencies. My life was scheduled around other people's needs.

Even when I was home, I wasn't home.

This time was different. This was mine. Not ours. Not temporary. Not a compromise. Mine.

And when I sat in the quiet that first night, I felt something close to peace.

But let me be honest: peace didn't come right away.

At first, the quiet was disorienting. It made me question everything.

Who am I when no one is calling my name? Who am I when I'm not fixing, managing, rescuing, performing? Who am I without the titles: wife, mother, boss?

I had to sit with that.

And sitting with it meant grieving the versions of myself that had shaped me and also outgrown me.

That apartment became my sanctuary. Not in a Pinterest-perfect kind of way. But in the way a room becomes a mirror. In the way a space reflects back your truth.

I filled it with light. With warmth. With music. With quiet. I bought lots of plants. Printed photos for my walls. Lit candles that smelled like cedar and bergamot.

And little by little, something in me began to soften.

Not because life got easier. But because I was finally creating space to just be. Not hustle. Not prove. Not perform. Just be.

Virginia Woolf once wrote that a woman needs money and a room of her own if she is to write fiction.

I'd take it further.

A woman needs a room of her own if she is to hear herself again. To return to the sound of her own voice. To choose her next chapter with intention, not obligation. To write her own story. One line, one box, one boundary at a time.

I didn't know exactly what was next. But I knew one thing with full clarity: It would be chosen by me. And that alone felt revolutionary.

But freedom comes with grief. For a while, I wrestled with an identity crisis. Who was I now? No longer a boss. No longer an entrepreneur. No longer a wife.

And motherhood? I knew I was still a mother, but it didn't feel like it. The house was quiet. No one needed me.

For years, my identity was wrapped around titles. Tasks. Being who everyone else needed me to be.

And now, it felt like all of it had been snatched away overnight.

I probably should have taken time to properly grieve. To process. To sit with all that had happened.

But I did what I've always done: I pushed it down. And dove headfirst into my next project.

I took everything I had learned, every spreadsheet, every system, every scar, and started building an app. A childcare solutions management system. I called it the fairy godmother I wish I had when I was running my centers.

Closure

I spent my last remaining funds building it. I partnered with a brilliant engineer out of London. The vision was clear. The app was elegant. Everything was clicking.

Until it wasn't.

He got an offer he couldn't refuse in New Zealand. Moved. Disappeared. The project stalled.

Then came the knockoff attempt. A competitor in Canada pretended to want to buy me out, but he was just fishing. He already had something similar, but it lacked the boots-on-the-ground insider details that only real operators would understand. He wanted my secret sauce.

And he got too close.

Eventually, I found another engineer who got it. He was excited. Aligned. But he was wrapped up in a long-term commitment that wouldn't free him up for months.

So I waited.

And in that waiting, something unexpected happened.

I was tapped to become the executive director of a nonprofit organization called Black Theatre United.

Founded in the summer of 2020, the summer of reckoning, by some of the top names in the industry, the organization was born from purpose and urgency. But it needed help. Infrastructure. Systems. Fundraising. Programs. Business development.

Closure

They needed someone to build. To hold. To lead.

It was way out of my comfort zone. But it was nothing I couldn't do.

I said yes. As an interim.

That was three years ago.

Sometimes freedom doesn't come with fanfare. Sometimes it shows up in a room full of boxes, a carton of takeout, and a candle flickering in the dark. But you'll know it when it arrives because for the first time in a long time, you'll be home.

*****

Reinvention sounds like a pivot. Like a career move. A makeover. A "new chapter." But for me, it's been something deeper. Something quieter.

Reinvention didn't come to me in a flash of inspiration. It came in pieces. After the breakdown. After the burnout. After I let go of the things I once believed defined me.

The pieces looked like this: Learning to sleep past 6 a.m. without feeling guilty. Sitting in silence for ten minutes without reaching for my phone. Saying no to opportunities that looked good on paper but felt wrong in my gut. Choosing rest over productivity on a random Tuesday afternoon.

It was in the small decision to stop scheduling every minute of my weekend. In learning to grocery shop without a list, just to see what I was drawn to. In taking walks with no destination, no fitness goal, just to move my body and clear my head.

It was in the moment I realized I hadn't posted anything on social media in three months and didn't miss it. That I was living my life instead of documenting it for other people's consumption.

The reinvention was in printing photos for my home instead of sharing them online. In holding sacred moments close instead of turning them into captions. Because the best parts of life can't be filtered, edited, or explained in 200+ characters.

I used to think reinvention was about becoming someone new. Now I know it's about remembering who you were before the world told you who to be.

I was never one of those little girls who dreamed about being something specific, like a pilot or a musician or dancer. I dreamed of meeting Prince Charming and having a family of little princes and princesses. Success to me looked like a beautiful family.

That dream shaped so much of what came after. Even when I built Smarter Toddler, it wasn't really about being an entrepreneur. It was about creating the kind of environment I wanted my own children to experience. It was about building a family in a different way.

Closure

Ah, but family comes in many forms. The one you're born into, and the one you create along the way. Smarter Toddler was the family I created. And yes, it was a business, but ultimately it was more than that. It was a vessel. A container. A space that brought together people who otherwise might have never crossed paths. It was culture. It was art. It was community.

So when that chapter closed, at the same time I was going through a divorce, moving out of the home where my children grew up, during a global pandemic, overwhelmed doesn't even begin to do it justice. I felt like I had to start from scratch.

I remember being on the phone with my attorney, trying to make sense of everything unraveling at once, when she said, "Well, Kettia, you're just going to have to reinvent yourself. And if anyone can do it, it's you."

Those words rang in my ear. But I remember thinking: What does that even mean? Do you just wake up one day and declare a new you? And who is that person?

So I went on a journey to find out.

Did you know that the self-improvement industry is a $46 billion-dollar behemoth and is projected to reach over $90 billion by 2033? That's a lot of ways to be told something is wrong with you. You could be "working on yourself" 24/7 and still feel stuck.

Closure

I realized fairly quickly: the answers were not out there. They were in the silence.

"The quieter you become, the more you can hear." - Ram Dass

You ever find yourself turning down the radio when you're lost in traffic so you can concentrate? That's what reinvention has felt like for me. Tuning out the noise so I could focus.

I carved out space to mourn my old life in very practical ways. I blocked out entire Saturday afternoons with nothing scheduled. No plans, no productivity goals, just open time to feel whatever came up. Sometimes I cried. Sometimes I slept. Sometimes I just sat in my garden and watched the plants grow.

I gave myself permission to grieve the version of the future I had imagined. The family business that my kids might inherit. The marriage that was supposed to last forever. The version of me that always had the answers.

I started journaling, not the organized kind with prompts and structure, but just stream-of-consciousness writing. Three pages every morning, no editing, no audience. Just me getting the swirling thoughts out of my head and onto paper.

I stopped performing and started being by making tiny choices throughout the day. When someone asked "How are you?" instead of automatically saying "Great!" I'd pause and give an honest answer. "I'm tired today." "I'm figuring some things out." "I'm okay, thanks for asking."

Closure

I started saying no to invitations that felt obligatory. Book club meetings where I hadn't read the book and felt like I was just showing up to be social. Networking events that drained my energy. Coffee dates with people I didn't really want to spend time with.

I changed my digital presence too. I stopped posting the highlight reel of my life. No more carefully curated photos of perfect moments. Most of the time, I didn't share anything at all.

For so long, social media had trained me to perform my life, to curate, to showcase, to project an image of having it all together. But when I began this quiet season of reinvention, I became protective of my peace. I didn't stop living. I just stopped broadcasting.

I printed photos for my home instead of sharing them online. I held sacred moments close instead of turning them into captions. Because the best parts of life can't be filtered, edited, or explained in 280 characters.

Reinvention, for me, hasn't been a single act like a career change or a spiritual awakening in Bali. It hasn't been a checklist of bucket list items or a personal brand overhaul.

It's been a devotion. A return to what's real. To what matters. To me.

Closure

I didn't eat, pray, love my way into some perfectly healed version of myself. I met myself in the discomfort of the unknown. I learned to sit with uncertainty instead of rushing to fix it.

I acknowledged my fear. I forgave myself for the marriage that didn't last, for the mistakes I made, for the moments I didn't show up the way I wanted to.

And I extended to myself the same grace I had always been so willing to give to everyone else.

We love our comfort zones. They're familiar. Predictable. But if I had stayed in mine, I would have stayed stuck.

Reinvention asked me to grow. To evolve. To say yes to new things even when I didn't feel ready. To believe I was worthy of something I hadn't yet imagined.

The journey wasn't about finding some new version of myself that was completely different from who I'd been. It was about peeling back the layers of who I thought I was supposed to be and remembering who I actually was underneath all of that.

I didn't have to become someone else. I just had to remember who I was before the burnout, before the titles, before the world tried to define me.

Before I learned that love had to be earned through performance. Before I believed that rest was something you had to deserve. Before I thought that asking for help was a sign of weakness.

The woman I found in that silence? She was someone I recognized. Someone I'd known a long time ago, before life taught me to be anything other than myself.

EPILOGUE

The Becoming

Freedom, I learned, doesn't announce itself with fanfare.

It shows up quietly, in the moment you realize you're eating dinner at 9 p.m. because that's when you got hungry, not because someone else's schedule demanded it. It arrives when you buy a car online at midnight, sign your own name, and sit in the driver's seat laughing at the audacity of starting over.

That first year alone taught me what life looked like without constant crisis. My house became my sanctuary, not a showplace, not an investment, but mine. I hung art where I wanted it. I left books scattered on every surface. I learned that popcorn and wine could be dinner, and nobody died from my choices.

The phone calls that once sent my nervous system into overdrive became ordinary interruptions. Unknown numbers meant car insurance surveys, not emergency repairs. Weekends stretched out like luxuries I'd forgotten how to enjoy. I woke up on Saturday mornings, made coffee, and sat at my kitchen table without rushing anywhere. Sometimes I read. Sometimes I just let the quiet fill the spaces that had been cramped with other people's urgencies for so long.

The Becoming

I started running again, not training for anything, just moving my body because it felt good to remember I was still here, still capable. No finish lines. No race bibs. Just the rhythm of my feet on pavement and the radical act of doing something purely for myself.

The most profound shift was the smallest one: setting my phone across the room at night instead of beside my pillow. For years, I'd slept with the ringer on high, ready for 2 a.m. emergencies. Now I went to bed knowing no one needed me to save them. That peace was something I hadn't known I was missing until I found it.

Divorce had stripped away my marriage. The lawsuit had stripped away my business. Bankruptcy had stripped away the illusion that I'd walk away with something to show for twenty years of building. But what remained was entirely mine: my time, my peace, my choices.

This wasn't the dramatic transformation you see in movies, no eat-pray-love montage, no sudden enlightenment. It was quieter than that. It was the slow, steady work of putting myself back at the center of my own life.

The becoming wasn't about finding a new identity. It was about remembering who I was before the world told me who I needed to be. Before I learned that love had to be earned through performance. Before I believed that rest was something you had to deserve. Before I thought asking for help was weakness.

The woman I found in that silence was someone I recognized, someone I'd known before the armor, before the titles, before the endless proving. She was softer than I remembered, but stronger too. Strong enough to rest. Strong enough to receive. Strong enough to say no to anything that didn't serve her peace.

I used to think success meant never letting anyone down. Now I know it means never letting yourself disappear.

The girl who left Haiti at twelve to chase the American Dream became a woman who built businesses, raised children, survived lawsuits, and learned that sometimes the bravest thing you can do is walk away from what's killing you.

But the woman who emerged from the ashes? She chose herself. Finally, fully, without apology.

And that choice changed everything.

www.ingramcontent.com/pod-product-compliance
Lightning Source LLC
LaVergne TN
LVHW091546070526
838199LV00023B/551/J